THE
MOTLEY FOOL
INVESTMENT
GUIDE

HOW THE FOOL BEATS
WALL STREET'S WISE MEN
AND HOW YOU CAN TOO

DAVID AND
TOM GARDNER

SIMON & SCHUSTER

New York · Toronto · London · Sydney · Tokyo · Singapore

For Dad

 SIMON & SCHUSTER
Rockefeller Center
1230 Avenue of the Americas
New York, NY 10020

Copyright © 1996 by David Gardner and Tom Gardner
All rights reserved, including the right of reproduction
in whole or in part in any form.

SIMON & SCHUSTER and colophon are registered trademarks
of Simon & Schuster Inc.

Designed by Victoria Hartman
Illustration by Jill Weber
Manufactured in the United States of America

20   19   18   17

Library of Congress Cataloging-in-Publication Data

Gardner, David, 1966–
    The Motley Fool investment guide : how the fool beats Wall Street's wise men and how you
can too / David and Tom Gardner.
        p.   cm.
    Includes index.
    1. Portfolio management.   2. Investment analysis.   I. Gardner, Tom, 1968-   .   II. Title.
    HG4529.5.G37   1996
    332.6—dc20   95-45766
                                                                    CIP

ISBN 0-684-81594-X

Contents

Foreword

* * * *

All changed, changed utterly:
A terrible beauty is born.
—*Yeats*

In the spring of 1995, Iomega Corporation (NASDAQ:IOMG) came out with a revolutionary disk drive whose disks held seventy times the capacity of existing floppies.

Between the initial announcement and the debut of its Zip drive, Iomega shares took off, running from $2 to $10 in a matter of months. The rise drew strength from the expectations created by the five-star reviews that computer industry rags lavished upon the new product, praise that was universal and without reservation.

But demand for the drive far outstripped manufacturing capacity, causing skeptics to conclude that little Iomega could never make enough Zips to turn a profit before the "big boys" showed up sporting copycat whiskers and claiming the market. Supporting the bearish view, Iomega was coming off two consecutive years of losses; it was fair to say then that the company's recent performance had been reminiscent of a young Elvis Presley . . . but without the voice or looks. Could Iomega's single great product justify a market valuation five times what it had been 6 months before? Some said the stock was going back to $2.

Simultaneously, with far less of a splash, a revolution started.

Unlike many grassroots revolutions, it didn't begin slowly in some rural backwater, or on a stump in a city park. Quite the contrary: Though quiet, it was instant and it was national. In metropolitan centers east to west across the union, private investors started polling their local computer stores, inquiring about their current stock of Zip drives and their backlogged orders for the product. ("So how far would I be down the waiting list at this point?")

Using computers outfitted with modems, they then signed online to publish this information in a public discussion of Iomega available to anyone Foolish (yes, that's a capital F) enough to listen. Concurrently, an anonymous engineer took a simple tour of the plant in Roy, Utah, and observed the Zip manufacturing process. From fifteen minutes of observation, he contributed his own numerical estimates of Iomega's production, apparently doing it so well that company management itself joined the discussion at that point, making a public accusation that he—a complete outsider—had provided inside information! (The charge was later retracted.) Further, another fellow on the East Coast had his parents, who lived an hour away from the factory in Utah, drive to the company's headquarters on a Sunday afternoon in order to report how many cars appeared in the company parking lot. (It was full.)

What resulted from the collection and online publication of these seemingly inconsequential details was a national public conversation of a kind that had never taken place before, that had never been *possible* before. And it created an almost overnight survey of Zip drive sales, one that clearly demonstrated Iomega's success in meeting the demand to an extent far exceeding general expectations.

How well the company was doing—a subject of so much speculation among benighted *offline* investors—had a sure answer among enlightened onliners.

The information was provided so quickly and so exhaustively that no Wall Street analyst or firm could ever have pulled it off. (In fact, at the time no Wall Street analysts were yet following Iomega.) But within a week, Wall Street institutional traders were gravitating to the discussion; a single spot in cyberspace had become *the* place to go for understanding and valuing IOMG. This was confirmed by a Dow Jones reporter who, in the midst of doing a story on the "Iomega online phenomenon," discovered with surprise that all four of her regular Wall Street sources were getting their information from something called The Motley Fool.

In less than 2 months, the stock zoomed from $10 to $30 as brokers, banks, pension funds, and investment newsletters piled in.

We know the story pretty well because we dreamt up, created, and continue to operate The Motley Fool, and we bought Iomega at $15 based almost completely on our readers' research. But cribbing in this case was fair play. You see, through our writings and our online portfolio, we were the ones who had inspired many of them to take their financial futures in their own hands in the first place, encouraging them to renounce the mediocrity of their mutual funds in favor of the greater risk and reward of common stocks. And together, we had a terribly fun time making a great deal of money.

That was and is the revolution, because somewhere in the midst of it we realized that all of a sudden the world had changed, and changed utterly. The Iomega story (which has since been repeated in our forum many times with other stocks) demonstrates that, thanks to online communication, it is now little-guy investors—not huge brokerage firms—who hold the most valuable cards. Consequently, over the next decade we think you're going to see Wall Street beating its path to Main Street.

The Motley Fool Investment Guide will show you offline how to do the same thing that we've been doing online. This book will enable even the rankest novice to invest expertly on his or her own, enjoy the heck out of it, and *beat* the pants off the market averages . . . all things that too many people think takes an expert, a Wise man, or a market insider to do—those Foolish enough, that is, to believe that the market can be beaten at all.

If you harbor the faintest intellectual curiosity, relish—not wilt from—risk and challenge, instinctively enjoy taking responsibility for your own future, and own a modem, today's investment environment is for you.

Though now that you have our book, the modem's optional.

PART I

WHO, WHAT, WHY, AND HOW

"Fool"?

. . . . .

Take heed. . . . The wise may be instructed by a fool. . . .
You know how by the advice and counsel and prediction
of fools, many kings, princes, states, and commonwealths
have been preserved, several battles gained, and divers
doubts of a most perplexed intricacy resolved.
—*Rabelais*

Fool?

Not a very *wise* choice for a name when you're trying to ply your trade in the investment world. For decades financial professionals have done their best to sell customers on their Wisdom. Whether it's the pinstripe suit, the avuncular smile, the firm handshake, or the advertising jingle ("Rock Solid, Market Wise," comes to mind) your typical broker, money manager, or financial planner has striven for an image that smacks of success, intelligence, experience, respectability—in a word, Wisdom.

And for years they've all been making a fair amount of money off of fools. You know about fools. You may even have been one yourself at some point. Ever listened to a salesman on the other end of a phone long enough that the voice-activated vacuum cleaner he was trying to sell you began to make sense? You were being foolish. Ever bought a stock on your dentist's recommendation without even looking to see if it was listed? How very foolish of you. Or what about when you snapped up shares of International Dashed Hopes Load Fund just because your broker said it was the top performer in its category last year? Terribly, terribly foolish.

Basking in the excesses brought about by this folly, the financial establishment hadn't banked on one thing—that one day the tables might turn when some Fools (and that's a capital "F," maestro) actually showed up.

◆ ◆ ◆

The Wise would have you believe that "A Fool and his money are soon parted." But in a world where three quarters of all *professional* money managers lose to the market averages, year in and year out, how Wise should one aspire to be? In what other realms could such a compelling paradox exist, that the paid professional can do no better than—in fact, cannot even do as well as—dumb luck?! And this general ineptitude has been made more ironic by the appurtenances that typically attend the Wise: expensive suits and gold cufflinks (to impress their clients), Swiss watches (to convey the importance of their time), mahogany desks (to rest at between rounds of golf), and other similar displays designed to impress and intimidate their customers. Ah, the many-splendored totems of those who were paid too much to make too little.

In fact, we got to thinking after a while that we should just go ahead and call ourselves Fools, since our attitudes and approach to life were so radically different from what was being passed off as Wisdom all around us. So we launched our original *Motley Fool*, taking the name from a nondescript quotation from Shakespeare's *As You Like It:* "A fool, a fool! I met a fool i' the forest, a motley fool." We'd always loved Shakespeare's Fools . . . they amused as they instructed, and were the only members of society who could tell the truth to the king or queen without having their heads lopped off. *The Motley Fool* began as a monthly newsletter, then transformed into a daily feature on a national online service, and now you have the most potent distillation of our Folly, a single tome containing all the Foolishness we can pack into it.

Our goal was and is very simple: beat the market and show others how to do it—the more novice, the better. In our brief Foolish history, we've enabled thousands of average people who didn't previously know a dividend from a divining rod to invest their own money without the help of Armani suits, and *crush* Wall Street at its own game.

Our approach is best characterized by its hostility to conventional wisdom. For example, the Wise will tell you just to invest your money in mutual funds. (This "double dip" enables them to charge you for that advice *and* then charge you on an annual basis for the funds' management fees.) We, on the other hand, are telling you to buy stocks. They'll tell you, "All right, take on the risk of buying stocks. But if you're going to do that, just buy safe ones and hold on." Poppycock. We're telling you to add some more volatile growth stocks to your portfolio, or you'll probably end up as flotsam left in the market's wake. And we're also telling you—horror of horrors—that you should consider *shorting* stocks, a devilishly fun attempt to profit off the *decline* of a stock rather than its rise. To the Wise, there is no more risky, bad-faith investment decision than shorting stocks. To us, there are fewer better opportunities available to the individual investor today. And the outrageous list goes on.

In what follows, we hope to teach you, to amuse you, and ultimately to make you good money at the same time.

But first we should introduce ourselves.

Who We Are, by Way of Explaining What This Book Ain't Going to Do

We're David and Tom Gardner, brothers, and the original editors of *The Motley Fool*. We originally began investing when we were given a bit of money of our own to invest, upon turning eighteen.

What we did with that money was what our father had always done before us: invest it in stocks. It takes some casual investors a lifetime to wean themselves off the numbing teat of mutual funds; we never knew the temptation. Our very first purchase was shares in a trucker called Leaseway Transportation (since acquired by a larger company). One hot summer we watched it go from $26 to $42, where we took our profit. The stock had been culled, using a few elementary measures, from the pages of *Value Line,* that redoubtable seven-inch-thick investment research monstrosity that we rarely use anymore because online resources are so much more powerful and timely. We cannot remember the exact rationale for the purchase of Leaseway, but that's not the point anyway. The enduring lesson for us was that if you're willing to take a risk, and if you play your cards right, you can make money in the stock market without paying the Wise for the privilege.

In this book we're going to break down the reams of writing that we offer on a daily basis in cyberspace into their primary components. The idea, as the man says, is not just to hand you a Twinkie . . . rather, we're going to teach you how to locate your own Twinkies so that you'll learn to feed yourself for years and years . . . prior to dying of a massive heart attack.

We want to help you help yourself make money. This was our intention back in 1993, when we launched *The Motley Fool* as an investment newsletter. Ye Olde Printed Foole—as we fondly refer to it—contained our stock picks, one monthly investment article, and a patchwork quilt of content in keeping with our motley interests. We mailed out unsolicited copies to a few thousand unsuspecting people and wound up our first month with exactly thirty-eight subscribers. We were depressed.

What we needed was visibility. So we decided to start a conversation about stocks on what at that point was a small but fast-growing national online service called America Online.

Through the power and beauty of el cheapo modems, we connected to America Online over local phone lines and started typing. We offered our investment opinions and advice in response to requests from complete strangers, doing our best to provide them with as much information about their own holdings as they could handle. In so doing, we discovered some wonderful things (like how many people were willing to volunteer their own investment research for the benefit of many) and some bad things too (see appendix on Zeigletics). But what we mainly did was acquire new subscribers. Within a few months, our little gabfest had grown into the most popular financial discussion on America Online. The company approached us about opening up an actual business on its service, where we could get paid for doing interactively on a daily basis many of the same things we were doing just once a month, noninteractively, with Ye Olde Printed Foole. Even better.

Throwing away printing and mailing costs forever, we went into the electronic publishing business.

By December, already having grown more popular than Morningstar (the big mutual fund research firm) the word started to get around. Soon we were AOL's most frequented service in Personal Finance. Why? Well, it didn't hurt that our Fool Portfolio, a real-money portfolio invested exclusively in stocks, rose 11.03 percent in our first few months online, while the S&P 500 (the index used most frequently to track money managers) gained just 0.19 percent. (We closed out our first year up 59 percent, almost 40 percentage points ahead of the market.) Lots of people were signing into our area to find out what was up.

What was up was that our stock-picking technique—the Fool Ratio—was working. The better it worked, the more Fools came to the forum. And as more came, there was more talk, more information shared, and more opportunities discovered and explored. Fools helped Fools (and themselves) make money. We all prospered without the Wise. Now, you can too!

Folly

· · · · ·

Foolery, sir, does walk about the orb
like the sun; it shines everywhere.
—*Shakespeare*

The too-earnest reader will no doubt wish at this point that the
moneymaking grub be served. This isn't that sort of book. If
you're interested in fast cash, you can find many other books to sate
your appetite. Books with titles like *How to Make $1,000,000 Auto-
matically in the Stock Market* no doubt contain the magical formula
that will enable you to become rich beyond your wildest dreams faster
than you ever could have imagined. And you can do it, it seems, without using your brain!

This book, dear reader, is written for those who drop—not slam—
their token in the bus meter, who remain seated when the FASTEN SEAT
BELTS sign turns off, who walk down to the final car of the subway train
because it's the one with the fewest people. In short, we write for
those who aren't in a hurry, those who actually think before they act,
those who are willing to exercise their brains. And, to stay in character,
we really should begin the book by talking about Folly. It's what we're
actually all about once you get past the juggling balls, the pointy caps,
and the red-and-green-checkered pantyhose.

The True Wisdom: Go Against Your Instincts

Foolishness is not a luxury. It is a necessity; it attacks conventional wisdom. Folly is particularly crucial today because through the miracle of
modern communication more bad thinking now circles the globe
quicker than ever before. "For every 10 bytes of value online there
seem to be 10,000 bytes of drivel," writes *Smart Money*'s technology

commentator Walter Mossberg. Too true. And if we're not careful, true wisdom—those proverbial 10 bytes of truly good ideas and approaches—will get lost in the 10,000.

It may take a Fool to notice this, but despite the continual advances in knowledge earned through scientific experiment, archaeological discovery, and globalized computer networking, one thing that has assuredly *not* increased over time is the collective true wisdom (or common sense). So while modern technology has determined that we'll continue to pile up more and more information, technology has no good mechanism for ensuring that we even maintain our common sense. In fact, it may be leaking away right now! One cannot help but notice that the ancients—Western and Eastern—were far more interested in studying the nature of wisdom and folly than we are, despite the abundant resources of folly in our time. What happens when you combine a rich history of literature and thought on the subject with a modern populace largely ignorant of its substance? Answer: received "truths" that no longer have much truth or meaning behind them but are accepted by wide swaths of the population as conventional wisdom. It is these sorts of situations that put Fools everywhere on red alert.

Good straight wisdom is a dear commodity. Benjamin Franklin had it, for instance. A glance again through *Poor Richard's Almanack*: "Three may keep a secret if two of them are dead." "He that speaks ill of the Mare will buy her." "He that's content hath enough. He that complains has too much." What makes these aphorisms tokens of true wisdom is the way they contradict our basic instincts. For instance, when we hear that the content man has enough, we naturally assume that the discontent man does *not* have enough. We are told, instead, that he has too much. Our foiled expectations force us to consider this new possibility, and after further reflection on our own experience we recognize that one or another of our grumbling acquaintances does in fact suffer from having too much, not too little.

True wisdom leads to that kind of insight by challenging our preconceived notions or expectations. A Fool has no quarrel with this wisdom. It is a universal good, beloved by all.

In the end, every great investment method succeeds not because of its numerical gizmos, magical formulas, or other assorted whizbangs. Rather, it succeeds by using some of the very commonsense wisdom we're talking about. Good investment practices can almost be called studies in good character. Warren Buffett's investment career, for instance, is not so much about balance-sheet analysis as Buffett's own humility, patience, and diligence. Peter Lynch's approach is not so much about price-to-earnings ratios as it is about perceptiveness, optimism, and self-effacing humor. The greatest investors are often outstanding human beings, insofar as they exemplify the highest achievement in one or more human characteristics like patience, diligence, perceptiveness, and common sense.

Because remember: Dealing in money, the investor constantly must avoid his own *instinctive temptation* toward fear and greed. Fear and greed will ruin your investment returns. It is perhaps an underappreciated trait of great investors that in putting up consistently superb investment returns, they are demonstrating their relative imperviousness to many of the less optimistic aspects of human nature.

This, then, is the true wisdom, to resist one's baser instincts. "Do every day one or two things for no other reason than that you would rather not do them. Thus, when the hour of darkness comes, it will not find you unprepared." So wrote the psychologist William James, another fellow who was more concerned with character than the minutiae of his respective discipline. James knew that in order to succeed we must vigilantly toil against our own wills.

Resist to subsist.

The Conventional Wisdom: "Go with Your Instincts"

Having set forth true wisdom, we are now left to examine its bastardizations. Revisiting an earlier point, true wisdom or common sense may be not much more than a husk in our present age, with so few having awareness of or appreciation for its rich history. Another form of wisdom, however, is alive and well: conventional wisdom. It is this counterfeit and useless form of wisdom—the conventional, or worldly, wisdom—masquerading as the real thing that has roused Fools throughout the ages in a call to arms.

For—say it again—the be-all and end-all of Folly is its attack on conventional wisdom.

We can best summarize the present-day conventional wisdom in this way: We live in a world that does its level best to convince us to follow our own instincts. "Follow your instincts," "Just do it," and "Because you deserve the very best" have been among our most popular advertising slogans. A fashionable Yuletide ad jingle these days urges us to treat ourselves to a gift; this, in the season whose whole meaning—even its secular one—is supposed to be about giving to *others*.

Even more disheartening, the means for the distribution of conventional wisdom are more powerful than ever before, thanks to the mass media. That's because *mass* media, by its very definition, has the power to broadcast to the masses. Never in the history of the world has any tool had the power to create so many like minds, as has television. This is obvious, a commonplace. What is not immediately so obvious is how bad so much of the thinking being inculcated on the minds of the American people is. In the investment world alone we have a financial network that features popular regular fare like "Buy! Sell! Hold!" where a few unFoolish random callers get to ask some bloke they've never met before—and who hasn't the slightest grasp of their own personal situations—what they should do with a given stock in their portfolios. The bloke, usually an analyst of some sort, gives preprogrammed answers of two or three sentences' duration, passing along his almighty, destiny-controlling Wisdom about Motorola or Apple to the unwashed anonymous masses. This is about as close as television ever gets (or can get) to interactive education.

And don't even get us started on Dan Dorfman, the television commentator who for years on a daily basis has blared analyst and "insider" opinions and rumors about a stock, almost unfailingly moving the market a few points up or down. For example, Dorfman suggested ten stocks as winners for 1995 on December 1, 1994. As of this writing, the Dow Jones industrial average is up over 28 percent in that period, and Dorfman's picks are up 22 percent. Those who have actually tracked the performance of the Dorfman stocks know how incredibly *good* this performance is for his stocks, and therefore how regrettable it is that some people listen to the guy. But as we were saying, this is mass media, baby . . . the market moves not just because Dan happens to open his mouth, but because he does so on national television.

What you end up with is a large segment of the population that is extremely receptive to the repetitive, conventional pabulum that television features because they believe that conventional wisdom is wise. That's why for market researchers and brokers and financial planners, these people are the easiest (and the most profitable) game in town.

One can learn a great deal from the Wise, though. In fact, the careful investor can learn so much through a brief analysis of common human error that we can't resist but putting it right here up front in the beginning of our book. We'll close our chapter on Folly by examining the two brightest pots of gold that marketers try to convince us we will find at the end of the rainbow if we'll only "just do it . . . follow our instincts . . . because we deserve the very best." Both can be poison for your brokerage account, and they are opposite but deadly investment mistakes. We're talking about the two idols, Wealth and Security.

Wealth

Let's take Wealth first. Everyone wants to be just a *little* bit richer, right? We've just about never met anyone who thought he had enough, whether we're talking about billionaires or mendicants. In the investment game, this leads people to take stupid gambles.

Most of the time, these people are younger people; the race for Wealth remains one run most fervently by greenhorns. (Security, as we shall see, is quite the opposite.) Unsophisticated first-time investors often almost instinctively swing for the fences. They've heard about that IBM stock their grandfather once bought and unloaded a few decades later for forty-five times his money. They figure the fastest way to make ten times their initial investment is to buy a stock at $5 that might go to $50, rather than one bought at $50 that would have to hit $500. In fact, perhaps one of the few negative side effects of Peter Lynch's *One Up on Wall Street* is that he induced a generation of readers to shoot for his fabled "ten-bagger" (a stock that makes an investor ten times her original money). Many people shooting for ten-baggers wind up buying pathetic penny stocks sold them by people who don't have their best interest at heart, even though Lynch is the last one who'd ever advocate such a decision.

We started a wonderful discussion in our online area entitled My Dumbest Investment. In it, we encouraged readers to provide a brief story of the worst investment they'd ever made, and what they learned from it. From the day we started it, it was one of our service's best offerings. We learned a lot.

Take the dentist from Illinois, who wrote of the year 1986, when he was a young, happy-go-lucky investor getting ready to invest in a company called Microsoft. But just then, *RINNNNNGGGGGG!* He got a call at work from an investment banker claiming to have just bought an expensive car with the money made off an investment in (whispered) *platinum.* The poor and self-admittedly naive dentist was convinced by this fellow to put his money into platinum on "margin," meaning that he effectively borrowed extra money beyond what he had in order to heighten his stack of chips on the table. "A few days later my first margin call came in as the bottom dropped out. I had to put several thousand dollars on my credit card to cover my losses." The lesson learned from his Dumbest Investment was an excellent moral to learn so early in his investing life.

Or take the screenwriter from Los Angeles who noticed in an issue of *Smart Money* magazine that a recent recommendation in its pages had dropped from $2 to just 25¢ per share in value. Excited, he didn't even bother to check out what the company, Memorex-Telex, did.

"Now, imagine this," he goes on, "I thought if I had bought it at $2, I would now be down, what, 87 percent or so? But what a deal it was now! A mere quarter! If they thought it was a good buy at two, it must be outta this world at 25¢!!!

"When a few months later I received the notice of the company's bankruptcy from my broker, I ruefully rubbed my chin, downed a Manhattan, and considered searching for a tall building." With the characteristic good wit that pervades the Dumbest Investment discussion, the writer concluded, "But I have a family. And, fortunately, I didn't throw away our nest egg. No, I saved that for some other dogs that maybe I'll write about later on."

The stories go on and on, as they will forever. There was the high-school student doing a summer framing job for an oil tycoon. The tycoon was praising a company traded on Canada's penny-laden, corruption-ridden Vancouver Exchange. Only problem was, kid didn't know the exchange's reputation or anything about money, in fact, except that this "tycoon" had made a lot of it. So the kid bought New Dolly Varden Minerals at $2.25, just before it dropped to $1.25. He then doubled his holding. It dropped to $0.25. Having lost 90 percent, he told us he was just hanging on to the thing, since it would "cost more to sell than just to keep."

There was the fellow who kept adding to a stock holding in a since-failed consumer electronics company, even as it kept dropping further and further. His wish: "May Crazy Eddie rot in jail for years to come."

There was the guy who, enticed by expectations of big returns, was convinced by his financial planner to make a large investment in a real-estate limited partnership in the mid-'80s. He lost it all. "To add insult to injury, I actually paid this guy for his advice, plus invested the rest of my savings in his 5 percent load funds that did a whole lot worse than a simple Vanguard Index no-load." (For more information about mutual funds, and what the heck "no-load" means, see part II, "Mutual Funds: Love 'Em or Leave 'Em?")

And finally there was the photographer who, "completely ignorant" about managing money, got to talking with his father's broker at his father's funeral (no joke). Soon after, he'd opened up a margin account so his broker could trade currencies for him: Swiss francs, yen, German marks, Eurodollars. "Five months later, the 'new' broker handling my account (never did find out where the original broker went, all my calls were never answered) called to tell me I should close out what remained of the account, or write a *new* check to continue trading. I closed: 88 percent loss."

The point of these stories is not that brokers and financial planners are evil. Not at all. Some are very good. Some are good, and just plain wrong sometimes. Every investment entails a measure of risk. The only point we're making is that in every case, the correspondent was taking on stupid risk—either because of having done no research, or having been baited by a sales pitch, or both. Why? In order to achieve get-rich-quick returns, in the chase for Wealth.

The lessons are probably self-explanatory: Don't invest in anything you don't understand. Manage your own money if you have the time and instinct. Don't fall in love with (and keeping adding to) any given investment. Lots of other people do stupid things too.

The overarching point is that it's those very get-rich-quick returns that will always remain attractive to our human nature. We will be tempted by the conventional wisdom to shoot for the big bucks by "going with our instincts," sometimes on our own initiative, sometimes at the urging of others (who may see us only as so much fodder). Our natural human instinct is toward Greed. It is this very instinct that one *must* resist in order to become a good investor.

Fortunately, you now have some Fools on your side who are aiming to help you do just that.

Security
Opposite Wealth, however, is another *bête noire,* another gorgon from which to avert one's gaze: Security. This one seems on the face of it to be far less threatening or objectionable than the impulsive chase for Wealth, better known as Greed. How can we seriously advocate that a desire for safety be placed in the same Circle of Hell as one of medieval Christendom's Seven Deadly Sins?

Easy . . . we're now talking about the two biggest threats to your (or your family's) long-term investment survival. Chasing Wealth, you may run headlong into Madame la Guillotine. But chasing Security is no less deadly a pursuit, akin to inhaling carbon monoxide in sufficient quantity to bring about your eternal rest.

In our first-ever issue of our defunct printed publication, we printed this contrarian line to which we still very much subscribe: "The least-mentioned, biggest risk of all is not taking enough risk."

The investment community today is infatuated with "risk avoidance" (or "risk aversion"). The primary aim of investing, the Wise tell us, is Safety—holding onto your precious dollars. Whatever happens, you *don't* want to lose what you've already earned through the sweat of your labors. Now, a perfect Fool might point out that you are *constantly* losing what you've earned, since even the low inflation of the present day is continuously eroding the value of cash. In fact, Treasury bills (the *Safest* investment of all) held from 1926 to 1989 *increased the real value of your investment less than 7 percent,* according to a study by Ibbotson Associates. In 64 years! Now, of course, with Treasury bills you were ostensibly up every year, and indeed some years you thanked your lucky stars that you avoided going down 20 percent in stocks. But here you are at the end of your investment lifetime tearing out whatever's left of your hair over the Grand Mistake you've made, all to appease the local deity Safety (who for all those years had such an alluring smile—flossed regularly).

The possibility that one might actually make good money sometimes does not seem to enter Wall Street's thinking—among the more respectable element, anyway. And to be sure, most business schools today teach the Efficient Markets Theory, which, when you boil it right down, says that no one can consistently outperform the market over time. (Note: Please keep your eyes closed and pay no attention to those who are outperforming the market. And don't bother telling the profs, either . . . they're probably in league with the mediocre fund managers.)

The cynic may step right in and suggest that many investment "pros" never *will* consistently or impressively beat the market, due to various handicaps that include the requirement to diversify large portfolios, timidity, a lack of imagination, the inability to short the market, and graduate study at business school. Given this, why NOT make the *sine qua non* Safety? Like the wastebasket by your desk, it's an easy target. And it seems to keep the customers happy . . . those who don't know what they're doing, anyway.

Speaking of which, we have heard money managers musingly opine, "You know, if the market goes up 25 percent one year, and I go up 15 percent for my clients, no complaints. If the market goes up 5 percent one year and I go *down* 5 percent, I get all sorts of calls." This is quite true to the experience of many money managers, and is a perfect example of our illustration. In both situations, of course, the money manager has underperformed the market averages by 10 percentage points . . . which, to Fools, is the most relevant year-to-year consideration. But in one situation the manager is humored (possibly even complimented), while in the other he's berated.

So, if *you* were an investment professional in this environment, wouldn't you (further evidence) make the *sine qua non* Safety? The pieces of this puzzle interlock quite snugly.

Now, since we advise whole-hog investing in the stock market, we do need to propound two things about playing it safe Foolishly. First is, invest money that you can afford to wait on. The stock market is risky. We like that very much; it helps us make money, because you almost *never* get something for nothing. But over a given period of time, your stocks could get mashed. Just over 65 years ago, thousands of people lost most of what they had by investing in the market. So if you get melted down on Meltdown Day, we want you still to have something left to slap back down on the table. Invest money that you plan on keeping in the market for at least 5 years. (We recommend a lifetime.)

Second, we invest in good companies. We generally avoid buying stock in companies that are losing money, companies that are cash-flow negative (we'll explain this later), companies with just one product, companies featuring a less-than-respectable-looking management, and a bunch of other yardsticks offered later in the book.

And that's about it. Beyond the two points about Security just covered, we advise staring down your nose at this slovenly creature, or the financial adviser who reflexively strikes the low-risk Safety gong. Yuck. With low risk come low returns . . . the numbers shown above regarding Treasury funds are not much better for low-risk mutual funds; their performance as a group is abysmal. The whole point of buying this book is to educate yourself profitably. We expect that even at this early point, you've already graduated beyond most of the rest of the world; most of the rest of the world is going with its instincts, and blaming someone else when it fails.

Now, before we close the curtain on Folly's chapter, we need to stick in a word about people who require income and high degrees of safety. These are typically older people. Just as chasing Wealth attracts the young in huge numbers, chasing Security can be a fervent hobby among the advanced. We've heard before from readers of our service, "Hey, the Fool investment approach may work for younger people who can take some risk. But I'm seventy-six years old. What about somebody in my situation?"

Well, we certainly advocate first of all that you get to know your own situation very well and act accordingly. If you don't feel competent to analyze your own situation, hire a financial planner to help. If your money is tied up in an annuity and you expect to need its every interest payment over the 5 additional years you expect to live, you should let that money stay put. On the other hand, if your situation is one that requires some income but allows you to contemplate risk in search of greater investment rewards, we think you're crazy to be just sitting in high-interest-bearing securities. These securities—whether bonds or mutual funds or preferred stock or real-estate investment trusts or what have you—*all* underperform the market historically. So if you're looking out beyond 5 years—but with income needs—you're probably going to do much better by staying invested Foolishly (in good stocks) and annually *selling off* a portion of your nest egg to meet your income requirements . . . better than any other single investment approach.

Just to make that clear: If you have a $50,000 annuity paying you a flat annual interest of $3,000 (a 6 percent interest rate), consider that you could instead have that money invested in the stock market (historic average return is about 10 percent) earning on average (therefore) $5,000 a year. Assuming an average year, you can sell $3,000 to provide you your income and still wind up with $2,000 to spare, available for reinvestment to produce an account value of $52,000 to begin the next year. Sure, some years your stocks will lose money and you'll have to take that $3,000 straight out of capital. But except under the worst market periods in history, which occur very rarely (and from which we will all *always* eventually recover), you'll end up well ahead even despite the occasional horrible 2- or 3-year run. Because some years will be wonderful.

This is the thinking that has us talking down Security and suggesting that people consider keeping their money in the market for their own good, even—perhaps, especially—when keeping their money in the market runs against their native instincts. As has been pointed out by many, the market is the best game going because it pays good stakes and the odds are stacked in your favor. Fear sometimes causes people to lose sight of equity investing's superiority, always (it seems) at the wrong time . . . when the market has just hit bottom. Don't let human nature sway you. Consciously taking on smart risk remains the best way to succeed in investing . . . and in Life too, we believe.

◆ ◆ ◆

In summarizing our Folly chapter, we hope we have demonstrated that conventional wisdom—what we call capital W Wisdom—provides society with stale half-truths that encourage us to follow our instincts. Folly, an ever-radical force for reformation and enlightenment (and a heck of a lot of fun, too), attacks Wisdom by providing its adherents contrary truths that enable us to resist our own base instincts. We've addressed the complementary bugaboos of Wealth and Safety, one which tempts us to take too much risk, the other to take too little. We've explained who we are and told you what we believe. Now, let us show you why you should join us online if you haven't already.

❄3❄

Get Online!

· · · · ·

Computing is not about computers anymore.
It is about living.
—*Nicholas Negroponte*

One of the more radical developments over the past decade, which has only just hit a head of steam in the past 2 years, is the creation of a new medium: "cyberspace," some call it, or to others just "online." New media do not come along every decade; this particular arrival is the biggest thing since TV showed up at the 1939 World's Fair. The online world has heretofore been the primary means by which we have spread our Folly; it also happens to be the single greatest tool for the individual investor today. This chapter is written mainly for the 90 percent of U.S. households that have not yet hooked into the new online medium. If you're already an experienced "Internaut" (an active explorer of the world's information archive, primarily the Internet), you can just skim this section for jokes.

The Communication—Not Information—Age

A neat thing happened a few years ago, and not many people noticed. To this day, many still have not noticed. The neat thing has to do with computers.

Most computer users had originally purchased their machines with the intention of accomplishing certain tasks constituting their daily work assignment. The bread and butter of these computers were standard "applications" (or tools) like word processing, spreadsheet and database analysis, and point-of-sale merchandise management. These applications were mainly designed to help a single user working by himself to get his work done. And not much else.

The "neat thing" that happened a few years ago is that people started using computers not as super-brain machines enabling them to plan or run their business but rather as *communications* devices. People actually started hooking their machines together in order to gab!

Over the past few years, the population and its gab have increased exponentially, due both to an increased awareness of the benefits of cyberspace and an ongoing improvement in the technology. What was once displayed on monochromatic low-resolution screens at 300 baud (300 bits per second) now appears as high-resolution video transmitted at speeds of 28,800 baud and up. More striking than the technological improvements, however, are the ongoing diversification and general improvement of the content available. To a certain extent the online revolution has begun to stratify our society, elevating those who recognize the benefits of gabbing online over those who do not.

Gabbing can sometimes be just gabbing . . . weightless gibberish of no particular relevance or lasting significance exchanged between two or more parties. We will continue to see this as long as there are two people in the world with computers, a phone line between them, and time on their hands. But anyone who thinks that preteen kids shouting at each other in cyberspace "chat rooms" represents the sum total of online communication possibilities has been duped. Gabbing can be worth a lot more than that.

Gabbing, for starters, can be fun. As just pure fun, and when done right, good gab can be reason enough to sign online. Hook up your computer and you can find somebody somewhere to talk about anything you want, from alpha particles to zoo jokes, 24 hours a day, 365 days a year. Your circle of friends will expand to all fifty states and around the world.

But gabbing can also foster and cement social ties of personal or business benefit, as we discovered when we set about building a volunteer staff to support our online service. Within four months, we had hired over fifty talented people from all across America to execute various responsibilities on a daily basis (writing, editing, managing, etc.). These people remain the life's blood of our service, enabling us to accomplish more than we ever possibly could have as two sleep-deprived brothers trapped in a small room with a large computer. Most of them we have never even talked to on the phone, let alone met face-to-face. Though we may not be familiar with all their faces, or even (often) their full names, we are amply aware of their competence. In this brave new world (positive Shakespearean connotation intended), they are our employees, and we've built a wonderful business with their help.

The possibilities of good gab are not limited to online publishing companies, of course. Classified ads posted by individuals to the Internet are among its most popular offerings . . . and they're free. And in niches across the online world—some hidden, others out in the open—professionals consult on a daily basis about issues and topics related to their fields. They "network" in the truest sense of the word.

If you've never been online, imagine reading a magazine where instead of just reading articles, you're able to talk with other readers of the magazine at the same time. Imagine the new opportunities for understanding, discussion, and friendship that could create. One-way publishing and broadcasting is yielding to two-way interactivity, and the world will never be the same.

The most exciting, most dynamic, most mass-market-driven use for computers today is communication. The majority of people, whom we'll continue to refer to as the Wise, still don't recognize this . . . to their detriment.

Benefits to Investors

Perhaps the first true benefit of being online that we ever encountered was the ability to type in our own trades in our own brokerage account. Discount brokerage houses like Charles Schwab championed this drive to introduce hands-on tools for the individual investor. Even better, in most cases discount brokers grant a discount off the normal commission rate for placing such trades. Suddenly, the power for initiating trade executions was in our hands, and our broker was "paying" us to do it. How novel! Our interest in the online world had begun.

Supplementing online trading was real-time investment information, including stock quotes and company news. A number of services now provide this information, at varying rates and of varying quality. (Some of it is so well presented that even those who have zero experience with computers can begin understanding and using it within minutes, so long as they have their minds set on learning.) Over the last year, we've spent most of our online working hours on America Online, where we grab fifteen-minute-delayed stock quotes and instantly available company press releases. As publishers, we have also developed our own quick little summary of the stock market's daily trading action (biggest movers, etc.) which we post within two hours of market close. Our Daily News brings the most important and interesting financial information to readers well before their morning paper ever arrives . . . if they even still subscribe to one. We're using the power of real-time information and the power of disseminating that information on a national basis at the mere click of a button.

Another great thing about the data available online is that good services update their research data (earnings estimates, fundamental financial statistics, etc.) every day, putting it right at your fingertips. The result is a net gain for individual investors: more data, coming faster, better organized for retrieval, and costing progressively less over time. An excellent example is afforded us in the evolution of the encyclopedia.

Starting out as huge shelf-long multivolume sets, encyclopedias generated good business for decades because repeat customers came back every 5 or 10 years to buy updated versions, while libraries generally purchased the most up-to-date. But the additional expense of buying supplements, or (God forbid) a whole additional twenty-three-volume set, put many people off. With the recent development of CD-ROM, encyclopedia publishers have now managed to put their entire opus on a single CD-ROM *and* improve the offering by incorporating animation and sound. Additionally, you can search these compact-disk encyclopedias by a word or words, effectively creating the ultimate index: one that contains everything in the work itself. But even CD-ROMs have to be updated and repurchased from time to time. And even the storage capacity of a CD hampers publishers looking to integrate more memory-eating video into their offerings. So enter the online world. Now publishers can update their encyclopedias on a *daily* basis without costing customers any extra expense or inconvenience. And publishers can house truly massive amounts of data on big computer servers that exceed a single CD-ROM's storage as much as the population of China exceeds that of the block on which you live.

The same is happening, and will continue to happen, with financial information. The most up-to-date info no longer appears in your printed monthly, and you'll be hard-pressed to call it up on your TV right now . . . supposing you should ever want to do such a thing. Nope. It's all going online.

But in the end, what really makes for the most compelling reason for investors to explore cyberspace is the opportunity to learn in ways more efficient and entertaining than ever before. Our experience has demonstrated that "group education" succeeds wildly online (so long as you pick a good group). In recent years, American educators have tried to bring students together to learn cooperatively in teams, attempting to get away from the more individualistic learning dynamic that prevailed earlier in the century. They need only turn to cyberspace to see it actually working on a grand scale (see the Foreword on Iomega), among people who in many cases will never even meet each other.

Again, here's how it works, roughly. As an investor interested in stocks or funds, by tapping into something like The Motley Fool Online you can, with the help of your fellow investors, stay as current on your own holdings as you desire—daily, weekly, or every hour on the hour. Let's say you own some stock in Apple Computer. You can sign online and locate a "message board" expressly dedicated to Apple stock. This is a public discussion, often followed by hundreds or thousands of readers, completely based upon these readers voluntarily providing the latest on the company's news and products, news on its competitors that may affect Apple, investment tips about good entry and exit points on the stock, general investment advice, and maybe a decent Silicon Valley joke or two thrown in. Whether you live in Georgia, Minnesota, or Hawaii, you'll be crossing paths with people who actually happen to work for Apple, fund managers, industry insiders, brokers, and a swarm of fellow individual investors (some of whom are extremely savvy). You'll find that when the printed financial dailies report news on Apple, your message-board correspondents will probably already have posted it. They may even have been anticipating it for weeks. And it's all brought about by a group of strangers. They are investors—bulls and bears—who become a sort of community unto themselves, with distinct personalities, shared interests, and a common history based on the news developments and price fluctuations of Apple and its stock.

In fact, the opportunity to stay informed about your investments, while at the same time learning more and more about investing in general, so far surpasses anything previously available that it's not unlike comparing our current picture of the universe with those days when everyone was sure that the sun circled the earth. Typifying the sort of messages that come in to Fool HQ every week, one of our readers wrote: "I have a hard time just trying to keep my usage from going over two hours a day. I am not complaining too much, though, since I have seen a 25 percent rise in both my investment account and IRA account [over the past 5 months], versus a *decline* in the previous 12 months. And it's no accident either. The free flow of data, news, ideas, opinions, and even rumors helps me make my investment decisions."

We've seen this process repeat itself over and over with thousands of people, and truth be told, the same thing has happened to us.

Once online, we doubt you'll ever turn back.

The Comeback of the Word

To digress for a moment: One of the beauties of the online world is actually its widespread use of text. The medium in its present incarnation is helping to restore the power of the written word. In fact, those who are reaching the most prominence in the new medium are, at heart, writers. But so is everyone else online. People communicate online today by typing back and forth to each other . . . it's a constant *pas de deux* of reading and writing.

Like many media mavens and education experts, we believe that while a picture may be worth a thousand words, the right thousand words can change the world. You want that in technical terms? Text-based learning works better than image-based learning. Our online materials—the stuff that can help you make money—it's words, sentences and paragraphs, not pictures, not videos. And we're *not* sorry, because we think that words work better.

Television has presumed to "inform" us through the exclusive use of sound and images, at the expense of written words. This just won't work. Imagine if art historians seriously claimed that we could learn a tremendous amount about Renaissance Italy by gazing at the *Mona Lisa;* we may learn a lot about art there, but not much history. We may, likewise, learn a lot about television itself when watching it, but we collectively come away without understanding what the fuss is really all about.

Fortunately for the next generation—the one that hasn't even hit first grade yet—a new educational force is at work, and it has the potential to dominate. It combines the surefire efficacy of traditional book learning with the dynamism and attraction of video and animation. It's called online. And it's getting better every day.

What the Online World *Doesn't* Do Too Well

After that rousing exhortatory speech, we feel it incumbent upon our Foolish selves to point out something that computers and the online world do *not* do well. The online world has still not come up with a pleasing way to present a book-length work. That's why we're publishing this in traditional book format. You still can't beat it. In fact, we have yet to meet a single person who derives gratification from rocking back in a lounge chair and reading his laptop computer a few hours at a time. And it's certainly not comfy to do at the beach (or even possible, given laptops' dim screens) . . . and, hey, if you can't read it at the beach, it ain't for readin'. In his fine book *Being Digital* (1995), Nicholas Negroponte speculates that designing a computer that looks, feels, even *smells* exactly like a book is just a matter of time. "Multimedia will become more book-like, something with which you can curl up in bed and either have a conversation or be told a story. Multimedia will someday be as subtle and rich as the feel of paper and the smell of leather." We shall see.

Now that you know where to go and how to get there, let's begin at the beginning and talk a little about (gasp!) mutual funds.

PART II

MUTUAL FUNDS: LOVE 'EM OR LEAVE 'EM?

·4·

Hey, Maybe You *Should* Just Buy Mutual Funds

• • • • •

Life is constantly providing us with new funds.
—*Henry Miller*

As we race headlong into the twenty-first century, mutual funds—the showpiece of the hour—are growing at a phenomenal rate. In 1980 over $145 billion were invested in mutual funds. Today, with over $2.5 trillion invested, U.S. income, equity, and bond fund assets have grown at an annual rate of 24 percent, twice the industrial growth rate per year over the same period. And more than 60 percent of those dollars were delivered unto them in the last 3 years. Unbelievable!

The personal savings rate, which has climbed 6 percent annually since the 1950s, sits now at a level never equaled in American history. Young people are conquering the technology of today, pausing to teach their elders and stashing away monthly installments into mutual funds. When youth saves, a country's prospects brighten.

But why do Americans choose mutual funds? Why aren't they falling for the latest round of penny-ante pyramid schemes: wireless cable start-ups, futures contracts, ostrich farms, Vancouver Exchange stocks? Why? Because mutual funds are safe, understandable, trackable, and well marketed. The larger fund families—the Fidelitys, Vanguards, Templetons, and Bergers—provide far more consistent returns than that which is being shark peddled out there to the Orange Counties of America. And funds can be held accountable. They can be monitored daily, weekly, monthly, and annually against the market's average performance. You'd have to be very foolish not to recognize the comfort in lumping one's money together with thousands of other investors, passing it to select managers whose performance can be measured, and going on with daily life.

Contentedness and confidence in the long-term profitability of your savings—those are the cornerstones to investing Foolishly. And mutual funds, which sprung up in an industry that had previously been doing a poor job of providing reassurance, have filled the void. There are really three overriding reasons that the mutual fund has blossomed into a multitrillion-dollar industry today. Let's spend the rest of this chapter learning them.

Why Buy Funds? The Broker Made Me Do It

Many investors just plunge their savings into mutual funds in order to avoid one of the financial world's less pleasant relationships, that between the full-service broker and the individual investor. Invest your money in a mutual fund with clearly defined costs and you need fret no more over fair commission rates, or whether your broker is overactively trading your account, or how your portfolio is stacking up against the competition. Full-service brokering of stocks is responsible for all of these ambiguities, possibly designed to bewilder individuals into accepting "standard" fee scales.

Any Fool, however much bewildered, knows that most brokers are rewarded for activity, not productivity—how often they trade, not how well. It's a bit like motivating an employee to *do* things rather than to *get them done*. It's a preposterous model and the chief reason that Americans will continue to move money away from investment firms into no-load mutual funds in the coming years.

No-load mutual funds are those that can be bought directly from fund companies for no additional commission, or "load." No-loads contrast with loaded funds, which brokers are paid a commission for selling. Because there is no difference in overall performance between the two, the future obviously lies with no-loads; most people would rather avoid situations like the one described below.

Consider this scenario: A broker calls you during dinner for the fifth time this month, pushing Huge Fruit Inc. (OTC:HUGE), a little-known California outfit involved in "agribusiness biotechnology." HUGE is trading around $3¼ and the cold-calling broker is cocksure that the company's LemonLarger engineering project is going to be a smash success. "Got any idea how many gallons of lemonade can be squeezed out of a fifteen-pound citrus?"

You don't, but you figure it's an awful lot.

You've been mulling over this recommendation for weeks now, and you're about ready to take the plunge. A stock that's selling at $3.25 a stub seems appetizing; you'll be able to gobble up more shares. And if in the coming years neighborhoods across the nation are to be serviced by giant-fruit stands, God only knows how much money you'll make. Meanwhile, the broker keeps pushing proofs over the phone to you: "Hey, once they've successfully engineered the oversized pineapple, for example, a multibillion-dollar fruiting operation like Dole either crumbles internally or buys Huge Fruit out at a premium. That's what technology is: cannibalization. Companies like Huge Fruit swallow their slower-moving competitors going forward. Thirty bucks a share isn't out of reach in the next 18 months, and that's just the beginning. But you've got to get in early to profit."

A $30 stock, did he say?! At $3.25 per share today, 1,000 shares would cost you $3,250. You multiply 1,000 shares times the projected price of $30. Wow! $30,000 for a gain of $26,750. That's over eight times your original investment—not bad for a fool. And it'll be damned fun cheering for a man-sized grape.

What you may not have realized in between your hesitation and the word "Buy!" is that you'll pay the broker exactly the same amount of money whether Huge Fruit Inc. goes to $30 per share or goes under, taking your $3,250 investment down with it. Anyone who's watched $3 biotechnology stocks come down the pike and get truck-squashed knows the amount of risk you're shouldering with Huge Fruit. But your broker isn't taking on *any* risk. In fact, because commission scales can be variable, the excitement that he's generated over HUGE may well have opened the door to charge you a bit more for his efforts. If he's shrewd enough to have sold you on a company whose financial statements you've never seen, whose business you're not familiar with, then he's got to be shrewd enough to see that he can ratchet up his fees on you.

One Fool we know claims it wasn't until he dug diligently through the morass of poorly fashioned monthly brokerage statements that he realized he was paying his broker $400 per trade while for years dramatically underperforming the market's average annual performance. He wrote us: "I didn't have any idea then that I should be setting expectations, and comparing them to the S&P 500's performance. I had no clue whether 5 percent per year, 10 percent, 20 percent per year was reasonable, nor what I should pay a broker in commissions to garner those returns. But now, Fools, *now* I know!"

Most fully served individual investors neither have any idea, nor ought they to, whether commissions on a trade like that in Huge Fruit, Inc. should sit at $50, $150, $450 . . . or $0—the preference of a Fool who doesn't trade nickel-and-dime stocks! As with all hard selling, the fair price is whatever a customer is willing to pay. Not surprisingly, some brokers make small fortunes persuading customers that those two-bit fruit enlargers, diamond miners, and international oil drillers are going to swallow up the market giants tomorrow. After all, if the stock's going to rocket up ten times in the next year, what's the big deal if you overpay 100 bucks on the launching pad?

What has most damaged the reputation of the full-service brokering industry is that incentives are tied only to a broker's deftness in getting you to buy and sell stock. Payment has *nothing* to do with the thoroughness of his research, the soundness of his logic, nor most importantly, his performance. This isn't to say that there aren't thousands of terrific brokers who do a stand-up job of outperforming year after year while teaching their clients how to understand stocks. The problem lies in a system that protects the countless many who neither outperform the market nor have any vested interest in doing so.

Fools may be forgiven for wondering whether the full-service brokering of stocks in its present form—absent performance incentives—will outlast even the VCR-tape rental industry. It'll be fun to watch. The middlemen who survive will be those who broker information, expertise, and bottom-line accountability. And the majority of individual investors will continue to rush their savings into no-load mutual funds—investment vehicles that they can hold accountable. They won't stand for anything less.

Why Buy Funds? High-Volatility Heartache

Imagine yourself holding on tightly to those shares of Huge Fruit Inc. as it bounds between $5 and $2 every few months. When it trends up to $5, your $3,500 investment at $3¼ (you paid $250 in commissions, ouch) blips up to $5,000, and you can't keep quiet about your winning investment at cocktail parties. *"Yep, m'broker says it's going to $30,"* you trumpet from one corner of the soiree to the next. But then, when HUGE bends back below $2 and your investment contracts to less than $2,000, you can't tell whether it's your liver, kidney, small intestines, gallbladder, or all of them, but something's hurting. Stock volatility, relative to its ebb and flow, can transform modesty into pomposity and digestion into heartburn.

Mutual funds are often the tranquilizing alternative. By virtue of their diversification, they're perceived to be less volatile than the average equities portfolio of a private investor. It's calming to know that you sit alongside thousands of other investors owning minute positions in hundreds of companies. That's participating in America's robust corporate growth going forward and sharing the risk. If the weather gets worse, we'll all pop open umbrellas together! And you could only profitably duplicate that diversity using stocks if you had a couple hundred million dollars in the coffers. (Hey, if you do, put this book down.) Essentially what a Fool notes here is that the larger mutual funds, by virtue of their reach and dimension, *are* the market. And since most investors are content to just shadow the market indices, these funds serve their purpose.

What exactly is a market index? you ask. The Dow Jones industrial average and the Standard & Poor's 500 index (also known as the S&P 500) are the two primary indices against which investors compare their investment returns. The Dow is a compilation of thirty huge American companies: Coca-Cola, Disney, McDonald's, Eastman Kodak, Sears, Exxon, to name a few. The S&P 500 tracks five hundred industrial, transportation, financial, and utility stocks (e.g., semiconductor, trucking, insurance, and heating companies), weighting companies to account for their relative size. AT&T, Apple, Chrysler, Intel, Marriott, Pepsi, and Nike are among the more familiar issues in the S&P group, some of which are also Dow stocks.

Regardless of their compositional differences, the S&P 500 and the Dow have pretty much walked in step since 1930; each has compounded average annualized growth of 10.5 percent per year. At that average rate, $10,000 invested in 1930 is now worth over $3 million, *after* taxes. It turns out you didn't have to be a railroad baron to prepare for the future of your great-grandchildren, eh?

In that spirit, the Foolish approach to investing rests firmly on the belief that your portfolio ought never to keep you up at night. Were the market to collapse, dipping 30 percent in 6 months and pulling your holdings underground, you shouldn't lose a minute of sleep over it. To illustrate our point, let's consider the best recent example of a market meltdown. Over 21 cruel months from early 1973 to mid-1974, the S&P 500 fell from 119.6 to 63.38. That's a 47 percent devaluation! The market was cut in half. *Biff, bam, POW!*

Look at your own investment portfolio today and ask yourself what would happen to your life if, over the next 2 years, *your* savings got cut in half. How much do you have? $800? It's now $400. $25,000? You're down to $12,500. $3.6 million? Nope, $1.8 million. Could you bear it enough to hold tight even while money managers were throwing themselves in front of bicycles, jumping off one-story buildings, and chomping down Flintstones chewable vitamins hand over fist?

If you couldn't, either your money isn't invested logically, or you shouldn't be holding your savings in the stock market. Because if you sell at the market's darkest hour in decades, when what was once whole is now grimly half, you're going to lose a little fortune. Composed investors held on tight through the early 1970s, and today, when you look at the market's growth from 1973 to 1995 (including that 47 percent gutting between '73 and '74), you still find 10.5 percent annual growth, the same average growth that the market has seen over the past 60 years . . . the same vehicle that turned $10,000 just sitting there into $3 million. If the S&P 500 isn't up at least 10 percent compounded annually from today's perch, take the Fools by the arm 40 years from now on Spacestation *Harold* and demand from us a free Tang spritzer.

By buying into the bigger families of funds, you essentially guarantee that you'll be able to participate in America's robust corporate growth in the decades ahead—the growth in companies like Williams-Sonoma, Dell Computer, Microsoft, The Gap, Broderbund Software, and yes, Viacom, beloved owner of this text. And you'll be able to sleep late and peacefully on Sunday morning. The household-name mutual funds virtually guarantee you long-term portfolio stability, low volatility, limited risk, and unscathed stomach lining.

And that's the second reason mutual funds are so popular.

Why Buy Mutual Funds? So Little Time . . .

You didn't see it? You didn't catch the news? You're not tuned into the stock market twenty-four hours a day? You have a fully developed life beyond the financial markets?! Well, then you missed the Huge Fruit Inc. news story that crossed the wires earlier this afternoon.

> RIVERSIDE, CAL.—(THE DAILY NEWS WIRE)—Jan. 8, 1996—Huge Fruit Inc. (OTC:HUGE) announced that the Food and Drug Administration (FDA), at a meeting yesterday afternoon to consider the LemonLarger® application, recommended rejection of the company's EnGene technology™ used in the genetic engineering of enlarged fruits and vegetables. After further review of additional materials provided by the company, the FDA cited widespread spinal dissolution in laboratory rats exposed to Huge Fruit's altered lemons. In heavy, late-afternoon activity, Huge Fruit Inc. is trading at $11/16, down $2¼, or 76 percent on the day.

One thing you probably didn't realize when you threw some "play money" into Huge Fruit Inc. is that unfamiliar ventures pushed on you by a broker over the telephone demand *more* research time on your part, *not less.* Imagining a glass of lemonade in every hand at Yankee Stadium, all pressed from a single immense lemon, is entertaining; unfortunately, it doesn't count as research in The Fool's School.

You wonder: *What possibly could have helped me dodge this lemon? Risk comes with the territory, no? What could I have done?* Those are fair questions. While the swift and sharp decline in the value of HUGE shares might not have seemed inevitable initially, more research may have made it so. Did Huge Fruit Inc. have other genetic engineering plans brewing in the backhouse? Were alternative streams of revenue being developed? Did the company have a load of cash on the balance sheet and negligible long-term debt?

Given the market's reaction to the announcement—the 76 percent loss of value in a single afternoon—the answer to all of the above questions was probably "Nope." That's a real shame, too. Those are issues that your broker should've addressed in detail over the phone. It would've taken you or him less than an hour of work to uncover. A Fool knows, though, that what often gets lost in dealings with salesmen *is* the research.

Assuming that you don't have the time outside of your work and family life to scrutinize dozens of stocks, mutual funds have to look pretty darned enticing. When you join throngs of individual investors who've turned their money over to "professional" management, you've freed up time, eluded the bogeyman, and absolved yourself of the responsibility to research the stock market. A sigh of great relief is in order here. Sigh, Fool, *sigh*.

On a recent train trip to New York, we overheard a retired father confess to his middle-aged son, "I don't know how my funds are doing, but I know they're up, and the money's safe. Somebody told me one of them is up 14 percent, but does that mean for the last year, or since January first, or for the year to come? I don't know. But the money's safe."

Never underestimate the beauty of delegating the management of your assets to a trained professional at a reasonable price. The right mutual funds bring security, profitability, and independence. By passing on the responsibility of money management to the "pros," you can get back to your own business, or your walking tour across Montana, or your child's Little League games.

When you put all that in the context of those Orange County and Barings disasters, with "traders" forfeiting some or much of what they had—and of what others had invested in them—via currency fandangles, option bloopers, and the latest beast, the derivative, you no doubt understand why individuals are casually plunging their money into pooled, sleepy investment vehicles without checking back on them but once or twice a year. After all, there's nothing wrong with moderate annual portfolio growth on top of moderate annual salary growth. It beats the hell out of Huge Fruit.

◆　◆　◆

To date, the best alternative to sitting through brokerage cold calls during dinner and spending weekends digging into financial statements, and suffering $3 stocks that turn nest eggs into eggshells . . . to date, the best alternative is the mutual fund. Large, popular mutual fund families have historical returns that are clear, risk levels that are estimable, and future returns that can be tracked every day against the S&P 500's performance. Going forward, counting in decades, you can bet that by buying a few of the popular equity funds, you're going to outperform virtually every other non-stock investment vehicle, and the $10,000 of today most likely will be $4.5 million in the savings account of your great-grandchild.

But if you're still going to invest through a friendly full-service broker, be certain that you're at least getting the same treatment as mutual funds afford. Are you on the receiving end of:

- historical returns that are clearly reported?
- risk levels that are estimable?
- future returns that can be tracked against the S&P 500?
- a portfolio that is guaranteed to do no worse than mirror the market's average annual returns?

If your load of savings isn't at least mimicking the S&P 500's performance (after the deduction of all costs), you've blundered as an investor. And it is on that note that we move forward into chapter 5 and what must seem like unlikely advice, given our above treatment of mutual funds.

Maybe You Should
Avoid Mutual Funds

* * * * *

Probably the only place where a man can feel
really secure is in a maximum security prison,
except for the imminent threat of release.
—*Germaine Greer*

Why Avoid Funds? Market
Underperformance

It's the most damning statistic in the world of finance: over 75 per-cent of all mutual funds underperform the market's average return each year. The tags "professional investor" and "institutional investor" have become forever associated with the word *submediocrity* in the minds of Fools. Look at the results of some research on the mutual fund industry carried out by lecturer Robert Sheard. A former instructor at Georgetown University in Kentucky, and now a full-time Fool, Sheard went digging through the Reuters Money Network's database to re-search the 5,845 funds that they've been tracking. A closer look at the numbers revealed the following:

1. Of the 5,845 funds, only 2,615 have a 3-year track record, and of those 2,615 funds, 80.5 percent of them lost to the S&P 500 re-turn of 7.86 percent annual growth.
2. Only 1,936 funds have been around for 5 years. Of those, 79.9 percent lost to the S&P 500 return of 10.78 percent annual growth.
3. Only 780 of the funds have a 10-year track record. Of those, 87.3 percent lost to the S&P 500 annual return of 13.82 percent.

Nearly 90 percent of all funds that have 10-year records underperform the market. Good God! Imagine that—all those oft-quoted "professionals" in wing-tipped shoes, with hundreds of millions or billions of dollars to invest, losing to the market average year after year, after year. It's like finding out that 75 percent of America's English professors would underperform their students on the Graduate Record Exams (GREs). Who's teaching whom here? Who's managing your money?

Given this data, you'll understand why Folly says that all investors in the country must track their annual results against those of the S&P 500. Simply stack the total dollar growth of your portfolio versus the gains in the S&P 500. At this writing, the S&P 500 listed in the financial pages of any newspaper, sits at a level of 580. If you were to begin investing today, you would track the percentage gains or losses off 580 versus your own bottom-line profits. It's absolutely imperative that you fit your own investment performance into this overall context. Guess what? If you haven't been tracking your investments, don't be surprised to find now that your broker-managed portfolio, or your collection of mutual funds, has done poorly relative to the indices. "Professional" investors collectively have been underperforming the market for decades. In fact, they were and are doing it so consistently that to expect better of them is like expecting anyone to knock out George Foreman on Fix TV—oops, we mean, Pay TV.

Say it aloud once more for good measure: Since the real emergence of mutual funds in the early 1970s, over 75 percent of them have underperformed the S&P 500. Consider then that every time you drop a dollar of your savings into the pond of mutual funds, there's a 3-in-4 chance your frog won't o'erleap the stock market's average growth per year. Damned discouraging frog.

Why Do Most Funds Underperform?

As odd as it may seem, some of the challenges money managers face are quite similar to those confronting individual investors, namely a lack of time and a willingness to accept humdrum, average returns. If you're of the mind that mildly below-average returns on your own investments are bearable, given how little time you have to dedicate to portfolio management, rest assured most mutual fund managers probably feel the same way. Fund management teams have *much* else to do besides picking winning stocks. There are accounting tangles, legal matters, advertising plans, corporate development challenges, and these guys are often out on the road peddling their wares; there's an entire business to run *outside* of finding great investments for their shareholders.

Factor in, too, the Securities and Exchange Commission's (SEC) requirement that no single holding in a mutual fund exceed 5 percent of the fund's total assets. A mutual fund manager, therefore, must diversify into at least twenty holdings. Twenty great investment ideas each year? That's about ten more than Warren Buffett believes anyone should be expected to come up within a lifetime.

Further consider that this accelerated growth in mutual funds over the last few years has driven many of them up into the billion-dollar-asset stratosphere. Managing billions of dollars requires greater diversity of holdings. After all, 5 percent of $10 billion is $500 million, enough to buy a basket of small-capitalization companies outright!!

Fund managers also broaden their portfolio base because they know better than to create the impression that their fund is underdiversified. A Fool notes that, in the celebrated circles of the Wise, prudence in investing *is* overdiversification. Spread your savings thin and you'll be safe. We may even be to the point today when were a middle-aged man, with no prior investing experience, to don suit and tie, produce and air on CNBC a thirty-second video of himself strolling around a cardboard set, reiterating, "We are Wise, cautious, prudent, and deliberate money managers," he could be investing a quarter of a billion dollars in less than a year. Just name it The Wisely Diversified Fund.

But the most wondrous and least pardonable form of overdiversification is the common redistribution of large amounts of shareholder money to the fund's management team and outside directors. Overcompensation for management is a laughable example of the laundering of shareholder dollars that goes unchecked. Remember, a $10 billion mutual fund with a standard 1 percent management fee (seems reasonable, doesn't it?) will take in $100 million. That's a lot of money to spread around. The distribution of it to a mutual fund's outside directors, those who by law are not allowed to be involved in the day-to-day management of the business, is just too unthinkable to let slide by here. Each year these people are getting paid hundreds of thousands of dollars to meet for a couple hours to provide vague expertise in long-term strategic planning and joke about protecting shareholder rights, while getting belly-rubbed in a massage parlor in Tahiti. It's absurd. There just can't be an easier six-figure salary in the United States.

Mind you, a Fool finds nothing improper with paying someone millions of dollars to manage a burgeoning conglomerate that outperforms its industry. Honest success need be rewarded. Does anyone think Michael Jordan is overpaid, given what he's done for Nike, Gatorade, the Chicago Bulls, the city of Chicago? There's nothing wrong with paying for performance. It's when fat cats peripheral to the business make loads of money while the operation underperforms the averages—precisely what is happening in the mutual fund business—it's only then that a Fool has to get up on his orange crate in the town square.

The final and most entertaining reason that 75 percent of all mutual funds perform sorrily stems from an unusual matter peculiar to the mutual fund industry called "window dressing." Window dressing is the quarter-end ritual during which mutual fund managers belatedly window-shop for the best and brightest stocks of the quarter. Why? To make their portfolio look impressive. In March 1995, when a stock like Cisco Systems (NASDAQ:CSCO) had risen 45 percent for the quarter, you can be sure that mutual funds were lining up to get a few shares of CSCO on their account statement. Why? To let their shareholders know that they were in on one of the hottest stocks of the quarter. That they took a position after the great run-up and perhaps made nothing on the transaction, or lost money, isn't what matters. What does? Appearance—image is everything. In other words, in this industry it can be as effective to look like you made money as it is actually to have done the deed. Until, that is, some Fool (it could be you) points out that the king (or the fund manager) has no clothes . . . and no profits either.

Why Avoid Funds? So Little Time . . .

When you consider how many publications dedicate themselves to the analysis and tracking of what are primarily lousy investments, you can understand why we have a tough time determining just what are the opportunity costs associated with mutual fund investing. What were the costs for medieval cartographers who spent their lives mapping out a flat Earth when the Greeks had shown the planet was spherical? Can a value be placed on pointlessness?

Look upon mutual funds in this light: Imagine yourself in a university physics exam. The professor passes around copies of the test, then stands in front of the class and announces, "You have two hours. Oh, incidentally, 75 percent of the information in your textbook for this semester was inaccurate. Good luck!"

The same can be said to the reader of any of the hundreds of publications dedicated to the—at last count—over eight thousand mutual funds: 75 percent of your reading is fluff. And no Fool should waste his time trying to determine which minority of it was fruitful. Let us say this again just to be sure you've got it: If you play a game—say the shell game—where 3 out of 4 of the choices is a losing proposition, then your chances of winning are 1 in 4 from the start. Your chances of losing are 3 in 4. Makes you want to find a new game, doesn't it? Well, friends, that's the point.

Strangely enough, you don't hear that sort of talk about the mutual fund industry very often. But then consider how much money is riding on the profitability of the mutual fund. Newspapers and magazines create advertising-ready pages by doling out mutual fund advice. Among the widely distributed financial magazines today, a single page of advertising is worth $25,000. The challenge to an editor, then, is to build up as much material as he can around which to advertise. Ahh, wonderful mutual fund industry, you've doubled the information available to the financial publications of America. No matter if the information is bad, misleading, overoptimistic, or more harmful than helpful: It pays $25,000 per ad page! "Thank you, mighty universe of mutual funds," say the financial retailers coming out of the woodwork to sell funds with front loads, back loads, inter loads, high expense ratios, 12b-1 fees, skylark fees, redemption fees, signature fees . . . who can keep track of all the related costs? These days salesmen have a hand in every one of your pockets when they sell you a fund, and you'd be a fool to assume that they've done any meaningful research on their recommendation. Incidentally, there's no such thing as an *inter load, skylark fee,* or *signature fee,* but how would most individuals know that?

A Fool must reiterate here that there's nothing wrong with paying for service, creating jobs that handsomely reward hard and profitable work . . . but what about paying handsomely for nothing, or worse, underperformance? With over eight thousand funds to research, with brokers selling them on commission, and with many funds sticking their customers with hidden costs, individual investors are really back where they started with Huge Fruit Inc. Namely, weary. They now have to research not simply the investment, but the myriad costs associated with it *and* the salesman who's cramming it down their collective throat. Absurd, really.

Why Avoid Funds? Ingredients, Please!

If Fools are to accept the credo, "Don't ever invest in something you don't fully understand," then 99 percent of all mutual funds should be crossed off the candidate list. Mutual fund prospecti feature a wonderfully rich language, Prospectish, that is indecipherable, uninformative, and legalistic. And the idea that you can ever get a serious grip on a fund through the fundamental analysis of its individual holdings is bunk. You'd be analyzing stocks right through till the next appearance of Halley's Comet.

Sad to say, sometimes even the most scholarly fund investors among us, those who willingly forego summer barbecues to huddle over investment tomes, get backhanded by fund managers who take extra risk on the sly, deviating from their proposed course. What!?! You didn't know that your mutual fund was dabbling in derivatives? You weren't aware that management was experimenting with some option trading this quarter? You didn't hear that Joe, the new intern at Strategic Diversified Wisdom Fund, decided to try his luck at some "currency swapping"?

Pity those well-read mutual fund investors who found out back in the first quarter of 1995 that, while the S&P 500 was racing to new highs, their large-cap, blue-chip, stodgy, old-money mutual fund collapsed because the fund deviated from its proposed course and plunged headlong into Mexican investments. Have sympathy on your neighbors who, after combing through dozens of mutual fund prospecti, settled on one that decided to—*aww*, what the hell—*go for it* in derivatives. The Fool can name names: Fidelity's Asset Manager Fund wins the bobo prize for being a *non*-emerging-market, conservative fund that got walloped for testing the Latin American waters in 1993. That's right, ladies, gents, and Fools, a *non*-emerging-market fund. Manager Bob Beckwitt increased his exposure to Mexico subsequent to the signing of NAFTA. By year's end the fund was 20 percent invested in Mexico (!)—half in bonds and the remainder in stocks and peso-denominated cash. An additional 5 percent of the fund was exposed to the Argentinian austral and similar Latin American currencies. A *non*-emerging-market fund.

Beckwitt's fund lost 6 percent for the year in 1994. His Asset Manager Growth Fund fared even worse, posting a year-end loss of 9 percent. A 6 percent loss, a 9 percent loss, that's not so terrible . . . right? During that year, the S&P 500 *rose* 7 percent and beat those funds by 13 percentage points and 16 percentage points, respectively. For investors Foolish enough to compare their holdings to the S&P 500, *that* hurt!

But if that looks bad, consider the Piper Jaffray Institutional Government Income Fund. Hands down, it won Bonehead Derivatives Move of the Year in 1994. The fund supposedly sought current income consistent with *"preservation of capital"* proposing to invest in U.S. Treasury bills, notes, and bonds *"guaranteed as to payment and interest by the U.S government . . ."* Sounds pretty conservative. But then, head manager of the fund, Worth Bruntjen, went ahead and bought an array of long-mortgage derivatives, including inverse floaters and principal-only (PO) securities. ("Definitions, please!" You don't need 'em.) Bruntjen also had the fund fully leveraged, keeping it 150 percent invested in 1994. Versus S&P 500 gains of 1.32 percent, the Piper Jaffray Institutional Government Income Fund lost a heartrending 28.5 percent. In a single year. At that rate, the fund would turn $1 million into less than $1,500 in 20 years. Now *that's* investing.

Therein lies a primary reason to avoid mutual funds. You can't see the *business* in which you're investing. And when you can't see what's going on with your money, it doesn't matter how wise or Foolish you are, you can't evaluate a fund's holdings or its strategy. You can only pay your money and take your chances.

And what tool for fairly valuing mutual funds has replaced the good old homegrown fundamental analyses that turned enormous profits in stocks for the great investors of the past? Price studies. The most popular and least meaningful technique used to value mutual funds today is an eyeballing of their 1-, 3-, and 5-year records. Compare it to a baseball game, a Boston Red Sox–Minnesota Twins game. Disregard whether the game is being played at Fenway Park or in the Metrodome, who's pitching, whether any players are injured; in fact, disregard altogether who's on the teams. Now pull out your Elias Sports Bureau manual and find out how many games each team has won over the past 5 years. Whichever team has won more, price studies suggest, should win the game. It's ludicrous.

Oh, but before putting money down on that analysis, *do* check to see if the Sox pitching staff is into inverse-floating derivatives.

Running Historical Numbers

Let's look at some of the numbers together to paint a prettier picture of what happens to our dollars when we hold them in the light of compounded returns. We'll work off a base of $10,000, showing pretax profits:

Year/Vehicle	Growth Rate	$10,000 Becomes . . .
I. 20-Year Period		
Huge Fruit Inc.:	−95.6%	<$0
Piper Jaffray Fund:	−28.9%	$11
Treasury Bills:	3%	$18,061
Bonds:	5%	$26,533
Average Mutual Fund:	7%	$38,697
The S&P 500:	10.5%	$73,662
II. 40-Year Period		
Piper Jaffray Fund:	−28.9%	$0
Treasury Bills:	3%	$32,620
Bonds:	5%	$70,400
Average Mutual Fund:	7%	$149,745
The S&P 500:	10.5%	$542,614
III. 60-Year Period		
Treasury Bills:	3%	$58,916
Bonds:	5%	$186,792
Mutual Funds:	7%	$579,464
The S&P 500:	10.5%	$3,997,023

That's the sort of chart that should be stamped on the inside of every investment text published; it oughta be drilled into the minds of business school students and memorized alongside Frost poems in grade school: $10,000 in Treasury bills for 60 years is worth half as much as $10,000 in mutual funds for 40 years.

But most astonishing of all is the 60-year performance of the S&P 500 versus your average mutual fund. The former blossoms into nearly $4 million, while the latter fails to reach $600,000. Pretty damning evidence for an industry that spends billions of dollars each year selling itself to individual investors.

Fools don't wile away many hours wondering whether Wall Street is right when it tells us that we ought have our money broadly diversified in mutual funds, bonds, gold, and T-bills. Fools already know that all of these have underperformed the S&P 500 year after year after year. Sixty years of history is pretty damning evidence for bonds, gold, and T-bills, and the last 20 years have convinced us that mutual funds are an investment opportunity that isn't one.

We close this chapter by calling on all mutual fund managers to waive management fees every year that they underperform the S&P

500 by more than, say, one percentage point . . . that they underperform the S&P 500 . . . the S&P 500 . . . 500 . . . 500 . . . Echo . . . echo . . . echo.

We didn't think they would listen!

But in the next chapter, we'll prove that being average is really quite simple.

The Vanguard Index
Trust 500 Portfolio

• • • • •

Averageness is a quality we must put up with.
Men march toward civilization in column formation,
and by the time the van has learned to admire the masters
the rear is drawing reluctantly away
from the totem pole.
—Frank Moore Colby

Imagine a single mutual fund whose eminently trackable performance virtually matches market-average growth year after year,
whose holdings are clearly outlined for you in advance, and which demands virtually no research. Imagine no more. Your dream is real and
available in Vanguard's Index Trust 500 Portfolio. This *many*-billion-
dollar fund simply duplicates the holdings of the Standard & Poor's
Index by buying all five hundred stocks, and is thus able to match (and
compound) the index's growth year after year.

When you consider that mutual funds have consistently underperformed the stock market, Vanguard's S&P 500 index fund really starts
looking attractive. It demands no research and outperforms the majority of funds on the market. For this and the reasons outlined below, we
don't really think there's any other fund out there worth buying.

No Salesmanship

Remember that friendly broker a couple months back who kept calling
when you were giving the kids a bath, or working out in the yard, or
just sitting down to dinner? You know, the one with that biotechnology

stock that was going to radically alter the way we live? Yes, you know, the one who kept calling and calling and calling, getting increasingly impatient as he touted Huge Fruit Inc., the couple-dollar stock from the company with only the best of intentions. Remember the hassle? Remember that you lost half your investment? Well, we certainly hope not, since we hope that you've never had any such experience.

Those hazards and hassles don't happen with the Vanguard Index fund. This operation goes a long way toward wiping out the broker and mutual fund world's shoddier practices. With no hard selling, no hidden fees, and no confusing monthly statements, the fund truly has been fashioned after the finest of business models: The buyer comes first.

Full Disclosure

Remember that day down at your local bank when they just wouldn't let you out of the building unless you bought into a couple of their favorite heavy-load funds? You know, when they water-pistol-whipped you at the door, tied your feet together, put a sock in your mouth, and forced you to sign sheets of paper against your will. Ah, yes. And how'd those heavy-load mutual funds do—the ones "committed" to only the safest of domestic investment products? Yes, that's right, the ones that instead diversified into Costa Rican corn futures, leveraged options, and a nice load of Canadian penny stocks? Remember, the mutual fund that dropped 29 percent before you limped back into the bank and begged them to free you from the investment? Again, we certainly hope you don't.

The Vanguard Index fund, a no-load fund, doesn't hog-tie you into a lot of investments you hadn't prepared to make while sticking you with a variety of hidden costs down the line. The fund buys only the five hundred stocks listed on the S&P 500, companies like Coke, AT&T, Pepsi, Colgate Palmolive, Gillette, Chrysler, Toys R Us, Nike. These are all American companies that have flourished as industry leaders and which, as a group, will accurately reflect U.S. growth going forward. True, you don't get the excitement of mid-dinner phone calls and bank tellers threatening you at squirt-gunpoint. With Vanguard those thrills are gone. What you get in their stead is a mutual fund that paces the most profitable vehicle for investing in the twentieth century: the U.S. stock market.

Hassle-Free Performance

Wouldn't it have been nice if all our dreams of a technological world had turned out as planned, with greater efficiency leaving us more free time? In many ways, we've ended up with a professional life that claims as much, more, or far more of our time than it did in the pre-Pong world. In this regard, one of our core Foolish beliefs is that investing ought to be a profitable and time-saving venture, meaning that every step of the way, investors should be evaluating how much of their time they're spending and for how much long-term profit.

When you look out over Wall Street, crowded in now by more than eight thousand mutual funds, doesn't the Vanguard Index fund look ever inviting? You literally have to do no research to participate in America's corporate growth at a moderate pace. Take a look at the index fund's 5- and 10-year performance:

The Vanguard Index 500 Fund

	5-year	10-year
Vanguard Fund	12.43	14.48
S&P 500	12.62	14.78

You can see that Vanguard slightly underperforms the market, due to the expense of running the fund. However, this annual 0.20 percent (over the last 5 years) will have a negligible effect on your returns over time. What you see above is a fund that has outperformed most of the competition, but for a second here, look beyond the performance. This fund demands zero research. Zero. And the historical returns of the S&P 500 can be traced back 60 years.

When we consider the research responsibilities of mutual fund investing, we can't but conclude that the work is not commensurate with the return. Even if many mutual funds matched the performance of Vanguard's Index fund, Fools would still have to sort through the prospecti, still have to bone up on our Prospectish, still have to keep an eye on the operation to be sure that management hadn't fled to warmer climes, still have to be vigilant of the sorts of investments the fund was now making. After all, what's in a name but a name? If management leaves, maybe the Prudent Sage Fund, which had matched market growth for a decade, then collapses under the weight of an overexposure to Moroccan bean futures—a thing you hadn't known existed. There's much to keep your eye on, no?

But in Vanguard's Index fund you find 10.5 percent growth back-tested 60 years, zero research commitment, a full knowledge of what investments the fund is making (simple long positions in five hundred of America's greatest companies), and—not to be underrated—time to spend on other things.

We know we're repeating ourselves here, but all things considered, how Foolish can you get?

Abiding Expectations

Going forward, one of the most important investment lessons we hope to illustrate is that you need to set expectations for profit growth.

If you haven't done this already, you now should break out your port-folio's total and compounded growth for the last 5 years. If you haven't matched or, better yet, outperformed the S&P 500's performance of around 12.5 percent, there's absolutely no reason you shouldn't redis-tribute all of your savings into an index fund. That's stock-market aver-age growth, a beautiful thing stacked up against other investments over time. And all with zero effort, hassle-free. It's such a win-win scenario that it hurts us to think of all the money being lost in the Huge Fruits and Wisdom Funds of America.

The Switcheroo!

Surprise!

It's time for the old hidden-ball trick, razzle-dazzle, end around, the hocus-pocus-double-dealing-hoodwink-snooker play. We know it well. Thus far we've done our level best to convince you to invest in stocks and then not to, to convince you to invest in mutual funds and then not to, and most recently, to persuade you to buy the Vanguard Index Trust 500 Portfolio fund and now . . . not to!

We end this chapter by rescinding everything that, up to this point, might be confused with a buy recommendation. Don't buy just any stock because the market does well (e.g., Huge Fruit). Don't buy mu-tual funds because you've lost money in stocks (Wisdom Fund). Don't buy the Vanguard Index fund because your mutual funds have been un-derperforming the market (Vanguard Index Trust 500). Don't buy any of these. Why? Because there are far more profitable approaches to in-vesting that take no more time.

What we have built together, thus far, is the bottom step of the Fool-ish investing ladder. We ask: Is there any reason to garner less than market-average returns, which have rewarded at the rate of about 10.5 percent per year for six decades running?

Resoundingly, no!

Step onto that bottom rung and start climbing. Two decades from now you ought to be staring 10.3 percent growth (the market average minus Vanguard's .2 percent annual expense) compounded on your savings, at the very least. For those with $20,000 to invest, that would grow your portfolio into $142,000 over the next 20 years . . . and more if you were Foolish enough to put some money away weekly, monthly, quarterly, and annually for your future.

Should you be happy with 10.3 percent growth per year without carrying out a lick of research? Compared to what's being foisted upon many individual investors by the institutions, most definitely yes, you should be pleased. Investors should not settle for market underperformance over any protracted period of time. And there's nothing at all wrong with 10 percent annual growth, eh?

But, what if you jangle bells on a cap every so often? What if you too have been known occasionally to wear red-and-green-checkered pantyhose? Then no, dear Fool, you shouldn't be satisfied with mediocrity. Throw away all thoughts of index funds and market-average growth. With no more research time and no greater risk, we think you can slam past the indices that most money managers lose to each year.

PART III

THE DOW DIVIDEND STRATEGY

Stepping Away
from Vanguard

• • • • •

The difficult and risky task of meeting
and mastering the new . . . is not undertaken
by the vanguard of society but by its rear.
—Eric Hoffer

So now once again, we opt to pull apart, analyze, and ultimately denounce the very things we just celebrated, endeavoring to uncrown King Vanguard, so lately enthroned. That's evolution.

In chapter 3, we applauded mutual funds for providing a dependable way to turn a profit on your savings. Far more fructiferous than the nickel-and-dime, hot, and hyped Huge Fruits of "corporate" America, funds give their shareholders diversity, long-term profitability, and comfort. They're the response to those many cold-calling full-service brokerage firms that haven't yet proved to lowly Fools that they comprehend the notion of "service."

Service (n): an act giving assistance and *advantage* to another

That means putting your customers' well-being, their short- and long-term prosperity, before your own—a pretty good business plan. It's one the industry doesn't always have pegged as its priority, though.

But don't confuse our criticism of poor service in the world of brokering for a promotion of the mutual fund construct. Why not? Because the vast majority of mutual funds, while profitable, underperform the market's average return each year. We reiterate that over 87 percent of all mutual funds with a 10-year track record have failed to be just average! So the next time you find yourself at a shivaree in the company of five fund managers wearing ascots and sipping demon rum with the Wise, ask them if their annual returns have matched those of the Standard & Poor's 500 over the past 5 years. Four of them, at least, will hang their heads and skulk. Fool, think how overpaid they are, given that you and I can essentially duplicate the S&P 500's returns without doing a lick of research. Investing in the Vanguard Index Trust 500 Portfolio fund takes no time, no research, no Pepcid, and puts you out front of 80 percent of the competition.

But now we'll push the ante up once more by knocking the crowning cap off the head of Mr. Bogle (Vanguard's redoubtable founder) and strongly advising against your investing in the Vanguard Index fund. While no one ought to accept anything less than average returns, we don't think private investors should settle for mediocrity either. Give us an opportunity to prove to you that without much more than an hour of research per year, you can quite easily outperform Wall Street's well-heeled stewards.

Vanguard Hype: The Efficient Markets Theory

The Efficient Markets Theory (EMT), a very Wise approach to the stock market, is the philosophical underpinning of Vanguard's multibillion-dollar Index fund. It posits that the stock market is an efficient thing, wherein all present prices properly reflect the underlying, fair-market value of stocks. What the heck does that mean? Stocks, EMT theorists tell us, are always fairly priced; the only thing that bumps them up or knocks them down are unforeseeable events—mergers, new partnerships, announcements of new products or services, and so on. Because these price stimulants are "unforeseeable," the Wise tell us, all future movements on the stock market are random, unpredictable. Investing is guesswork. You can't consistently beat the market; it's impossible.

It's unfortunately not surprising that this mumbo jumbo has found a home in America's finer, greener universities and business schools, where increasingly the notion of excellence and incentivization has given way to a soft, sleepy relativism. Forces that we can't control determine everything, the Wise tell us. And that being the case, there's no reason to study individual stocks and the businesses behind them, nor to prepare, nor to aim high, aspiring to outperform. Hmph, teach that to your kids?

It also doesn't amaze a Fool that this jerry-built theory is being inculcated on investors by index fund marketers. Vanguard's promotion of the Efficient Markets Theory is philosophy by convenience, since the "why bother?" attitude bolsters its multibillion-dollar business. If the best that private investors can do is merely the average, and the worst is unthinkable, Bogle's low-cost index fund looks mighty attractive. How opportune!

It's a radical proposition, perhaps, but it's one that Fools are comfortable propounding: Mr. Bogle has been making brilliant sales pitches in teaching the "No Sense in Trying" approach, *not* teaching brilliant investment lessons. Remember that were the market truly efficient, every perfectly valued, publicly traded security would inch forward .03 percent per day en route to annual returns of 10.5 percent . . . *every* market day of *every* market year of *every* market decade. It doesn't happen, and it's the inefficiencies that have Fools rummaging around looking for market outperformers.

Many have gone before and go with us. The market has been beaten consistently and significantly by the high-profile likes of Peter Lynch, Warren Buffett, and George Soros, to say nothing of the tens of thousands of Fools who do time in our online forum. And this plays out because the stock market isn't propelled by synergistic forces driving toward greater efficiency but rather by divergent ones ever generating greater complexity. Pricing in a barter market like the stock exchange isn't the upshot of one mind, one approach, or one analysis, but the consequence of many different attitudes, valuation models, degrees of expertise, and varieties of expectation.

Consider the Intel (NASDAQ:INTC) debacle in the winter of 1994. After rounds of heated argument conducted on the Internet between technologists, investors, and insiders, Intel revealed that its Pentium chip did produce calculative errors at the seventh decimal place. The stock sold off to a split-adjusted low around $28 a share. The questions swirled: Would Intel have to recall and replace all of its Pentium chips? Would Microsoft look to partner with a different supplier? Would the courts bubble over with lawsuits from Pentium users whose businesses relied on flawlessly accurate measurement: engineers, construction companies, chemists, and others? Intel: a brand name forever scarred?

Now consider the myriad reasons why the hundreds of thousands of institutional and individual investors tracking Intel bought and sold this fantastic stock during the upheaval. Some felt the company was in serious trouble; others thought the market had overreacted to the news and that the stock was underpriced; some routinely picked up more INTC shares in their employee stock plan; others cashed out, needing capital to buy a home, a stereo, a DeLorean. Fools recognize that there are an untold number of reasons that stocks are bought and sold at given points in time and at given prices. It's a blooming, chaotic, complex market with few pockets of efficiency—quite a bit like life. And Intel's stock provided a great example of that untidiness of open barter markets; within half a year of the Pentium "disaster" and after few truly significant news items, the stock of the greatest semiconductor chip maker in the world was trading at $57 a share—a clean double. A 100 percent return . . . not bad for 6 months' time.

In this and countless other instances, Mr. Bogle's position that the markets are efficient, that future moves are unpredictable, and that every investor in the nation simply ought to buy an index fund and accept market-average returns is simplistic (and boldly opportunistic). He has either confused the concepts of mean and deviation, or he's a tremendous salesman—or both. It's been one of the great pitches, predesigned or not, in the financial industry over the last 20 years, attracting tens of billions of dollars of business for Vanguard. A Fool hopes the logic will be looked through now. The Index fund is no more than a nice toehold for private investors en route to market outperformance.

Beating the Market Average

We don't want to light into John Bogle and the Vanguard Index fund mentality too fiercely, though. There's an extraordinarily important and rudimentary lesson that the vast majority of private investors have yet to learn: If you can't beat 'em, join 'em. If you've had trouble historically with your investments, Vanguard is there for you.

That said, if you can beat 'em, Fool, go ahead and beat 'em. The book would end here if we thought we couldn't direct you to significantly better than average returns in the remaining pages. By the end of part III, in fact, we hope to have put you in position to nearly double the S&P 500, posting annual returns in excess of 20 percent per year. The process should be relatively painless—nay, agreeable—it'll demand little research per year, and present you little, if any, long-term risk.

Out of Funds into Stocks

· · · · ·

The best servants of the people, like the best valets,
must whisper unpleasant truths in the master's ear.
It is the court fool, not the foolish courtier, whom
the king can least afford to lose.
—*Walter Lippmann*

The remainder of our investment guide is going to concentrate wholly on building investment portfolios that outperform market average. You'll be surprised at just how simple it is for the individual investor to top mutual fund managers, of which the majority lumber from one investment opportunity to another, follow the herd, are undertrained, underperform the norm, and in many cases, end up so because they have tens of millions of dollars to invest. It may seem counterintuitive, but it's true: *You* have the advantage.

But beating Wall Street is going to take some motivation and mobilization. You're going to have to move out of mutual funds, to forget about them altogether, and put your savings into stocks, the most profitable investment over the past six decades. An awful lot of Americans believe that investing in real estate is the best way to compound extraordinary long-term returns, meaning that an awful lot of Americans haven't studied performance numbers for the twentieth century. Equity investments are not only more profitable than real estate, they are more liquid. You can sell any listed U.S. stock at the going market price tomorrow morning at 10:00 AM. Not so for that 120 acres of dry land 300 miles northeast of Yellowstone, nor that townhouse with one bathroom and seven spacious bedrooms. Not so, in fact, for any property on the market. Real estate is more cumbersome and less profitable than stocks.

Briefly below, we'll detail some of the initial challenges you'll encounter, and some of the initial steps you'll have to take to begin managing a market-beating portfolio, Foolishly.

1. Making the Switch to Stocks

First, we need hammer out again that our aim is to outdo the 10.5 percent annual growth that the S&P 500 has compounded over the last 60 years. Beating the S&P 500 is the goal of every institutional investor on the planet; sadly, for the majority of them, that's nothing more than a pipe dream. Ask any number of fund managers whether they could garner better returns with a $50,000 portfolio or a $5 billion portfolio; they're fibbing if they don't name the former.

It's no easy road for fund managers, though for the most part they're amply rewarded for poor performance. Why is it tough on them? Not only will they be critiqued weekly with that multi-hundred-million-dollar portfolio—the chief reason that funds underperform the market—but they'll also find it difficult to invest in the most rewarding operations on the planet: small, growth companies on the U.S. market. Try investing $250 million into a company with $50 million in sales, and see what happens. A fair comparison might be managing a million dollars and being forced to invest it all in oranges down at the farmer's market.

The smaller investor can, however, make money on underpriced oranges, or underpriced automobiles, or underpriced land . . . or best of all, underpriced listed stocks. If you're an individual investor with so much money that every time you invest in a small company, you drive the price out of your range, like those oranges and pots of gold above, put down this book. You don't need to walk around being Foolish, and you don't need us! For everyone else, however, read on. The niches of inefficient pricing on the stock market are so various, so broad, and so exploitable for the individual investor, it's just maddening to see so many substandard returns year after year. Too many investors accept mediocre performance because they think the market indecipherable. Hooey! It's not an exaggeration to say that fifth graders can wallop the market after one month of analysis. You can, too.

2. Your Savings and Your Broker

The first thing you have to do is get your capital over to a discount broker. (Appendix A: "Stocks 101: A Primer for Those Who'll Admit They Need It" goes into more detail on the subject.) Discount brokerage firms are businesses that simply take your investment orders and carry them out. You tell them to buy shares of a public company, and they do so promptly. You won't get any advice from discount brokers and, most important, you won't *pay* for any advice—an offering for which financiers have conveniently overcharged decade after decade. Don't be convinced that what they're offering is worth half what they're asking. Your savings are worth more than that.

Now, what sort of money should you put away in the stock market, and how? First of all, only invest money that you can put away for at least 3 years. And if you can leave it there longer that's even better. Just look at Warren Buffett: His patience is prodigious! It's the single strongest card that individual investors can play: patience. Stay in front of the eight ball; pick your buy and sell points without anxiety; and invest only what you can leave untouched for at least 3 years. The Dow stock investment approach—a market-beating one—that we'll lay out in a subsequent chapter posted 13.75 percent total growth over its worst 3-year period in the last 25 years (1988–1990). That's 4.3 percent annual growth; not great at all, but certainly not risky. How'd it fare from 1973 to 1975 when the market suffered its second-worst three-year decline of the century? It was up 95.8 percent, or 25.1 percent annually. Again, don't invest in the stock market unless you can put your money away for 3 years at least, and if you can, don't invest in anything else!

Once you're ready to tuck away the money, it's time to decide which discount broker to use. We're not going to run through the gamut of them here; you can get all this information in our online forum. But we do caution you to read through the fine print in every advertisement and brochure upon which you rapidly move your eyes. Yep, they're a bit tedious. Remember, though, that often what looks cheap isn't really terribly cheap. The advertising in financial newspapers is notoriously slippery, contradictory, and self-promoting. There're some silly-looking sharks in them waters. Read carefully.

To get you started, let us examine the differences between discount brokers and the so-called deep discounters. Both take buy and sell orders and promptly execute them; they're large enough that they don't have trouble handling transactions on heavy volume days. But one way they differ is in their pricing scheme. The discounter charges about $70 per trade, where the deep discounter charges a mere $30.

Why the big difference? Well, discount brokers dole out more service: access to Dow Jones News Retrieval via telephone at all hours, software, which allows for trading by personal computer; a variety of other twenty-four-hour information services. Deep discounters cut things down to the bone—no bells, whistles, or thrills, no added value.

For many portfolios, the difference between $30 a trade and $70 a trade is quite significant. Run the numbers on your own portfolio, and then determine what sorts of services you'll need to make prudent investment decisions. It will vary from one portfolio to the next.

3. Accounting Software

The only way you're going to know that you're outperforming the S&P 500 is if you load some accounting software onto your computer and stack the growth of your portfolio against the market. You simply have to know how your investments are performing relative to the stock market; otherwise, "What do you really know?" Stick close to this sort of reasoning:

> *When you can measure what you are speaking about, and express it in numbers, you know something about it; but when you cannot measure it, when you cannot express it in numbers, your knowledge is of a meager and unsatisfactory kind: It may be the beginning of knowledge, but you have scarcely, in your thoughts, advanced to the stage of Science.*
>
> *—William Thomson*

When you properly account for your portfolio's growth and compare it to market-average growth, you take a giant step toward mastering the art of investing. The best software out there today is, of course, Quicken. It has dominated the financial applications market, and it makes it pretty easy for you to professionally account for your savings without undue hassle. You can also do this with a spreadsheet, of course. Heck, you can do it all on paper if you like, though we don't recommend it!

Now, it's true that accurate accounting, telling it like it is, can be painful at times. But remember, with Vanguards Index fund, there's no reason to do worse than average. Tap your heels together three times fast and repeat: There's no reason to do worse than average. There's no reason to do worse than average. There's no reason . . .

Don't forget: When accounting you'll want to remember to figure in *all* of your research costs as well. Yep, that $500-per-year newsletter/ fax service, that $250-per-year financial newspaper, that six-hour phone call with the CFO of Huge Fruit Inc.—all of these should be deducted from portfolio returns. If you can't beat the index fund after all costs are deducted, you've blundered.

So, account, account, account!

4. Using Online

Moving your money from mutual funds to a discount broker and into stocks isn't an easy, painless process. Much anxiety can accompany these steps. One of the beauties of online communications is that you can collaborate with thousands of other investors across the country who are in similar situations. The Motley Fool Online has hundreds of thousands of readers who contribute valuable information and share their experiences with the various discount brokers, accounting software packages, dividend reinvestment plans which allow you to begin investing with $50 (see appendix A), tax matters, investment approaches, home and car buying, and so on.

The information flows through our forum at the rate of two *Motley Fool Investment Guides per day,* rivaling the total research output of the Fidelity Fund family. And all of the information sits permanently up in our area, where you can sift through it, printing and saving the best stuff and skipping over the rest. We venture to say that any question on any financial matter you have will be answered promptly in our forum, and at no greater cost than the standard online hourly rate. It's an unbelievably valuable resource—even if you're using some other less Foolish financial forum—and it's a resource that every individual investor ought to use. Bar none.

Financial newspapers and newsletters can't respond to your questions, while most investment gurus won't respond to them for less than a basket of gold . . . and may well not provide suitable answers at any cost. Finding the right discount broker, the right software, even the right approach to investing has never been so simple or inexpensive as it is now in the digital world.

5. Moving Forward: The Attitude

It is so much in the financial services industry's best interest to race you through the above procedures at their proposed price that Fools may be forgiven occasional bouts of nausea, amusement bordering on mania, or severe *disillusi wisdomata.* There's a basic business principle to keep in mind at all times: Let no one rush you.

No one.

Far too many individual investors find themselves thrown out on

Wall Street, trading weekly, daily, hourly, juggling a mishmash of investment vehicles, falling behind in their accounting, and leaving out of their lives much of what is inspiring, rejuvenating, fulfilling, and non-financial. If you get a chance, drop by the local offices of any of the big discount brokering firms in the nation that provide access to news, the trading desk, and real-time quotes. Therein, you'll often run into bedraggled, wild- and watery-eyed traders—men and women, young and old—with phones on either ear. These are not stock-market *investors* but rather bettors, players. Our model, however, is designed for those aiming to prepare for their future, the future of their family, the generations beyond.

Investing Foolishly has you being so daft as to look fully three decades forward and three back. And yet it can enable you to spend no more than from 1 to 20 hours per year on your investments. Do you believe Warren Buffett when he claims to spend *no* time following the stock market? We do. And we like to contrast his savings account with that of the two-telephone trader.

There is no hurry to investing, and more often than not, there are losses to be had from impatience. *Take your time* locating the best discount broker, playing the stock market on paper, and tackling the accounting software, which will make it very clear how your money is doing relative to the entire stock market. If you can consistently outperform the market—and we think when you've finished the next chapters in this book, you'll find it quite simple—you'll have bested the most profitable vehicle for investment in America. Even though part III shows you how to do it in less than an hour, we *still* emphasize Patience.

The Dow

• • • • •

*If there were only one religion in England there would be
danger of despotism, if there were two, they would cut
each other's throats, but there are thirty, and they live in
peace and happiness.*
—Voltaire

Our first step out into the world of maximal investment returns
takes us to some of the largest corporations on the planet: the
stocks that make up the Dow Jones industrial average (DJIA). The Dow
is the most familiar of market indices, the one that the network news
commits a good four seconds to every night of the week. "The Dow
was up 4.65 points to 4346.73," Tom Brokaw recites, leading into
another pet-food commercial. So little has been taught to U.S. citizens
about investing and the stock market that most viewers probably better
understand, and care more about, the pet food.

What is the Dow? It's one of Wall Street's measuring sticks, an index
comprising the shares of thirty public U.S. companies in industries
ranging from agricultural equipment to automobile manufacturing to
oil exploration to fountain beverages. The unique factor that binds the
thirty companies together is their hugeness. Each company has more
than $7 billion in sales over the past year, landing it in the top fifth per-
centile of publicly traded U.S. companies. Most of them have a slew of
wholly owned subsidiaries sporting brands that you might not associ-
ate with the parent company. Did you know, for instance, that Eastman
Kodak owns, manufactures, and markets Bayer Aspirin and Lysol household cleaner? How about that Philip Morris doesn't retail only ciga-
rettes but also sells macaroni and cheese under its Kraft brand? Or that
Woolworth owns Foot Locker? Billion-dollar companies are by necessity diversified into a variety of businesses and involved in a multitude

of investments that often aren't readily apparent to consumers or investors.

There's an easy way to measure the actual dollar size of these giants by calculating what's called their "market capitalization." Market capitalization (market cap) tells you the total dollar value of any public company. The point of sizing up the Dow companies is to give you a sense of just how dominant, how enduring, how formidable they are. Capitalization is tabulated by multiplying 100 percent of the ownership (the number of shares of stock) times the price of the stock (the cost of one share). Essentially, market cap shows what it would cost to buy out a public company in its entirety. The market caps of the Dow Jones industrials range from $2 billion in the case of Woolworth to over $97 billion for General Electric.

"What do they look like alongside mutual funds?" you ask. Consider Fidelity Magellan, the largest mutual fund on the planet, with assets of $40 billion—just about half the value of General Electric or IBM. When you buy the Dow stocks, you buy a vast, rich variety of businesses stacked under a single corporate name. The larger the capitalization, the lower the risk. And if you can wallop market-average growth while minimizing your risk via well-capitalized stocks, well, all the better. That's why a Fool advocates that the first handful of investments any individual makes should be picked out of a group of the thirty Dow companies. Even in the land of the Wise, where volatility and risk are poison, the multibillion-dollar, internationally diversified Dow stocks are digestible. True, there have been some precipitous falls—IBM's crash from over $170 a share to below $50 in less than a decade comes to mind. But the majority of the Dow stocks, and the group as a whole, have punched in strong, dependable growth for years.

In fact, when you hold the thirty Dow Jones industrials up to the light, behold a curious vision. The index over the last 60 years has compounded annual growth of 10.5 percent, mirroring the returns of the S&P 500 index since 1930. And there's the truest efficiency to the market—the stability of long-term growth. In any given year the market may fall 5 percent, 10 percent, 20 percent. In fact, since 1930, the Dow Jones average has fallen more than 20 percent five times, so it's true that there is short-term risk everywhere on the stock market. But Fools who look decades, even generations hence, see long-term reward unaccompanied by long-term risk.

Four Dow Samples

Let's look briefly at four of the thirty Dow companies—Coca-Cola, Disney, IBM, and Merck—just to give you a feel for their diversity.

Coca-Cola (NYSE:KO), a 110-year-old company, is the largest beverage provider in the world, with $15 billion in sales over the past year, and more than 60 percent of that business coming outside of the United States. Coca-Cola markets products under the following brand names: Coke, Diet Coke, Sprite, Minute Maid, Tab, Fanta, Mello Yello, Nestea, Five Alive, Hi-C, PowerAde . . . and yes, sadly, Fruitopia. When Coke launches a new product, it's instantly got hands-down the most sophisticated distribution and marketing plans in the industry.

Disney (NYSE:DIS), over 60 years old, is one of the leading entertainment companies in the world with over $10 billion in yearly sales. The company manages theme parks and hotels (Disneyland, EuroDisneyland, Tokyo Disneyland), is involved in audio production (Hollywood Records) and video production (*Home Improvement, Siskel & Ebert*), runs its own cable television channel (the Disney Channel), has a book publishing wing (Hyperion), owns an NHL hockey team (the Mighty Ducks), recently gobbled up Miramax Films (*Cinema Paradiso; My Left Foot; Sex, Lies & Videotape*) and, of course, runs The Walt Disney Studios (*Lion King; Beauty and the Beast; Aladdin*). Think of the cross-promotional possibilities here: Disney builds a movie which spawns a book which spawns a miniseries which spawns a compact disk which spawns a theme park character which spawns concessionary sales at hockey games . . . which all turns back into the sequel. And each link of that chain is brought to you by Disney. Now that's integration, or, as they say at Disney, synergy!

IBM (NYSE:IBM), more than 70 years old, is the leading provider of personal computers in the world, with over $65 billion in sales over the last year. IBM offered its first computer in 1952, introduced floppy disk–drive technology in 1971, and revolutionized the personal computing industry in the early 1980s. Over 60 percent of the company's sales are international. In the spring of 1995, IBM reached into its back pocket, pulled out $4 billion, and bought Lotus Development, aiming to boost the software side of Big Blue. It all leads into what will be the great technology battle of the next decade: IBM versus Microsoft. (Microsoft's annual sales, by comparison, are currently far less: $5 billion.) With hardware manufacturing feeding into software development, IBM has some tremendous bundling and brand-building potential.

Merck (NYSE:MRK) is the world's largest pharmaceutical company, boasting sales over the past year of $15 billion, with 50 percent of its business abroad. Merck is over 100 years old and has been the purveyor of drugs treating cardiovascular ailments, schizophrenia, osteoporosis, glaucoma, asthma, hypertension, and numerous other ailments. Its two blockbuster drugs in the 1980s, Mevacor and Vasotec, broke new ground in the treatment of high cholesterol and high blood pressure, respectively. Merck has sizable joint ventures with DuPont and Johnson & Johnson, two other billion-dollar companies. Among these three giants, you have companies that know all the subtleties of the FDA's regulatory process and consequently show considerably higher approval rates from their offerings.

We could go on listing the accomplishments and activities of America's largest companies, but you get the picture. The Dow Jones industrial index houses businesses that provide the foundation for corporate activity in the United States and around the globe. Below we list the thirty current companies for your perusal.

Allied Signal	Goodyear
Alcoa	IBM
American Express	Int'l Paper
AT&T	McDonald's
Bethlehem Steel	Merck
Boeing	3M
Caterpillar	J. P. Morgan
Chevron	Philip Morris
Coca-Cola	Procter & Gamble
Disney	Sears
DuPont	Texaco
Eastman Kodak	Union Carbide
Exxon	United Technologies
General Electric	Westinghouse
General Motors	Woolworth

Why Invest in This Group?

Why? To outperform. There's no reason to invest in anything unless you believe that by doing so you can outdo the uneventful 10.5 percent in compounded growth you'll get via Vanguard. Don't buy speculative stocks, bonds, futures, commodities, gold coins; don't trade options; don't hop in on any cool-sounding, indecipherable wireless-cable deals. We don't think you'll outperform the market with them, and we've dedicated a section of our book (part VIII) to the matter. The unfortunate thing, of course, is that these are just the sorts of unstudied dice rolls that thousands of greenhorn investors casually toss each year. All it takes for some is a few moments of weakness on the line with a jelly-voiced broker. This isn't investing, of course, it's gambling—an excellent long-term approach to losing money.

Now, dear Fool, imagine instead a strategy designed to beat the indices by investing in a basket of the largest corporations in the world. Does that sound like an infomercial, or what!?! The comprehensive Foolish approach to investing in the Dow Jones industrials proposes to beat the market soundly while taking on negligible intermediate- and long-term risk. Does anybody think we won't see Coca-Cola, McDonald's, General Motors, Boeing, AT&T, General Electric, et al. in the year 2010? Investors in this group of stocks are a bit like children in a playpen; there aren't a lot of sharp objects, and it ought to be a lot of fun.

The second great reason to invest in the Dow companies is that you end up working from a small sample of potential investments. Perhaps the greatest mistake individual investors make is trying to follow too many stocks. Our three major U.S. exchanges—the American Stock Exchange, the NASDAQ, and the New York Stock Exchange—list over nine thousand stocks. It's tempting to spread open the financial pages on the weekend, peek in on thousands of stock quotes and muse, "I will conquer you all!" but it ain't gonna happen. Investors who try to manage too much research typically run unprofitable or underperforming portfolios. The Fool proposes that you start by staying on top of only thirty stocks, from thirty of the strongest, most profitable, and most immense companies in the world. Disregard the other 8,970 for now; you won't need 'em.

And the third great reason to invest in the Dow companies is that, as a group, they've met market-average growth for six decades running. Through an analysis of the historical performance of the thirty Dow stocks, we've screened out subsets of those that post superior returns each year, and we've identified the common variables that tie them together. The screen takes about fifteen minutes to run, demands no technology, is logical and quite profitable. It's the backbone of Foolish dividend investing, a model which by the end of each decade aims to double the annual returns of the S&P 500 and the Dow.

•10•

Doubling the Dow

· · · · ·

It's very good for an idea to be commonplace. The important thing is that a new idea should develop out of what is
already there so that it soon becomes an old acquaintance.
—*Penelope Fitzgerald*

By the end of this chapter, you'll have learned an approach to the
stock market that we expect will compound more than 20 percent growth annually, or twice the market's average return. It's the
Dow Dividend approach, which ought to be the foundation upon
which is laid the first brick in every individual investor's portfolio. The
most important of the three prongs of the Foolish investing fork (see
part IV, "Building a Foolish Investment Portfolio"), the Dow Dividend
model, has us placing two rather severe restrictions on ourselves. First,
we agree to limit our investments to only the thirty blue-hair stocks
listed on the Dow. And second, we agree to keep research time under
twenty minutes a year, or less time than it may take you to get through
this chapter.

Our Foolish Four Dow Dividend approach, with valuations based off
the dividend yield, a variable we'll define momentarily, has and should
continue to double up on the indices. Over the past two decades, it has
proffered 20 percent-plus in annual returns. To give you a sense of how
meaningful a difference that is, consider that a $10,000 portfolio in-
vested at 10.5 percent annual growth (Vanguard Index Trust 500 Portfolio fund) would grow into over $27,000 after 10 years. That same
portfolio invested for 10 years at a rate of 20 percent annual growth
would turn into over $60,000. So, in an average decade you'd make less
than $25,000 in the typical mutual fund, slightly more than $27,000 in

the Vanguard Index fund, and over $60,000 in our select group of Dow stocks. Doesn't take a Fool to pick from these three!

Defining Terms

The Dow Dividend approach, identified decades ago, was best iterated, back-tested, and popularized by one of our heroes, New York money manager Michael O'Higgins. In his book *Beating the Dow,* O'Higgins proposes a model that takes fifteen minutes of work per year, encourages investors to transact only about six to eight times a year, and drastically reduces the level of assumed risk. It's the least-research, lowest-commission, lowest-risk approach to beating the market that has ever been spelled out for individual investors. And it's further proof that the most rewarding strategies are often the simplest.

To invest successfully in the Dow stocks, you're only going to need to know a few basic principles. Just when the financial industry is throwing the kitchen sink at its "clients" to keep them guessing, Fools are working double-time to create and present methods for investing successfully that are workable, practical, and decipherable.

The Dividend

The first principle is the dividend payment. Dividends are the redistribution of a company's earnings directly to its shareholders. The most common form of dividend, and the one we'll concern ourselves with here, is the cash dividend. Let's look at an example:

Imagine that you, fellow Fool, are the founder and CEO of Grits 'R Us (NYSE:GRU), a $50-billion company that sells Southern food around the nation and the globe. Off those $50 billion in sales for 1995, the company turned a tidy 6 percent of pure profit, or $3 billion in cash. Let's further assume that there are 1 billion shares of GRU being traded on the New York Stock Exchange. This means that for every share of stock, there are $3 of earnings. Agreed? $3 billion in profits, 1 billion shares, $3 of profit per share.

Naturally, what your investors want is growth. They want Grits 'R Us to conquer the culinary world. If this year you turned $3 billion in profit, next year you'll be expected to turn somewhere in the ballpark of $3.45 billion, a 15 percent jump year over year. Searching the planet for and locating another $450 million in pure profit—that's no small task. And if your company does find it, the Street will come back hungering again, looking for $4 billion of earnings from Grits in the succeeding year.

Not surprisingly, what many monstrous companies come to realize is that they just can't meet Wall Street's growth expectations; they can't, for instance, achieve pure growth compounded annually at 15 percent or higher. At some point, they've exhausted their market. In the case of your company, you'll max out on grit sales sooner or later; your target customers probably aren't going to put the gruel down more than twice a day for you. The question then arises: Should you look for other businesses to diversify into? Conventional thinking dictates that the best way to locate new growth is to enter new industries. Should Grits 'R Us Inc. diversify into the world of computer software (GritSoft), and telecommunications (Voice-Mail 'R Us), and precious metals mining (Golden Grits)?

For many companies, and hopefully for your chophouse, the answer is no. Diversification at the industry level is costly, requires levels of shrewdness and discipline that few possess, and can serve in the long run to undermine the effectiveness of your core business. Your management team might spend so much time trying to manufacture and distribute the GritNet Voicemail Platform Equipment to the regional Bells that they forget how great a time commitment it took to market and distribute Southern U.S. food in the Pacific Rim. *Bonk!* Your international food sales lag just as you're having trouble convincing the telecommunciations industry that your voice-mail equipment is worth a damn. What happens then? GRU growth halts, your stock plummets, and *The Wall Street Journal* runs a front page story entitled GRITS 'R . . . IN TROUBLE? Diversification, you see, can be a most dangerous game. Pick the wrong ancillary business, and your empire may show signs of declining and failing.

Think then in what a difficult position the largest companies in the world find themselves. They're shrewd enough not to take too many risks trying to court totally new markets. But if they don't meet Wall Street's growth expectations, their stocks fall out of favor, their brand names get stung, and they don't have the same outlet for raising capital that they once did. Consider Woolworth (NYSE:Z), one of the Dow companies, which saw its stock fall from over $34 a share to $12¾ from November 1992 to April 1994. The fall lost a lot of money for Woolworth shareholders—from individuals to institutions to employees to company management. It also burned the Woolworth brand name, which will take years of work to rebuild. And lastly, it left the company without advantageous sources for raising capital. Remember that if Woolworth goes out onto the markets with a secondary offering of 10,000,000 shares at $35, it raises $350 million. But with the stock at $12, it lands $120 million. Even to public companies with $8 billion in annual sales, a *difference* of $230 million to invest in future growth and pay down existing debt can be quite meaningful.

So what are companies to do if they can neither meet Wall Street's growth expectations nor find moderate-risk, alternative businesses? They pay cash dividends to their shareholders. Compensating shareholders by paying out earnings directly to them is a way to moderate growth expectations. Shareholders who get the equivalent of a steady 3 to 5 percent each year off their investment just from four quarterly dividend payments don't cash out as readily when the company falls short of double-digit growth. The quarterly payments also attract older investors who, into retirement, need to generate regular income from their savings. Quarterly cash payouts from companies meet those needs. In many ways, the dividend acts as a safety net.

The Dividend Yield

All of the above leads gracefully into the second concept you'll need to grasp in order to invest Foolishly in the Dow stocks—the dividend yield. The dividend yield is a snap calculation that measures the payback per share relative to a company's stock price. Even that definition makes it sound more complicated than it is. Let's take an example:

If Grits 'R Us is trading at $50 a share and paying a $2 per share annual cash dividend, its dividend yield is 4 percent (2 divided by 50 equals 4 percent). And thus, if Grits is still trading at $50 a share a year from now and hasn't altered its dividend structure, holders of the stock will have watched the value of their investment increase by 4 percent.

	Total Shares	Share Price	Dollars Invested	Dividend Yield	Annual Dividend
GRU	100	$50	$5,000	4%	$200

Don't let those numbers confuse you; this is fifth-grade fare, and fortunately for Fools like us, that's about as tough as the mathematical work gets in this book.

Now, annual dividend payments of 4 percent, when compared to the market's average return of 10.5 percent, aren't terribly inspiring. If you put $5,000 into the Vanguard fund you could expect on average $525 annually, compared to that piddling $200 GRU payment. Why ever invest in the dividend-paying stock, then? Those who invest in dividend-paying blue-chip stocks do so expecting the stock price to rise in addition to the dividend payout.

Let's consider a live example: From earnings, Coca-Cola (NYSE:KO) as of this writing dished out 85¢ per share each year to its shareholders. If you owned 100 shares of KO, you could therefore expect to receive $85 worth of dividend checks in the coming year. Wall Street likes to relate that payment to the share price, in order to assess the annual percentage return from the dividend. At the time of this writing, Coca-Cola stock is trading at $63 per share. The dividend yield? 0.85 divided by 63 equals .013, or 1.3 percent per year. That's paltry compared to index returns, eh? But it's not too shabby when combined with KO stock appreciation; over a 12-month period from May 1994 to May 1995, Coca-Cola stock rocketed from $36⅝ a share to $61⅞ marking a 69 percent gain in value. With or without the dividend, that's a market-smashing return.

Question: What became of the dividend yield when Coke's stock appreciated in '94 and '95? Was it 1.3 percent the entire way? The answer is no; KO's 85¢ dividend represented a 2.1 percent payout when the stock was at $40, 1.7 percent when the stock was at $50, and 1.4 percent when the stock was at $60. You'll note that if the dividend remains the same, and the stock price drops, the yield grows larger. And vice versa—if the stock appreciates, and the dividend remains the same, the yield gets smaller. So, Fools rightly ask, is it better to buy Dow stocks when their dividend yield is historically high or low?

That's not an easy question to answer, and dividends themselves aren't static. Companies can reduce or raise their payout. For instance, Coca-Cola's international business over the last 18 months may have been so profitable that it can afford to boost its annual dividend. If it raises the dividend by 50¢ per share, making for a $1.35 payout, its dividend yield hops back up to 2.1 percent. Conversely in April 1995, Woolworth eliminated its dividend, announcing that it would use the capital, once slated for its shareholders, to restructure its core retailing business. The stock didn't move on the announcement, but the dividend yield dropped from 4.5 percent to nihil.

Businesses naturally adapt to economic, industrial, and managerial changes and in the process alter their dividends. The dividend range, thus, isn't simply a factor of the fluctuating share price. It can be altered at Company HQ. But while the dividend isn't a changeless thing, the U.S. stock exchanges are home to the most stable ones in the world. Don't expect too many payment cuts from the Dow heavies, unless they see extraordinary opportunities for growth that demand immediate capital, or (more likely) have encountered extraordinarily disastrous circumstances. Dividend hikes, the shareholder's best friend, are pretty well managed, too, with companies maintaining somewhat standard yield ranges. For instance, over the past 20 years, General Electric's dividend yield has never risen above 6 percent nor fallen below 2 percent.

The more dynamic half of the yield equation, then, is the share price, not the dividend. Yields fluctuate every market day of the year, as stock prices rise and fall. Because of this, studying fair-pricedness and looking for future market outperformers based on the yield is a fruitful venture. Their rising and falling tells investors a lot about the market's pricing of the stock. And a Fool's answer to the above question, "Should I buy Dow stocks with the highest or lowest yields?" is: Buy the highest-yielders, betting on great turnaround opportunities. Let us explain.

The Dow Ten

If you'd sorted out from the Dow group the ten highest-yielding stocks, bought equal dollar amounts of them in 1973, then adjusted your portfolio once a year, selling those that no longer fell into the group of ten while buying all that did, your return for the 22 years (1973 to 1994) would've been 17.23 percent per year. It would have taken no more than fifteen minutes per annum. The S&P 500's annual return during that time was 11.19 percent, meaning that Dow Dividend investors outperformed the average by 6.04 percent each year.

At first glance, 6 percent per year probably doesn't seem remarkable, but it's a lot more inspiring when you pause to compound the returns annually over a 20-year period. If you'd invested $10,000 in Vanguard's S&P index fund (its Index Trust 500 Portfolio) in 1973, at 11.19 percent growth per year, that $10,000 20 years later would have grown into $83,400. If, instead, you'd tugged on your belled Fool-cap, and dropped your $10,000 into the ten highest-yielding Dow stocks in 1973, making the necessary changes each year, that account would now be valued at $240,300.

That over $150,000 difference is what 6 percent a year can make when translated into cash and compounded year after year after year. Either you accept $83,000 from Vanguard, suffer through the less than $80,000 forked over by your favorite well-marketed mutual fund, or secure $240,000 Foolishly. We can't help noting that the worst performer out of that group, the mutual fund, far and away requires the most research. There are over eight thousand of them now! Vanguard, alternately, demands no research. And being Foolish with the Dow stocks, the largest, most resilient public companies in America, takes fifteen minutes of work a year and over a 20-year period has nearly tripled the Vanguard index fund. Now you can see why we reached over and tipped the crown off Mr. Bogle's head. These are the sorts of decisions even the merest Fools can handle.

The Top Ten Yielders

With fifteen spare minutes on our hands this afternoon, we decided to pull open *The Wall Street Journal*, scan the list of the thirty Dow stocks with prices and yields, and assemble the top ten yielders here for you.

	Yield	Dividend	Price
1. Philip Morris (MO)	4.87%	$3.68	$75⅝
2. Texaco (TX)	4.80%	$3.20	$66⅝
3. Exxon (XON)	4.52%	$3.15	$69¾
4. J. P. Morgan (JPM)	4.20%	$3.00	$71½
5. Chevron (CHV)	3.89%	$1.85	$47½
6. 3M (MMM)	3.25%	$1.91	$58¾
7. DuPont (DD)	3.04%	$2.08	$68⅜
8. General Electric (GE)	2.96%	$1.69	$57⅛
9. General Motors (GM)	2.96%	$1.40	$47⅜
10. Sears (S)	2.73%	$1.60	$58⅝

A call over to our friendly deep-discount broker with the request that he put $2,000 in each of these ten stocks would yield the following:

	Investment	Shares
1. Philip Morris (MO)	$1,966.25	26
2. Texaco (TX)	$1,998.75	30
3. Exxon (XON)	$1,953.00	28
4. J. P. Morgan (JPM)	$2,002.00	28
5. Chevron (CHV)	$1,995.00	42
6. 3M (MMM)	$1,997.50	34
7. DuPont (DD)	$1,982.88	29
8. General Electric (GE)	$1,999.28	35
9. General Motors (GM)	$1,989.75	42
10. Sears (S)	$1,993.25	34
	$19,907.66	—

Compounding out 17.23 percent growth off your $19,907.66 yields a portfolio worth $478,000 pretax after two decades. At $30 per trade and twenty trades per year, you'd pay $12,000 to your deep-discount broker over the 20-year period, but you'd end up with a pretax portfolio worth over $398,000. (The reason the portfolio is worth $80,000 less despite commissions payments of only $12,000 is the lost value of that $600 per year in commissions compounded; trading costs, as you can see, are significant!) Not bad, considering that the same amount of capital invested in Vanguard grew to only $167,000 and a money-market fund would have turned into $36,000, before taxes, over the same period of time. Ouch.

The Dow Five

In his book *Beating the Dow,* Michael O'Higgins proposed narrowing the list down to the five lowest-priced stocks of the group of ten. Why? He believed that investors ought to take advantage of the extra volatility tied to lower-priced issues. In an efficient market, the highness or lowness of share prices shouldn't necessarily have any effect on valuations. Percentagewise, a floppy disk shouldn't vary in price any more than an automobile. But in barter markets, where there's a necessary complexity or inefficiency to pricing, lower-priced issues show greater volatility. A $100 stock that climbs $1 is up 1 percent. A $25 stock that rises $1 is up 4 percent. Investors, not surprisingly, are in the habit of focusing on lower-priced issues, hoping to catch superior profits in a volatile upswing.

Over the past 20 years, the subgroup of the five low-priced high-yielding Dow stocks has returned *21.1* percent growth annually, nearly doubling the returns of the S&P 500 and the Dow Jones industrials, and over 3.5 percent better than the annual returns of the Dow Ten. By picking the lowest-priced stocks, you've narrowed your portfolio, reduced your commission costs, and improved your returns. Congrats.

So we took the extra thirty seconds to sort out the five lowest-priced issues of the ten top-yielding Dow stocks.

	Yield	Dividend	Price
1. General Motors (GM)	2.96%	$1.40	$47⅜
2. Chevron (CHV)	3.89%	$1.85	$47½
3. General Electric (GE)	2.96%	$1.69	$57⅛
4. Sears (S)	2.73%	$1.60	$58⅝
5. 3M (MMM)	3.25%	$1.91	$58¾

This hypothetical $20,000 portfolio broken out into the five stocks via a deep-discount broker produces the following:

	Investment	Shares
1. General Motors (GM)	$3,979.50	84
2. Chevron (CHV)	$3,979.50	84
3. General Electric (GE)	$3,998.75	70
4. Sears (S)	$4,045.13	69
5. 3M (MMM)	$3,995.00	68
	$19,997.88	—

Compounding out 21.1 percent annual growth off that portfolio of $19,997.88 yields pretax growth to $920,000 after 20 years. Adjust for $30 commissions paid to your discount broker at the rate of ten trades per year and you have a portfolio worth $856,000. Stack that up against the $398,000 from the Dow Ten portfolio, the $167,000 from the Vanguard fund, and $36,000 from a money-market fund, and you'll know why we think Mr. O'Higgins is the most underrated money manager of the late twentieth century.

The Foolish Four: 2-2-3-4-5

But 21 percent growth annually wasn't enough for Fools in our online forum, who began to pick apart the historical numbers, aspiring to construct more profitable models. In his text O'Higgins notes that the lowest-priced of the five stocks is often that of a company in real trouble, with a suffering stock to boot. Our historical tabulations proved him out. Ann Coleman, the talented editor of our *Weekly Fool* printed publication, ran the numbers in the fall of 1994 and reported back to the forum. Below are the 20-year returns of the ten highest-yielding Dow stocks, by price position. Keep in mind, although these numbers are all keyed to January 1, that's just a convenience. You can start investing with the Dow Dividend approach any day of the year; just remember to reevaluate and make changes one full year later.

#1 Dow	8.38%
#2 Dow	29.82%
#3 Dow	17.93%
#4 Dow	17.54%
#5 Dow	19.60%
#6 Dow	12.25%
#7 Dow	11.80%
#8 Dow	13.01%
#9 Dow	11.48%
#10 Dow	10.82%

Dow Ten	17.23%
Dow Five	21.21%
DJIA	11.19%

Over the past 20 years, the lowest-share-priced of the highest-yielding Dow stocks has returned compounded growth of 8.38 percent per year. That pretty much falls in line with the average annual growth of mutual funds, but it's below market-average growth, and thus unacceptable to a Fool. Again, don't invest in anything on the stock market that you have reason to believe will garner less than 10.5 percent long-term annual growth. In this case, with a 20-year history of underperformance, the lowest-priced stock doesn't cut it.

Gazing on the numbers a minute more, a Fool further notes that the second-lowest-priced stock, what Michael O'Higgins termed the "Penultimate Profit Prospect (PPP)," provided unbelievable returns over the past two decades. 29.82 percent annual growth is more than two and a half times the Dow Jones industrials growth per year.

So you have the lowest-priced of the group coming a cropper, and the second-lowest thriving. From these two bits of information, we fashioned our Foolish Four approach to Dow Dividend investing, by tossing out the lowest-priced stock and doubling up on the #2 position. Taking the necessary ten seconds, we constructed the following portfolio:

	Yield	Dividend	Price
2. Chevron (CHV)	3.89%	$1.85	$47½
2. Chevron (CHV)	3.89%	$1.85	$47½
3. General Electric (GE)	2.96%	$1.69	$57⅛
4. Sears (S)	2.73%	$1.60	$58⅝
5. 3M (MMM)	3.25%	$1.91	$58¾

We phoned up our deep-discount broker and made the following buys with our $20,000:

	Investment	Shares
2. Chevron (CHV)	$7,980.00	168
3. General Electric (GE)	$3,998.75	70
4. Sears (S)	$4,045.13	69
5. 3M (MMM)	$3,995.00	68
	$19,997.88	—

Looking back two decades, the Foolish 2-2-3-4-5 approach has compounded 25.5 percent annual growth. Our $19,997.88 portfolio would've blossomed into $1,878,000 in 20 years. The same discount-brokerage commissions on eight trades per year would leave Fools with a healthy $1,791,000 portfolio, enough to pay for the kids to drink beer for four years in college . . . and maybe not much else. The Foolish Portfolio would have increased over ninety times in value after 20 years, utterly phenomenal.

To recap, building a Foolish Dow Portfolio takes no more than fifteen minutes a year, demands no research materials other than one copy of *The Wall Street Journal,* is low in commissions, assumes minimal risk, on average triples per year the returns of your average mutual fund, and demands no more than a telephone or modem relationship with a deep-discount broker. It is also a logical approach, capitalizing on Wall Street's overreaction to bad news. When Grits R' Us suffers through its telecomm debacle, investors are quick to forget that billion-dollar companies usually bounce back. Fools, however, are quick to remember this, and pick up shares of GRU-like stocks in the darker hours.

Below, we summarize the performance of the six investment vehicles we've discussed so far. In the left column are the average annual returns for each over the past 20 years, and in the right column sit the results of those returns on a $20,000 investment over two decades (with commissions fully deducted, of course):

	Average Annual Growth	$20,000 for 20 years
T-bills/Money market	3.0%	$36,000
Average mutual fund	7.5%	$85,000
DJIA and S&P 500 (Vanguard fund)	11.2%	$167,000
The Dow Ten	17.2%	$398,000
The Dow Five	21.1%	$856,000
The Foolish Four (2-2-3-4-5)	25.5%	$1,791,000

That table should be photocopied—we don't care, go ahead!—and stapled on the inside of every business book in the country. Hand it to your spouse, pass it to your uncle, deed it to your grandchildren. Compounded rates of return tell the entire story.

It is our opinion that no one should begin investing in the stock market unless they have an understanding of the concepts outlined above and a familiarity with the compounded-return table presented here. The aim of maximal profit, minimal risk, minimal research, and maximal

Foolishness is achieved by the Dow Dividend approach. Call it shameless self-promotion on our part, but we think the next time a colleague or nephew or in-law asks you how you are investing your savings, you should shock them with the following reply: "2-2-3-4-5, I'm a Fool."

Why Does It Work?

It's not good to dive into an investment without fully understanding what it is you've invested in and why you believe it will be profitable for you in excess of market-average growth. It's no different with dividend-yield investing: Fools need to comprehend why it works.

The first reason this simple approach so soundly outperforms the market is because institutional investors are chained to a pretty hairy, hungry beast that demands to be fed often, and it's called Short-Term Mentality. A short-term mentality is a necessity for the Wise in Manhattan, where results are published daily, weekly, monthly, and quarterly. The adage "Cut your losers and let your winners run . . ." has been taken to the extreme. Stocks are termed "dawgs" for underperforming over a single month! It's this reaction to a beast clamoring for better performance *this week* that opens up opportunities for us. When the health care debate heated up in '94, there was no uglier sister out there than Merck Corporation (NYSE:MRK), which fell as low as $29, trading at less than fifteen times earnings. In the face of potentially having its prices controlled, what could Merck do for Wall Street this week, this month, or this quarter? And with the mutual fund battle to keep redemptions down by hiking short-term profits and showcasing only winning stocks at month's end, who wanted to step out and publicly champion Merck, a stock which had fallen fully 50 percent off its 5-year highs? Who dared confess, "We hold Merck"?

It took a Fool. In early August 1994, applying the dividend-yield approach, we bought Merck for a cost-adjusted price of $30.36 per share, in its darkest hour. Within 9 months the stock was trading at $50 a share, up more than 60 percent for us. Wall Street's desperately short-term approach, its need to advertise success at every turn, allowed Fools to step in and pick up a stock that more than tripled the S&P 500's returns over the next 9 months.

The second back upon which dividend investing rides is that of the retiree investor. Retirees typically invest their savings with the aim of garnering strong returns off little volatility. Elder folk are also looking to generate steady streams of capital. Without salaries, retirees rely on a regular influx of capital from their savings to pay bills, stock the refrigerator, and allow for the thwicking of golf balls, turning of cards, clicking of cameras, and subsidization of grandchildren . . . and occasionally, children.

Appropriately, they cotton to high-yielding Dow stocks. Recognizing their clients' needs, financial planners and brokers can't get into just any blue-chip stock; they need dividends substantial enough that the quarterly payouts will get their customers from one month to the next. They also want substantial enough growth to make the investment worth it. So they roam the beach, watching the handheld quote machine. And they wait. Finally, when the yield is attractive enough, they plunge in, and the turnaround is afoot. Filing in behind them comes Wall Street, clamoring to be a part of the rally. Then, lo and behold, all of a sudden it's okay to own stock in Sears, even if you're not a frequent shopper. When the Fool bought Sears in August 1994, a collective gag echoed throughout Fooldom. There was a great dislike for the brand, particularly in the wake of their auto center debacle. "Sears? Why!?!" the Wise screeched. That's precisely the time that yield investors jump. The stock is near to its annual low; the yield is high relative to other large-cap growth stocks; and the brand name is suffering. Ahh, bliss!

The final reason that the dividend-yield approach has been so lucrative over the past two decades is that it looks beyond the problem of brand-name weakness. When the company name is suffering publicly, investors can't help overreacting. But with a strictly numerical model, Fools just look past the gossip, recognizing that billion-dollar companies with, say, 10 percent profit margins and 50 percent of their sales abroad don't just fold. A damaged brand can tempt Wall Street into treating these stocks like small-capitalization issues. Can you hear the door of opportunity creaking open?

·11·

Arguments Against Dividend-Yield Investing

. . . . .

I like to do all the talking myself. It saves time, and prevents arguments.
—Oscar Wilde

There are plenty of arguments against the Dow Dividend, or Dow Yield, approach to investing, and it wouldn't be Foolish to ignore them. We do have to share our experience, though, that the majority of opponents of the model are industry players. After all, a model this simple and this profitable renders obsolete full-service brokering, financial magazines, newspapers, and newsletters, and undermines the entire mutual fund industry. If you hadn't yet heard of it, no wonder!

Only Four Stocks?

Individual investors are naturally uncomfortable about being under-diversified with their investments. Add to it that many have been weaned on the institutional investor's habit of broadening the holdings in order to maximize commissions. Remember that if you're invested in bonds, gold, stocks, options, futures, commodities, load mutual funds, and others, someone is taking a commission on each of those investments, and that someone would probably like to keep you as broadly diversified as possible. Apparently not everyone has read the reports published over the last decade which indicate that a portfolio of eight diverse stocks showed little more volatility than one housing dozens or even hundreds of stocks. Fools did. And we start by recognizing that broad diversity really does nothing but reward the seller of the investment products.

Further consider that the Foolish Four stocks you'd be purchasing don't really represent four typical companies. Chevron closes fiscal 1995 with over $35 billion in annual sales, General Electric with $65 billion, Sears with $55 billion, and 3M with $15 billion. That's $170 billion in annual sales. These aren't four companies with four management teams, Fools. These are four groups of dozens of investments each packaged under a single name. Consider that as we ponder the most successful investment we made in fiscal 1995—America Online, whose stock tripled in value in a single year—we do note that with two strong years in front of it, America Online will turn into a billion-dollar company. We'd have to find one hundred seventy such investments in a variety of industries to duplicate the depth of our four Dow stocks. Now that's diversity!

Only 20 Years?

Another accusation we hear is that the Dow Dividend approach has been back-tested only 20 years. What happened before then? And what guarantee is there that these sorts of returns will continue?

A Fool asks: Is there a guarantee of anything inside or outside of the financial world? Certainly not. What we do note, however, is that the 20-year history is 10 years longer than you'll get from 90 percent of the mutual funds on the market. In fact, the vast majority of mutual funds don't even have 3-year records for investors to consider. Scoping the historical numbers, you'll find that less than a few hundred mutual funds existed 20 years ago, compared with the eight thousand kicking around today. The Dow Dividend approach's historical returns are more constant and more convincing than anything you'll find in the universe of mutual funds.

Just to delve deeper, though, Kip Fisher, another member of our staff, ran the numbers back to 1961, and found that the Foolish Four outperformed the Dow Jones industrial average by over 8 percent per year, landing 18.35 percent compounded growth versus the market's average annual growth of 10.02 percent. Those returns are slightly lower than the past two decades, but Michael O'Higgins rightly notes that regulatory and socioeconomic variations have created a different market today than existed in the 1960s. Either way, the records astonish.

Overpopularity

One of the concerns oft-expressed in our forum is that enthusiasm over the approach will eventually dilute the returns. If everyone buys the Foolish Four, where will the profits go? At one point some investors actually requested that we not highlight this information in our forum. When you find something this good, keep it to yourself, they implored. It's not an unusual take on the stock market; much of the industry is built around secrecy. A lead selling point of Bloomberg Business News, America's high-end institutional financial service, is that you can build your own approach to the stock market without anyone else finding out about it. How Wise! With our nation's $3 trillion debt, aren't we all better served by collaboration, that which leads to greater sophistication and business savvy?

But strictly in terms of the annualized returns going forward, this is a legitimate concern. What happens if everyone Foolish buys? Rote, formulaic investing traditionally does get watered down. However, take a look at the one-day dollar volume of the four Dow stocks noted above. (Daily dollar volume gets full treatment in chapter 15.) The day this chapter was penned, Chevron stock traded $29 million worth, General Electric traded $105 million, Sears had volume of $60 million, and 3M was up on $41 million traded. The four stocks traded $235 million that day. Off 250 standard market days in a year that means that over $60 billion trades in the Foolish Four on average each year. Never mind what our publisher's projections show, sales of our book are *not* going to wreak havoc with that $60 billion.

Finally, more invested dollars simply mean that these companies will have greater access to new capital. More money leads to increased earnings growth which can lead to further stock appreciation. Popularity is not a curse for well-managed companies.

Not Enough Work

The most ludicrous and least potent attack waged on Dow Yield investing that we've come across is the one that says the approach is objectionable because it rewards investors for not working hard. Apparently some of the Wise would prefer to turn 10 percent annual profits on two hours of work a day, heavy commissions, and short-term capital gains taxes than to land 20 percent-plus returns annually off one hour of work per year, low commissions, little anxiety, and long-term cap gains taxes. Compare this Wise argument to the following:

Golf: "I'd rather kick and scream, break a club, and shoot a 97 than have an easygoing round and shoot a 75."

Travel: "I'd rather spend the decade and hoards of money trying to build my own airplane than pay $200 and fly a commercial jet from New York to Boston."

Mathematics: "I'd rather scratch the numbers down on paper, starting over again each time I err, than type the numbers into a spreadsheet and let the computer calculate for me."

It all makes it easy to be a Fool, no? Our aim with all of our investments is to maximize the profit, maximize the simplicity, minimize the risk, minimize the opportunity costs of investing, and markedly outperform the market's average. The Dow Yield approach achieves all these objectives and one more—it gives us another means for poking fun at the Wise, who have spent decades convincing private investors that they'll never be able to understand the stock market. Pa-tooey!

•12•

Alternate Models

• • • • •

Brevity is the soul of lingerie.
—*Dorothy Parker*

#2 Stands Alone

The most profitable alternate model, buying only the #2 (or PPP) stock, is also the most dangerous. No Fool would put all of his money into one stock, even if it did compound 29 percent growth annually over two decades. The perfect example again is old Woolworth, which fell more than 40 percent in 1994, even as it sat in the #2 spot at the turn of the year. The thought of watching your entire portfolio fall 40 percent while the rest of the market slugs through a mediocre year is not terribly comforting. Those who decide to go with this model do so at their own risk and should not name themselves Fools when the day is done.

Roll Your Own

A more attractive alternate model, playing on a similar theme, is the Rolling #2 model, which has you investing capital biweekly, monthly, or quarterly in the #2 stock. Since the positions change, sometimes daily, rolling into the #2 will put you into perhaps as many as a handful of Dow stocks in any given year. Back-testing this particular alternate model is well-nigh impossible. Fools like to keep things simple, eh? Just the thought of sifting through so many old newspapers or digging through so many databases makes a Fool's neck grow weak.

But the model is an interesting one for a few reasons. It might provide the necessary diversity. It could catch Dow stocks before they float to the sky. And it's a model well suited to investors who don't have lump sums of money to invest but rather salary payments to roll into the market on a regular basis. This is one model that we'll be tracking in the coming years.

The downside to the model, of course, is that you could possibly fall into ruin paying out those commissions. At $30 a trade, a portfolio that rolls into a new stock every two weeks will be paying out $780 in tolls per year, and double that when you start flipping out of and into new #2s in the second year. Furthermore, the model demands that you stay on top of exactly when you bought how many shares of which stock. If things get tangled, you may end up paying short-term taxes on mistaken trades. Sometimes it is just best to keep it simple.

Foreign Model

An alternate to the Dow model that has sent full-service brokers scurrying to create unit trusts to sell is the foreign blue-chip model. Studies have shown that the yield approach works on London's Financial Times index, posting comparable returns to the U.S. market. For a Fool, there is great significance in the word *comparable* used to describe the returns. With better returns from the U.S. model, why take your money abroad? Furthermore, why pay commissions for a full-service outfit to make these trades for you?

There are two other reasons to steer clear of the foreign model. The first is that dividends are considerably less stable in foreign markets. The United States has built a reputation for featuring companies that bend over backward to meet dividend expectations. Certainly there are advantages and disadvantages to this; would that Woolworth had closed out its dividend sooner and put some of that cash into rebuilding the business and paying down the heavy debt. But for investors who focus on the yield, greater predictability is a necessity.

The second reason not to venture out on the foreign markets is that there are a variety of unique circumstances that individuals aren't well prepared for: currency fluctuations, regulatory discrepancies, and the like. Add to it that those who do invest in the foreign dividend model primarily do it through full-service firms, meaning higher commissions and lower intellectual returns. This isn't one of our favorite variations!

The Un-Dow Model

The final and perhaps most attractive of the alternate models is the Un-Dow model, which is simply designed around locating other attractive blue-chip stocks based on dividend-yield valuations. Only thirty companies get into the select Dow group, but there are hoards of other well-capitalized, global, diversified, and profitable companies. Pepsi, Hewlett-Packard, Wal-Mart, Pfizer, and Chrysler stack up pretty well against Coca-Cola, IBM, Sears, Merck, and General Motors, respectively, no?

Without question, the same sort of valuations based on dividend-yield ranges can be run on large-capitalization stocks that don't sit on the Dow. In fact, there's reason to believe that some better bargains could be found outside of the Dow group. Greater scrutiny is afforded the Dow companies, and typically greater scrutiny can lead to more fairly priced issues. Off the Dow, Wall Street can easily lose sight of the dominance and resilience of billion-dollar operations. When the Motley Fool Portfolio picked up The Gap (NYSE:GPS) in the spring of 1995, we did so because the stock was trading near its annual low, near the low end of its dividend yield historically, and sat in an industry that had been discarded by the Street in favor of technology. It was a simple Un-Dow play that we hoped would markedly outperform the market. We picked it up during some of its less favored moments at $32½ per share.

The Un-Dow model is one that has been studied very closely in our forum, with variations based on the S&P 100 Large-Cap index that have compared favorably with the traditional model. It certainly convinces a Fool of one thing: Buying high-yielding large-capitalization growth stocks during down times is a model that is effective, broad-reaching, and one that won't get diluted anytime soon.

The research will always continue, of course. In August 1995 we launched our Dow 30 Area online, complete with profiles, financial tables, and annual returns for all thirty stocks, along with a list of the top five and ten highest-yielding Dow stocks. In this spot online, managed by top investor Robert Sheard, we also feature message-board discussion where thousands of investors gather to analyze the group, looking to increase returns by building more powerful and profitable models. We also field and pose questions daily about the approach, ways to improve on it, other possible high-yield strategies, how to invest in the group at the lowest commission rate, and the like. In the years ahead, we expect this will continue to be the premiere spot for discussion of Dow stock and dividend-yield investing.

To Conclude: Thanks, Michael!

There are so many wonderful features to the dividend-yield model that we have a hard time restraining ourselves. We believe this model to be the greatest investment approach ever presented to the individual investor. Michael O'Higgins is a name that should sit up there with Lynch and Buffett, among the group of smashingly successful institutional investors who have done much to assist individual investors. His model combines superior performance with simplicity, cost and time efficiency, low risk, and high Foolishness.

We are of the mind that every single investment outside of the Dow group that an individual makes should be compared to the performance and simplicity of Dow Dividend investing. For instance, how will your non-Dow stock stack up against the historical 25.5 percent annual returns of the Foolish Four? How much time will it take to adequately research the investment? How high will the commission costs be? How much greater risk is there in the investment relative to these multibillion-dollar, beaten-down blue chips? We don't actually propose that you invest only in the Foolish Four, because we think there is education and superlative growth to be had beyond the group. But again, we do believe that every single investment you make outside of this select group should be compared directly and continually with the Foolish Four Dow stocks. And in the end, if you do choose to dedicate your entire portfolio to the highest-yielding Dow stocks on the market, we expect that two decades hence, you'll be extremely pleased with the growth in your savings.

Thank you, Michael O'Higgins. We hope that the improvement made to Beating the Dow, which has pushed higher the average annual returns by over 4 percent, is sufficiently Foolish.

PART IV

BUILDING
A FOOLISH
INVESTMENT
PORTFOLIO

·13·

Building a Foolish Investment Portfolio

· · · · ·

It was the best of times . . . it was the age of
Foolishness. . . .
—*Charles Dickens*

Beyond the Dow: Why Go Anywhere Else?

There *isn't* a reason to go anywhere else. Fold closed this Foolish tome and venture off to another aisle in the bookstore, because now you have enough information to garner outstanding long-term returns on your savings. It doesn't matter whether you've stashed away $3,000, $30,000, $300,000, or more, putting money into the Dow approach will reward you handsomely in the coming decades. The strategy has outperformed the Fidelity Magellan Fund (Lynch's old haunt, and still considered one of the more popular growth funds—if not the most popular one); over the past two decades, it would have effectively doubled your initial investment every three years; it encourages you to save and invest prudently; and it will enable you to smile pityingly upon all who generate investment talk that is slick, confusing, or replete with gibberish jargon. For the record, English Financial Jargon (EFJ), or Wise-Speak, is a language to which Fools have found a one-to-one correlation with market underperformance. If you have to read something more than twice to figure it out—lose it! It's not worth the trouble.

When an investment strategy like the Dow Dividend approach demonstrates both resiliency through the stock market disaster in 1973–74, which sent stocks 40 percent lower, and then booming success through the '80s bull market, Fools sit up in their seats. And when it's simple enough for an adolescent to grasp, we can't resist waxing philosophical; George Sand must have been juggling some colorful balls and jangling bells on her cap when she wrote, "Simplicity is the essence of the great, the true, and the beautiful in Art." Let us add to that: Finance, as well.

Then, you ask, why bother reading more of this nonsense? Because holding to our aim of simpleton investing and high profitability, we *do* find cause for pushing out into the open seas in search of better investments beyond the Dow—*to outperform 25.5 percent in annualized returns.* It's really what the rest of the book is about, starting with this very chapter, in which we're going to get you starting to think about investing Foolishly.

That 25.5 percent proposition must seem irresponsibly aggressive to many of the pros on Wall Street who make their living convincing investors to dampen their expectations and limit risk at every turn via diversification into a variety of investment products, from each of which the institutions conveniently shave a nice commission. Broad diversity limits upside and hits investors over the head with its own pound-of-flesh, peril-high risk.

We think you might be able to fish out greater than 30 percent per year on your own without assuming considerably greater risk and without engaging in needless overdiversification. By mixing some smaller, more volatile, and less prominent growth stocks in with your Dow holdings, you'll be participating in our economy's most vibrant sector, that driven by entrepreneurial forces.

Now, the 30 percent annual growth aim doesn't mean we hope for 30 percent *each and every year.* Some years you'll lose money along with the market; others you might grow your portfolio value by as much as 50 to 75 percent. In its first year, The Motley Fool Real-Money Portfolio closed up 59 percent, returning us over $29,000 on our initial investment. If we can compound 30 percent annually—our aim—our $50,000 will grow into a pretaxed portfolio of $9.5 million two decades hence. No doubt between now and then, over one 12-month period, the value of our portfolio will decline by 25 to 30 percent or more, down with the market. Youch. There's no doubt, either, that we'll just hold right through it. Why? Because the same $50,000 settled safely into CDs at a bank—which *never* lose money—will blossom into a $90,000 portfolio in two decades. Which one of these blossoms is the rose: blind timidity ($90,000) or calculated risk ($9 million)?

Recognizing the Sacrifices

Thus far, we've offered up the Dow Dividend Strategy, a damned profitable approach, one whose annual returns would generate enthusiasm among high-risk venture capitalists. It requires less than five minutes of research per year, and it has you aggressively limiting your risk. As we head out over those turbulent waters in search of the strongest growth companies of the future, you should be asking yourself the following questions:

> Am I outperforming the Foolish Four after deducting all related costs—spreads, commissions, financial publications, et al.?
> And how much greater risk am I taking?
> How much time am I committing to this, and how much time do I want to be committing to this?
> Am I composed enough to manage investments that will naturally be more volatile than my Dow holdings?
> Do I care about this stuff?
> Do I understand this all well enough to grasp why some of my investments are more successful than others?
> Do I understand stocks and how they're valued in relationship to their companies?
> *Am I a Fool?*

Maybe the last one isn't terribly important, *maybe,* but the preceding seven definitely are. At intervals, you'll need to reassess your situation, carrying out some basic accounting and taking a periodic reality check. We've done this for years and feel confident that there *are* profits in excess of 25 percent annual growth to be had in the universe of small-capitalization stocks. And in our minds the opportunity costs of tracking growth companies are actually *rewards,* not expenses. You'll learn the ins and outs of business competition, you'll hone your critical thinking, and we believe you'll enjoy the process almost as much as the profits.

But there are some hard realities here that bear consideration. What'll it take to outperform Dow Dividend returns? Investing Foolishly will require that you commit more time to researching businesses, that you become thoroughly familiar with the concept of equity ownership, that you take on greater risk than you have with your Dow stocks, and that you find ways to communicate with other investors to share information, analysis, and opinion. That must sound like a huge undertaking: "Rome wasn't built by a working couple with two kids!" you protest.

Rest assured our approach is manageable and ought to share a symbiotic relationship with your professional career, each feeding off the other. You'll be investing initially in small-cap, acorn-size companies whose businesses you understand because they relate to your career and hobbies. And tracking them down will set you out in search of the highest-quality operations in America—companies manufacturing outstanding products, providing superior services, sporting strong brands, and growing with an in-house bias toward long-term excellence. No doubt it'll take effort, but it's a project that will pay hefty dividends in the years ahead.

What Consequences?

The first issue we'll need to address is risk. Small-capitalization growth stocks—the focus of part V—can fluctuate by 30 to 50 percent or more in a single quarter—occasionally in any month, week, even day. Our Fool Portfolio investment in America Online (NASDAQ:AMER), though astonishingly profitable in our first year, fell more than 25 percent in value *twice* during that year. Hey, losing 25 percent off the present value of your investment can be daunting. You invest $20,000, it falls to $16,000—*ouch!* You invest $10,000, now it's $7,500—*eesh!* But if you've picked high-quality, highly profitable companies in burgeoning industries, the volatility shouldn't faze you, as long as your company is still fundamentally sound. By the close of our first year (August 1995), America Online had risen more than 260 percent for us, from $14½ per share to over $52. You can imagine that those two 25 percent drops aren't terribly memorable.

But the only way to minimize and ultimately absorb the risk associated with equities investing is to carry out research that is thorough, creative, and logical enough that you're well prepared for a variety of scenarios. After all, some stocks fall 25 percent, then fall another 25 percent, then follow with another 25 percent drop. So how do we avoid these, as we build our Foolish portfolio?

The minimum time commitment on your part is the time it takes you to track each of your investments quarterly. Public companies are required by the Securities and Exchange Commission (SEC) to state their financial performance four times a year. The majority of companies run on a December fiscal year, meaning that their quarters end on March 31, June 30, and September 30, and December 31. It takes the accountants a few weeks to compile all the information, so you'll find companies typically reporting their quarterly numbers at the end of January, April, July, and October. In chapter 16 ("Making Sense of Financial Info"), we'll detail what you'll need to concentrate on in those reports; for now, we just emphasize that in the non-Dow stocks that Fools hold, you should expect to review the sales, earnings, and cash-flow numbers every three months.

Patience is your last challenge. The temptation to overanalyze your investments and hyperactively trade your account may seem immense at times. When you compete head-to-head with 25.5 percent growth, it's easy to get restless, believing that more activity should result in more profits. Some investors sketch stock graphs every market day of the year, claiming that price movements tell them more about their investments than the strength and long-term viability of the companies behind them. Over the course of a single day, one of their stocks rises $1, then drops $½, then lifts again $⅜, then a further $¼, then it gives away $1 before the close. So, that hourly analysis is supposed to tell us all something about the value and future direction of these investments? We don't buy it. We've come across no scientific studies showing that short-term price fluctuations are predictable. And even if we did, who would want to live their lives this way? Not us. Investment approaches that compel their adherents to track price fluctuations daily or hourly are bad investment ideas, for both their own bottom line and their quality of life.

Conversely, having the patience to wait for and wade through quarterly earnings announcements is a discipline that you'll have to master before being dubbed Fool. And even then, sitting through some disappointing quarters (often your best recourse) will demand ever greater self-restraint. If your company comes in with $100 million in sales for the quarter, and Wall Street was expecting $115 million, look out below. More often than not, your investment will take a hit, and oh how you'll be tempted to sell, on a dime. At those times, a Fool digs through the story to see if the sales letdown was a short-term anomaly, or whether it might signal structural problems symptomatic of some more permanent disorder. Being patient and careful has won—and always will win—on Wall Street.

And the rewards you can expect from well-chosen, well-researched, small-cap investments are extraordinary. In our first year online, four of our five small- to medium-size companies provided returns well in excess of 30 percent annualized growth. American Online (NASDAQ:AMER) grew 260 percent; Ride Incorporated (the snowboard manufacturer—NASDAQ:RIDE), Foolish for less than three months, had risen 51 percent; Iomega Corporation (NASDAQ:IOMG), also Foolish for less than three months, was up 60 percent; and Boston Technology (NASDAQ:BSTN), which we had only recently jettisoned, rose 48 percent for us. Not all of our holdings slammed forward, of course. Our fifth small-cap, Sonic Solutions (NASDAQ:SNIC), manufacturer of digital audio workstations, disappointed us with subpar performance in two bad earnings quarters and at year-end had hammered us with a 30 percent decline.

As we've stated before, our aim is to beat the Dow Dividend approach through a diversified Foolish portfolio heavily weighted in growth stocks like those just mentioned. So far, we've mostly spent time asking ourselves *why* we should do anything other than play the high-yielding Dow stocks. For most of the rest of the book, we're going to share with you exactly how we go about trying to crush the market. It's time to start focusing on how to build a Foolish portfolio.

Where to from Here: Investing Foolishly

If you envision our Foolish investment stepladder, you may wish to picture the bottom rung as Vanguard's S&P Index fund, with its solid 10.5 percent growth per year. But if you treat ladders the same way we do, you'll never waste your time or effort stepping on the bottom rung. Even though we love the way Vanguard's mindless fund drubs 80 percent of its peers, too many simple ways exist to beat it. Thus, the second rung—and a very comfy step it is—belongs to the Foolish Four and the Dow Dividend approach, which should grant its fans the same 25 percent annualized returns going forward that it has served up in the past.

If you're now ready to consider stepping up to the *third* rung, remember this: You're considering forsaking an investment approach that invests in safe large-caps that return you 25 percent per year with zero research. You'd better be willing to spend extra time and you'd better be ready to top 25 percent. If you didn't answer yes to both of the previous charges, you have no other good reason to waste your time doing your own investment research, unless you simply enjoy doing so for its own sake. But if you *are* prepared to go these extra miles, you must be thinking of investing Foolishly . . . you're thinking of building a Foolish portfolio.

So it's time you knew that we put three things in our portfolio. You've met one of them, and the other two are coming up. Let's talk about these right now.

Batting first are the high-yielding Dow stocks that you've already read about. These belong in *every* portfolio because they'll provide you robust strength in good times and strong protection in bad times. We typically make these about 20 to 30 percent of our overall holdings.

Batting second come growth stocks, particularly of the smaller-cap variety, since these remain the best-performing investment over the past many decades. Growth stocks make up 50 to 60 percent of our overall holdings. While many people shy away from the volatility and risk associated with small-stock investing, we're of the mind that good risk leads to good reward. Even though you'll suffer through some of your worst investment moments holding these stocks, you'd have to *not* be a Fool to avoid them. Part V analyzes the ins and outs of growth-stock investing.

And batting in the third slot are shorted stocks, the final component of the Foolish portfolio, and the subject of part VI. These make up anything from 0 to 20 percent of a Foolish portfolio. Shorting stocks is a simple technique designed to profit off of some select stocks' *declines.* This portion of your portfolio will of course cushion you against drops in the overall market, since you can expect your "shorts" to drop in kind. Ideally, though, you'll make money on these investments even in average to good markets, if you're good at identifying overvalued situations.

Part VII recapitulates the Foolish investment strategy, since we think reviews are important.

But before we go zooming off excitedly into parts V to VII, we do want to spend some time with first-time investors to begin thinking about their first growth stock picks.

Making Your First Stock Picks

As you've heard, part V provides an extremely thoroughgoing look at which growth stocks to pick, what to look for in their financial statements, how to value them, where to buy them, and when to sell them. But for now we'll pretend you're a complete novice and help you get started locating your *first* growth stock pick. "Where the heck would I find it?" you inevitably wonder. Good question.

Let's begin with where you shouldn't bother searching. In selecting your very first non-Dow investment, you should *not* pore through your financial newspaper, where you'd be faced with the prospect of looking over some nine thousand stocks, listed daily. You should also *not* use the free advice of your neighbor's ex, who at the post office this morning claimed to have overheard rumors of some buyout. Another place *not* to go: financial magazines and newsletters . . . and you can throw out the hot tips revved up on national, money-tawk television as well. No, dear reader, neither should you even consult The Motley Fool Online.

Your first growth stock investment should ideally come directly from your own expertise . . . out of your professional life. One of the fringe benefits to having a job, we've found, is that you get in pretty good touch with what's going on in at least one domestic industry. Take advantage of that, whether you're in automobile manufacturing, house-keeping, natural gas exploration, magazine publishing, parenting, con-struction, commercial banking, fiber optics—whatever. The public companies working in your industry are playing on your home field. You're employed. You're paying Social Security. Milk it.

Your Industry

If you're waiting tables in a restaurant, order up financial statements from Wendy's, Buffet's, Lone Star Steakhouse, Landry's Seafood Restau-rants, et al. If you're a computer programmer, scour the hundreds of small- and medium-size software companies, from BMC Software to Broderbund, Electronic Arts, Netscape, et al. If you're a lawyer—heck, you needn't worry about investing at all. Just keep inducing your clients to sue other people and take your 3 percent annual growth in CDs.

Kidding!

But can you hear the mating call of employment and investment? In fact, as you the investor learn more about your industry—what makes certain outfits better than others, how the companies generate profits, what their prospects are going forward, how much risk there is in the group—then you the *employee* become more valuable to your busi-ness. Nick Corcodilos, a former headhunter who manages our online job-hunting area, says, "Make yourself more valuable to your business by understanding what drives its profitability and how you can push that forward." Learning about companies in your industry improves the like-lihood of your outperforming the Foolish Four *and* will help you maxi-mize your value in the workplace.

Your Interests

The next box to pop open in search of great investments is the one stuffed with your hobbies, interests, and keepsakes. In many instances, the products and services tied to your private life may be nearer and dearer to you than your own career. Name your favorite hobby, and you're likely to find a pretty full range of businesses that have devel-oped in support of it. If you love computer games, Electronic Arts (NASDAQ:ERTS) has $500 million in yearly sales. If you love classical music, consider a company like Kimball International (NASDAQ: KBALB), manufacturer of pianos and organs with annual sales in excess of $800 million. If you love to read, look no further than the consolidation and competition in the publishing industry. Are you a basketball fan? Hmm, doesn't Nike own that sport?

Wherever you look, there's a public company filling in to serve the market, a public company that might make a wonderful investment. Searching for gems among the places, activities, and services that you prize is about as Foolish as it gets.

Your Insight

The third pathway—hemmed in by giant oaks—en route to that end-of-the-lane, whitewashed home shaded by apple trees (and to decent investment returns on your early investments, as well) involves nothing more than looking around yourself: What industries are thriving? What are people talking about? What products and services are your friends hooked on? Everything is fair game, from magazines to Rollerblades to computer-networking software, from telecommunications equipment to bowling alleys to TV sets . . . and you can even splash in some microbrew, too. Every one of us, regardless of our present financial condition, comes into contact with extraordinary products and services offered by public companies that would make for fine long-term investments.

The challenge is often just seeing with clear enough eyes. And our online experience has proven that your eyesight can get a lot better when it's backed by the efforts of thousands of *other* eyeballs, all looking to find the best new companies and products. If you're among the majority of readers that, studies suggest, doesn't read introductions to books, please do consider going back to the Foreword and reading about Iomega Corporation (NASDAQ:IOMG). The story of the way the Zip-drive manufacturer caught the investing public's imagination is terribly apropos here. We first heard about Iomega from the online buzz created by those who'd bought and loved its new product. We then read magazine reviews of the Zip drive, took seriously the growing need for memory capacity in a digital world, rifled through the company's financials, and bought a great stock. Ain't no hocus-pocus to any of this.

High Quality

Now that we've laid down what we think are the three clearest roads to finding potential investments—your industry, your interests, your insight—we're obliged to emphasize that finding the best *products* around doesn't mean you've found the best *companies* in which to invest. Beware the one-trick-pony business, aiming to thrust, say, a terrific new brake system for tractor trailers out to market, while showing no other products in the pipeline. Brake It Down Inc. (NYSE:UNE) goes public to raise cash; it generates awesome sales and earnings on its

Gimme-a-Brake throttle for a full year; it saves a wagonload of cash by not spending anything on research for future product lines; then money-laden management heads for the hills, leaving shareholders on a downward roll with bandless brakes.

An awful lot of the fireworks that greet initial public offerings fizzle quickly after liftoff. Know thy company, dear Fool. True, you can't hold yourself responsible for learning everything possible about a business. That's management's full-time job—to think strategically, plan prudently, pursue growth aggressively. But your analysis will improve your returns.

In making your first growth stock investment, your responsibility is to perform enough research so that you believe or don't that a given company will match up well against its competitors, outdo market-average growth, and remain focused on long-term prosperity. Warren Buffett has said, "You can't do good business with bad people." Investing is no different. After all, when you buy a small piece of ownership in an operation, you do business with the executives of that company. It's your charge to make some determinations about the quality of that team.

So look to high-quality companies succeeding in industries that you understand from your own experience, whether that experience comes from your job, your home life, or your vacation.

What You'll Need

Finally, in your efforts to build a Foolish portfolio, it'll help to have a few tools along the way. The brief closing section of this chapter may look much like a series of advertisements, so we'll state up front that Foolish palms aren't getting greased for the succeeding information. These are services we believe are extremely useful in the struggle to beat the market. They're reasonably inexpensive and provide valuable information that's easy to process. We now prove to the world how miserable we are at running a business by presenting them to you without taking a single, quiet commission for our labors.

S&P Stock Guide

The *S&P Stock Guide* is a simple little book that provides one long line of data on thousands of public companies. It is one of the Fool's favorite resources, for three reasons: It's easy to read and fun to flip through; it allows you to screen out companies in advance of sending away for financial information; and, what is sweeter, many brokers pass it out as a freebie to their customers. Some bit of Wisdom prattles on about how you get what you pay for in life. Sure, sure. This freebie has a lot of value packed into it.

To our eyes, the most useful stuff in the *Guide* details how financially strong a given company is. In chapter 16 we'll look deeper into this and define some of these terms, but for now suffice it to say that the *Guide* can help you answer the following sorts of questions: How much cash does a company have in relationship to its long-term debt? How do its current assets compare with its current liabilities? The first question helps you figure out how well the company is setting itself up for the long term; the second will aid you in analyzing short-term finances. Consider the two companies below, with the information the *S&P Stock Guide* would provide:

The Motley Fool Inc.

Current Assets:	$16.2 million
Current Liabilities:	$23.5 million
Cash:	$11.1 million
Long-Term Debt:	$22.0 million

Herb's Amazing Portable Automobiles

Current Assets:	$18.7 million
Current Liabilities:	$12.3 million
Cash:	$27.4 million
Long-Term Debt:	$2.1 million

Which of these two companies looks more attractive to you? The one with less in current assets than in liabilities, and less cash than debt? Or is it the other one? If we held a Nerf sledgehammer over your head and, in a gruff voice, demanded of you, "From these numbers, invest in either Herb or The Fool!," which would you pick?

Without being able to look at other factors, we wouldn't invest in either of them, of course, but if we were forced to at Nerf sledgehammer–point, we'd take the man with the portable cars. Fools know not to underestimate a company's ability or inability to generate cash internally from its business. The Motley Fool, in the example above—and these numbers are fictional, thank God—has nearly $11 million more debt than cash, and may soon have guys tapping on their door with blackjacks because of the excessive short-term liabilities. Conversely, Herb's numbers are quite the other way, a testament to his ability to develop a four-wheeled motored contraption that can be folded into a briefcase and taken in to work. Don't underestimate cash, and the *S&P Stock Guide* will enable you to ferret out the winners from the losers *before* you begin requesting financial information, saving you time and effort.

Now, if they'd only just put company phone numbers in the thing . . .

Zacks Analyst Watch

What we didn't note above when we talked about the need to track the quarterly sales and earnings performance of each of your investments is that you'll actually have to stack those performance statistics up against Wall Street's projections to get the clearest sense of how your company is doing. Later in the book, we'll present some fifth-grade math calculations and a short homespun investment theory to help pin down ways to value growth stocks. But for now you need to be aware that the big and small investing firms employ analysts whose job it is to know an entire industry and generate quarterly and annual growth projections for individual companies.

That means that every time Herb's Amazing Portable Automobiles announces its most recent three-month performance, investors across the country will be scoring the results against Wall Street's projections. And if Herb announces 50 percent growth across the board, with sales jumping from $25 million to $37 million, and earnings bumping up from $4 to $6 million, but Wall Street had expected 60 percent growth across the board, look out below. Expectations drive ahead of the market; when they aren't satisfied, the herd moves to other issues.

This being the case, it's extraordinarily important that you know what the growth projections *are* for the companies in which you invest. When Herb presents that latest quarter, showing 50 percent sales and earnings growth, and the published financial report contains nothing but rah-rah stuff about how you no longer have to park your car on the street, *you'll* understand why the stock fell from $10 to $8 a share.

Ah, but *how* will you know that the company underperformed estimates? You'll need an earnings service. We happen to use *Zacks Analyst Watch,* a monthly publication that costs us $250 per year and offers quarterly, annual, and five-year earnings growth projections on five thousand publicly traded companies. In the case of Herb's Amazing Portable Automobiles, you'll be able to spy the consensus earnings estimates of all the analysts that have been following the company. How much is this company expected to make when it reports earnings three weeks from today? How about the following quarter? What about the year-end estimates? And what is the 5-year projected earnings growth rate for the company? *Zacks* also smartly reports how companies did in their previous quarter, so you can check any company's performance vis-à-vis the estimates last time around.

Zacks Analyst Watch has been the most comprehensive, most accurate, and most valuable earnings service around, the ideal scorecard in a world where investors have to be on top of what Wall Street is saying about the growth potential of their companies. At $250 a year, it ain't cheap. But with the consumer-investor market broadening, and *Zacks'* market share ranging out beyond Upper Manhattan, we should see the price decline. In fact, right about the time we were concluding this book, First Call (the institutional information service) was beginning to publish its monthly earnings estimates on America Online for no more than the price of connect fees. Once again, this will be the wave of the future, providing information at your fingertips that was technically and economically unthinkable just a decade before.

Online Communications

It used to be that investors had to pay out a couple hundred bucks a year for a daily financial newspaper, then another few hundred in financial magazines and newsletters, just to feel in touch with the market. The digital world is changing all of that, distributing information across America with greater efficiency and less expense.

Consider that in what presently ranks as the most active online financial service in the world, The Motley Fool, we offer all of the below:

- Daily news, with a thorough stock market recap at 6:00 P.M. Eastern every market day
- Fifteen-minute-delayed quotes
- Individual message folders for ongoing discussion on over one thousand stocks
- Twelve hours a day of live interactive investment talk
- Two $50,000 model portfolios managed in full view for investors to analyze, track, compete with, or just duplicate (if they like)
- Two dozen industry analysts ready and waiting to answer questions on individual stocks and their sectors
- An entire school offering assistance on managing your 401(K) plan, retirement investing, portfolio management, tax strategies, and investment theory

And all of this at America Online's base rate (as of this writing) of $120 per year, nearly half the cost of traditional financial newspapers. And online connect fees are getting cheaper, while newspapers and magazines are not.

Great businesses are built on providing products and services that are more convenient, more comprehensive, of higher quality, and less precious than the competition. More information, better analysis, at a lower cost: It's a model that ought to be most familiar to those in the financial services industry, right? Businessmen should know the business world better than any, no? That certainly hasn't proved true in the cobbling together and distribution of financial information, which runs at such a premium that many individuals have heretofore been unable to access it.

You should take advantage of the greater sophistication that the digital world offers on the cheap. Financial newspapers, magazines, and TV programs pick and choose what *they* think to be the most important of news stories; they present what *they* believe to be the proper angle in their editorials. They offer opinions without having the capacity or the accountability to hear back from their often more sophisticated audience, and they do all this at rather great expense. Being Foolish means being digital.

Steering the Tottering Boat

With the outboard mounted firmly on the boat, you're set to cruise the open water in search of profitable fish, but don't forget whose hand is on the wheel. Yours. No one in the financial world has your and your family's long-term best interests closer to their heart than you.

Once you recognize that *you* are solely responsible for the investment decisions you make, you'll start making better decisions. Much of the Zeitgeist seems to flow around excuse building, which has our courts overwhelmed with nuisance suits and our universities blustering with complaint. Be contrary in this respect; if you plan to venture out from your Dow holdings, take it all head-on. Building a Foolish portfolio with Dow high yielders, monster growth stocks, and a smattering of precariously priced shorts can prove awfully profitable.

But do always remember that if your dory does start taking in water, you have the strongest, handsomest, and most dependable dock on the lake in Beating the Dow.

PART V

SMALL-CAP
GROWTH STOCKS

•14•

Why Small-Cap
Growth Stocks?

• • • • •

Think naught a trifle, though it small appear;
Small sands the mountain, moments make
the year, and trifles life.
—*Edward Young*

Small-capitalization growth stocks ("small caps") make up the second component of our three-tiered Foolish investment approach. It's not hard to figure out why. Since 1929, small caps have as a group well exceeded the overall returns of larger stocks. A study by Ibbotson and Associates, the esteemed Chicago research firm that tracks the performance of stocks and mutual funds, shows that from 1940 to 1993, small-cap stocks posted average annual returns of 15.9 percent, versus a large-cap return of 11.7 percent over the corresponding period. That may look like only 4 percentage points, but when you compound that return over those 54 years, the difference is huge. A $1,000 investment earning 15.9 percent annually is worth $2.89 million 54 years later; a $1,000 investment bringing in 11.7 percent over that time ends up worth just $0.39 million, or $390,000. So when you examine it historically, it's clear that investing in anything else means a lower, slower flight to fame and fortune.

Despite this, many people resist investing in small caps because of the inherent risk associated with them. You can make a lot of money in these stocks, and you can lose a lot too. That's because little stocks often react to dramatic news like gnats in the wind (whether the wind is blowing for or against them). But is that reason enough to avoid some of the best bets on the market? Nay. If these people didn't so

Wisely avoid these stocks, they'd understand and appreciate the value (pun intended) of strong small-cap representation in their portfolios.

That said, small-cap stocks are not the right choices for people who can't afford the short-term risks. Do not risk investing in small-cap stocks if you'll need the money to make your mortgage payments! It's the very same story if you're a retiree who cannot tolerate losing capital you need to live on. *Never* invest money you can't afford to lose in stocks.

But as we wrote earlier, consciously taking on smart risk remains the best way to succeed in investing. We embrace risk because the opposite is timidity, which is what most of the world is good at. Always remember, dear reader, that it wasn't the Wise who discovered the New World. Join us as we emulate Columbus and head for deep water.

Now, before stirring small caps into your investment cauldron, you must first thoroughly understand the ingredients and their effects. As the title indicates, part V attempts to convey to you every single Foolish thing you need to know about choosing, valuing, and investing in small-cap stocks. Handled properly, small-cap investing is tremendous fun and exceptionally lucrative.

Just What *Is* a Small Cap?

You probably already understand the "growth" part of "Small-Cap Growth Stocks." A growth stock is simply one issued by a company whose sales and profits have risen for the past few years and are expected to keep rising in the future. Market capitalization, on the other hand, demands some explanation.

The investment world is not terribly different from the scientific world in at least one respect: its affection for taxonomy. Taxonomy, the study of the general principles of classification, serves investors in all sorts of different ways. Once you've been prowling around the market a little while, you'll realize that everything is classified, categorized, sorted, and gets a sign hung on it. You can see it all around you in everything from the basics like a different ticker symbol for every stock, to today's elaborate mutual fund categories, to the different classifications of filings with the Securities & Exchange Commission (SEC). Not surprisingly, taxonomists have also classified stocks by "market capitalization." The market capitalization of a stock is simply the total number of shares of the security multiplied by the price per share. The resulting figure describes in monetary terms the total value of a company's equity. For instance, Gen X Stuff Inc. (NASDAQ:USLS), a marketer and retailer of merchandise with vacuous pseudothemes designed to help corporate partners sell product into the youth niche, just came public at $10 per share and now has 12 million shares outstanding. Power up those calculators, people. What's the "market cap"?

It's $120 million ($10 per share times 12 million shares). Many people simply refer to this figure as the "value" of the company, since any potential purchaser (supposing anyone would actually want to buy this enterprise) would pay around $120 million to own Gen X Stuff. (FYI: Most acquisitions of good public companies occur at a "premium" to their market-cap valuation, which means that purchasers offer an amount *higher* than the company's market capitalization in order to discourage competing bids—and to account for things like name-brand properties and other "goodwill" items.)

We typically divide up the market capitalizations of companies into four categories: large cap, mid cap, small cap, and micro cap. Everyone has his own definition of these categories, but the numbers below present a dependable enough guide, circa the late 1990s:

Large cap	Over $1.5 billion
Mid cap	$200 million to $1.5 billion
Small cap	$50 million to $200 million
Micro cap	Below $50 million

If you're interested in calculating and following some market caps on your own, you'll need a good source for a stock's total number of shares outstanding. Numerous sources exist, the most common of which is probably the *Standard & Poor's Stock Guide.* Total number of shares out also appears in the quarterly earnings statements printed in financial dailies, and you can obtain this information directly from companies as well, when you call them up and order their investor information packets (see the section at the end of chapter 15, "Your Call to the Company Requesting Info").

Now that we know our caps, we can talk familiarly about market capitalization with people who haven't yet read this book and don't know investing, and make them feel stupid. Beyond that enjoyable diversion, however, lies a useful way to generalize about any given portfolio. We can call your portfolio a "mid-cap portfolio," for instance, meaning that your investments are primarily in fairly well known companies whose market caps are somewhere around $1 billion. Or we might call one or another mutual fund a "micro-cap fund," suggesting that it sports a stable of relatively anonymous up-and-comers that *probably* are pretty volatile.

Generalizing about the capitalizations of stocks in a given portfolio often leads to useful insights. For example, big stocks generally fluctuate less than small stocks, in much the same way that airplanes are less affected by wind than are hot-air balloons. This points up a fact we will keep emphasizing as we proceed: Size correlates directly with inertia. As you've already seen, The Motley Fool's first-tier investment is high-yielding blue-chip stocks. We intentionally pile up this large-cap ballast in order to steady our balloon without compromising its ground speed. On the other hand, you'll meet some people whose balloons have no sandbags at all, wild-eyed people with hot-air portfolios full of penny stocks top to bottom. Look fast, 'cause if the wind shifts, you won't see them anymore. With such out-of-balance portfolios, they won't be able to right themselves if the market goes the wrong direction. Then again, you may have friends who make the opposite mistake, heaping their vessel with far too many sandbags. Their balloons never get off the ground. As is always the case in life, one must constantly work toward a happy medium, erring neither on the side of dearth nor plenty.

Why You Shouldn't Buy Small Caps

In Foolish style, let's first spend some time examining why you *shouldn't* buy small caps.

For one thing, you definitely shouldn't buy small caps if you don't know what you're doing. You'd be surprised how many newcomers plunge right into the market just because they happened to get a "hot tip" when they had a little money on hand, without having the faintest idea of what they're doing. The market, in this context, should be treated like deep-sea diving. Would you debark a diving bell at 500 feet without ever having read an instruction manual? We hope not. Fortunately, you now have your Foolish instruction manual for investing, and you've figured out that no matter how "hot" a tip is, there's homework to do before you make the buy. (Guess what: There's even *more* work to do *after* you buy a small-cap stock.)

You should stay out of small-cap stocks if you don't have the time or are unwilling to follow them. Small-cap growth investors must scrutinize their investments on a more regular basis than equity investors of any other stripe, just as you have to spend more time keeping an eye on a crawling baby than your typically immobile two-week-old infant.

Another reason to avoid small caps is if you instinctively shy away from risk. While we celebrate taking risk—the *right* risk—we don't look down on those who eschew it. Everyone is different, and the good news is that a motley variety of market-beating stock-picking approaches exists. So if you're not risk-tolerant by nature, don't try to be something you aren't. Avoid small caps.

We've already mentioned yet another reason not to buy these things: If you need the money elsewhere. If you're putting your lunch money (or its equivalent) down on the market, you're hoping to hit the Lotto jackpot. Again, the most frequent mistake new investors make is to invest as if they were playing the lottery—buy enough long shots and one of them has to hit! We've met plenty practitioners of this philosophy. (See chapter 21.) Both the lottery and this investment style are, as the Italians say, a "tax on imbeciles." Well, we say, "No new taxes!" Don't waste your money on Lotto. You'll lose. Lotso.

All right, that's quite enough on why you shouldn't buy small caps. If you've worked your way through the above and decided that you're still interested, then part V is for you.

Why Even the Family Goldfish Should Hold Some Small Caps: Getting in First

Having learned what "small cap" means and in which situations it should be avoided, let us delve more deeply into the advantages of small-stock investing and why even Irving, your family goldfish, should probably own a few of these shares.

The primary reason for buying small-cap and micro-cap growth stocks—aside from their superior historical performance—is that mutual funds and institutions cannot buy them . . . yet. Or even if they can, mutual funds and institutions cannot build up any meaningful holding. "Meaningful" here is defined as "in a sufficient quantity to make any noticeable difference to the fund's overall performance."

The reasons partly involve the natural dimensions of the situation and partly involve SEC regulations. The natural dimensions are obvious: At last count, the average mutual fund had about $425 million in holdings. So, let's set up our own fund for discussion's sake. We'll call it Joe Fund, and it's going to be absolutely average; it has $425 million in holdings and wants to make lots of money. If Joe Fund's manager (Joe) wanted to hold ten stocks, he would divide that money into ten parts, or $42.5 million each. Now, the total value (as measured by market capitalization) of many excellent small caps and micro caps is right about $50 million. Further, the management team of the typical micro cap owns 15 to 40 percent of the company, meaning that a large portion of shares are simply not available on the open market. Thus, you can see that any serious attempt by Joe Fund to establish a meaningful stake in these companies would more often than not involve virtual buyouts of the targeted companies! At the very least, if mutual funds were seriously to attempt to buy 20 to 30 percent of a stock they loved, they'd push up the price so quickly that the latter half of their buying would be at prices far beyond the attractive initial entry point. Not a formula for good investment returns . . . especially when it comes time to *sell* a big stake. The price could be driven down just as far and as fast as it was driven up.

So, what would *you* do if you were Joe managing the Fund and wanted to invest in small caps? You'd end up having to spread out your holdings into, say, fifty separate stocks, in order to avoid the dangers of buying "too much" of a company. Do you have fifty good investment ideas? We expect not, because you're human, after all. Well, so are money managers. We know of very few money-management teams— let alone individuals—who can effectively keep up with fifty or more investments. And every additional investment makes it that much more likely that an investment portfolio will do no more than duplicate the market's performance.

Add to all of this some SEC regulations and a fund's own chosen limitations as published in its prospectus, and you generally wind up with a portfolio that cannot put more than 5 percent of its assets into any given stock, and therefore isn't going to waste its time with tiny stocks that won't have any effect on its bottom line.

To reiterate: The first reason that you want to buy these stocks is that mutual funds cannot . . . yet. The idea is that the small investor *can* buy these stocks, getting in early on some of the great emerging growth stories of American business. Microsoft, Intel, and Wal-Mart all began simply as initial public offerings on the NASDAQ. Mutual funds couldn't really buy them back then, when they were small caps. Over the course of time, as these companies became mid-cap and then large-cap companies, mutual funds and institutions have moved in, in a multibillion-dollar way. The ideal for the individual investor in this situation is to have been the person *selling* the shares to the institutions when the big guys finally became convinced that one or another of these stocks was worth owning. (Although in the case of these three companies, the best plan of attack would have been never to sell at all—but that's a separate story—see chapter 18.) Institutional buying has driven many a small cap into mid-cap territory, and can in many cases be a very accurate contrary indicator (i.e., that institutions are finally buying indicates that the stock is "played out" and the Foolish investor does best to hop off the wagon).

Now it must be said that some of the best-performing mutual funds historically are small-cap growth funds. These include, among others,

Fidelity Low-Priced Stock Fund, Hancock Special Equities A, Heartland Value, and Oberweis Emerging Growth Fund, all of which have compiled market-beating records over the past decade. But what happens then? More investors hear of these funds and invest *their* money in them, too. The fund's assets swell, forcing managers either to invest that money into new stocks they don't like as much, or put more and more money into their favorite existing ones, at significantly higher prices in most cases. And if a small-cap growth fund's assets *still* continue to grow via appreciation, it often has to close itself to new investors altogether or risk walking away from investing in small caps anymore!

By investing directly in the stocks yourself, you gain the ability to profit hugely off of stocks that mutual funds couldn't buy for their customers in sufficient amounts. You get in before the big guys get in, and once they decide to get in, the big dollars they throw at your stock help push it up for you. The best timed buy of all is the purchase of a small cap just before the institutions "discover" it. We've doubled our money in a couple of months or less with stocks in small, emerging-growth companies like Applied Innovation, National TechTeam, and Scientific Technologies, each of which was an unknown small cap that suddenly became known right after we bought it. That that happened is pure luck, of course—no one can control just exactly *when* it is that the next Star Search will turn up one's own stock. But by concentrating a portion of your portfolio in excellent small companies in dynamic growth situations, you give yourself a great shot at beating Harry, your mutual-fund-owning neighbor who plays the tuba, by a wide margin.

Why Even the Family Goldfish Should
Hold Small Caps: Other Reasons

You already have a couple of good reasons for buying and holding small-cap stocks: They have been the best-performing category for decades, and you can beat the institutions into these stocks and then *use* the institutions to prop them up further. The good news doesn't stop there, though.

Here's something to recognize and applaud: Small numbers multiply much more rapidly than big ones. As we'll learn in chapter 17, "The Fool Ratio," we construct valuations for most stocks off earnings multiples. In other words, we believe in a very strict relationship between a stock's price per share, and its company's earnings (or profits) per share. If you do too, then you must recognize that when earnings double, a stock's price may very well double. The question is, which company is more likely to double in size in the next 2 years (all other things remaining equal)—a company with $10 million sales or one with $10 billion in sales? Right, the smaller one. It's a lot easier to triple and double again in size quickly when you're starting from a base below $100 million . . . a lot more difficult anywhere above that.

Earnings grow fastest among small companies. And what often accompanies earnings growth is share price growth. It's an argument made down through the decades, perhaps most convincingly and recently by Peter Lynch in his wonderful book, *One Up on Wall Street.* It didn't hurt that Lynch put his money where his mouth was. He's made a whole career off expounding his love of growth stocks and generating superior returns by investing in them.

Another reason to like small companies is that they are typically closely held by management. That means that the people running the company have a significant financial stake in the success not *just* of the company but of the stock itself. In fact, in many cases, the performance of the stock has a much *greater* influence on the wealth of the management team than does their annual salaries. This is a good thing, quite the opposite of Big Company America, where Forbes 500 operations pay their senior officers huge salaries—way too much, in fact—without in most cases involving them meaningfully in the ownership of the company.

Fools favor companies that are at least 20 percent owned by insiders, and the place you're going to find these companies is mainly among NASDAQ small caps. What this means is that if you invest in one or another hot dog stand, the guy running it probably cares even more than you do about whether or not the dogs are selling. He's probably running your business as if it were the make-or-break opportunity of his financial life. Hey, it probably is, since if he's like the typical small-company management, most of his wealth is tied up in his company's stock.

Because small-cap stocks have such a proven record of achievement, and because they'll always represent an exciting way to invest one's money, these stocks have garnered increasing amounts of attention from individual investors as well as the media at large. (Whether it's the recent ubiquity of NASDAQ television commercials or the emergence over the past decade of *Investor's Business Daily*, the names and profiles of good small companies are easier to come by than ever.) But while everyone's hearing about them these days, very few really know how to locate the best ones, how to value them, and which ones to buy and hold. Now, let's look at a Fool's first task, locating the best growth stocks. After that, we'll go on to learn how to read their financial statements, how to value them, and how to trade them.

·15·

Selecting the
Best Growth Stocks

* * * * *

I have called this principle, by which each slight variation,
if useful, is preserved, by the term Natural Selection.
—*Charles Darwin*

Convinced of our need to fight the good fight and buy up some of these growth stocks, our first task is to discover how to select the best ones. We're not going to learn which ones to *buy* yet, necessarily, only how to develop a list of quality stocks to watch.

One of the more common questions we get online is how we locate stocks. It isn't so much how do we decide which small caps to buy, but rather *where* we look to find them in the first place.

We have three primary sources. The first (though we use it the least) is your local grapevine. Friends of yours who also have an interest in doing their own investing can often provide useful first leads, particularly on companies you'd not heard of before. Sharing ideas on a regular basis with other motivated investors (via starting an investment club, or otherwise) can be profitable and enjoyable. Of course, you should treat these tips only as "useful first leads." Stock tips are a perfect example of "the grass is greener" phenomenon. It always seems like someone has at least one stock that's running faster and jumping higher than anything in your portfolio. And it seems like anything they might suggest would probably outperform anything you could come up with. Well, pilgrim, don't you believe it. Many a Wise man and woman (or their foolish counterparts) have run right out to buy up that high-tech stock they heard being touted at the last cocktail party. Or maybe it's the blue-ribbon retailer whose name was whispered over an expensive lunch. Come on, people. You'd kick the tires and look under the hood before you wrote the dealer a check, wouldn't you? Why would you ever invest in stock if you've never heard of the company and haven't checked it out? Just because your pal told you it was the next hot thing?

Highly, highly unFoolish.

Peter Lynch is a great believer in buying stocks in companies whose products you like, which makes a lot of sense to us. *However,* some people have taken his advice to an abusive extreme and just bought Sara Lee because they like the croissants, then added on Limited because they buy clothes there, then bought some Starbucks because of a nostalgic feeling regarding a good cup of coffee they once enjoyed after hours . . . all of this, without ever doing a lick of homework. Also highly unFoolish. You certainly should take advantage of shared investment ideas with your friends—including companies you've come across both by investment research *and* direct exposure to a product—but please always understand an investment before you undertake it!

A second primary source we use, ever more frequently, is the online world. As we wrote about in chapter 3, you have the advantage online of drawing on a national—rather than a local—community, including many people with greater knowledge of a company than you could ever possibly come by yourself. A community of people united for a common cause can achieve astounding results.

The investment advantages of this new environment cannot be overstated. If you consider yourself a serious investor—or even if you just want to be one—and you're *not* online, you're missing out. In the online world you'll meet people who work at the very company whose stock has caught your fancy, people who work for a competitor, analysts who follow the stock for Wall Street firms, savvy investors who enjoy sharing their investment approaches. In the online world, you can get closer to the source than any pinstriped Wiseman ever got. In fact, stick to your area of expertise and you may *be* the source. And it can pay off. Big.

Among our volunteer staff online we number several doctors, a railroad industry insider, a marketing executive with a Japanese technology multinational, a lawyer or two, a paper-and-forest-products industry analyst, a consultant, a microbrewer, a software developer, and more than forty others . . . the list goes on and on. These were all people we met online, and we signed them up to build The Motley Fool's Industry & Market Analysis section. In so doing, we leveraged the power of the medium to give our audience the opportunity to ask investment questions on a daily basis of industry professionals whose expertise they would otherwise never have come across. That's what we mean by "missing out."

Okay, the third method we have for finding stocks, and the one we continue to use most often, is the earnings page of any good financial daily. We prefer *Investor's Business Daily* (*IBD*), a name you'll read a fair amount in these pages because we believe that the present incarnation of *IBD* is the investor's best friend among financial newspapers. Not only does that newspaper contain more useful numbers than any other on a daily basis, it presents them in a way that simplifies the process of locating good stocks.

The earnings page, for example, first divides up all the companies that reported earnings the day before into two groups, the "Ups" and the "Downs." Because we're only looking at top-quality growth companies, we completely ignore the "Downs," those companies whose most recent earnings came in *lower* than the corresponding numbers from the year before. In general, about a third of all earnings reports are downs, which means that *Investor's Business Daily* enables us to scan the earnings page in two-thirds the time it would take using *The Wall Street Journal.*

Every single day, we comb through the "Ups" from top to bottom, scouring the list for companies whose earnings are up. Of course, this isn't *all* you're going to find out about these operations, but this is how you start. Soon, we'll fill you in on the eight principles that will help you sort out the likely winners from the likely losers, but let's take our baby steps first. When we find a company report that qualifies, we clip it out with scissors, glue the clipping to a sheet, and type the stock into our database.

Keep this up for 3 months—that is, one quarter—and you'll have encountered an earnings statement from virtually every U.S. public company. You should end up with a list of one hundred to one hundred fifty top companies, most of them unrecognizable names, that include some of the greatest newcomers to our stock markets.

Wow! That may sound like a lot to do. It certainly is about a one-hour commitment a day and a couple of hours on weekends to get it all in a spreadsheet. If you have the time to do this, we think your investment returns will justify the time spent. At the very least, you will wind up thoroughly educated.

If you do not have sufficient time or inclination to do this, you have a few options. If you don't have any time at all for this stuff, go directly back to "The Dow Dividend Strategy" (part III) and *do* collect $200. You definitely shouldn't worry about the material in this chapter; you have enough other things to worry about, and your Dow High Yielders will stand you in good stead.

If, on the other hand, you do have some time, just not quite enough, you have two alternatives. One is to play a hit-and-miss strategy, combing the earnings page when you can but not worrying about those days when you can't. Not everyone needs a hundred-stock database. If you spend, say, one hour one day a week, you'll still have twenty-plus companies to add to your list, and twenty potential new investment ideas in 3 months will suffice for most people. A second option, which you can combine with the first, is to take a group approach to this work. This is where the power of the online world comes in. Merge your list or spreadsheet of stocks with those of others. Let's say you commit to clipping earnings reports from interesting companies on Mondays. Find someone who'll do it Tuesdays, then you both find someone to do it Wednesdays, and so on. Combine your lists every weekend into one spreadsheet and e-mail it to everyone, and you have a good gig going. Cooperating never seems to occur to our species often enough.

Okay, you've now learned all the places we go to find stocks. The rest of this chapter explains how we go about selecting the best ones. Let's start by introducing Messages.

Messages Incorporated (NASDAQ:MESS)

NOTE: Throughout this section, we'll be looking at Messages Inc., an upstart company bringing some ingenious new ideas to a fairly dull, mature business. This fictional company, based in Reno, Nevada, exhibits dynamic growth of the very sort Fools favor, though the situation grows a bit more complicated (and educational) as we delve deeper. Messages won't be coming public anytime soon, probably, so we're going to fast-forward several years for the following chapters.

So, a friend turns you on to this new investment idea—a company you've never heard a thing about. That's quite surprising, given the story you now have before you. Messages Incorporated. It's the newest thing . . . recently mentioned on the nightly news, you're told. Hmm . . . . Well, at least your friend has been kind enough to provide you the company's investor information packet. Let's read the company description:

Messages Incorporated™ manufactures, markets, and distributes written communications included with traditional novelty items. The company's primary business involves tiny scrolls inserted into fortune cookies, except that **Messages** has radically redefined the meaning, function, and popularity of these items. In 1996 the company pioneered the use of flavored scrolls with the introduction of its new TastiScroll® technology, a line of paper breath fresheners. In late 1997 the company introduced new concepts for the messages themselves, creating the popular Info-Cookie®. InfoCookies, whose predecessors focused entirely on conveying "fortunes" of little redeeming value, now feature stock tips, lucky lottery numbers, winning picks for NFL games, and revenue-generating suggestions for entrepreneurs. The Info-Cookie won the Best of Show prize at the 1998 Consumer ProductFest, and helped **Messages** reach 25th on the year 2000 list of The Forbes 200 Hottest Small Companies.

The company forecasts dynamic growth into the twenty-first century on the wings of its two-tiered expansion strategy: (1) vertical growth, involving further development of message concepts for the InfoCookie (Braille messages, audio messages, custom birth and death announcements, etc.), and (2) horizontal growth, involving the deployment of messages over a wider range of consumer gift items (airline snackpacks, compact discs, piñatas, etc.). **Messages'** InfoCookie brand name poses, in the company's estimation, significant barriers to competition.

Messages™ is a registered trademark, and markets its primary product line under the service marks "More Than Just a Cookie" and "We're Talking to You."

With interest, you peruse further the company's news announcements and press materials. You notice that much of Messages Inc.'s publicity revolves around stories of people whose lives were radically changed by messages they'd read: those who made money on the stock tips, lottery winners, and entrepreneurs turned on to their winning product ideas by suggestions contained on the company's edible scrolls. Amazing. You wonder right away whether Messages has run into legal problems from people who may have acted on some of these moneymaking tips, failed, and blamed the cookie. But in a precedent-setting 1996 case, Judge Marcia Ito ruled the company "not responsible for losses incurred as a result of its products," adding that "these are basically just a novelty item, fortune cookies whose messages adults shouldn't take seriously." While the company itself might disagree with the reasoning, it obviously agreed with the ruling. Legal problems appear to be a nonissue for an investor.

Business is booming. The start-up company's sales have already reached $50 million over the past 12 months and are mounting at an impressive rate. A few analysts have trotted out impressive earnings estimates for the next few years, and is that at all surprising? Nope. The production cost of these tiny TastiScrolls must be negligible, while the faddish enthusiasm that the market has taken to the product has enabled this company to charge rates far above its production expenses. The company's common stock has done exceedingly well, and many are now speculating that Messages might make an attractive acquisition for a bakery products conglomerate, like Sara Lee.

Messages Incorporated grabs your attention even further when, a few days later, a *New York Times* op-ed piece skewers the company's newest business plan to make a large portion of the "Inspected by No. X" messages in new garments *edible*. The article contends that by conditioning consumers to blithely ingest their "Inspected" slips, the company will induce thousands of people to eat chemically treated paper that is not at all edible. That's because Messages' TastiScrolls are expected to penetrate only 30 percent of the "Inspected" slip market, meaning that *fully 70 percent* of these slips will be quite inedible. Reacting to the piece, the stock drops from $15 to $10 in one day, as critics suddenly reach a consensus that *The Times* has put a permanent kibosh on Messages' aggressive "horizontal" expansion plans.

Ah, but the competitive business advantages of the product eventually far outweigh short-term admonitions, and in the coming weeks the company continues to announce sales deals with domestic and multinational corporations. Corporate partners simply cannot deny the entertaining enhancement of including InfoCookies and other imaginatively placed messages in their products. The "brand enhancement" of inserted messages enables a diverse group of manufacturers to differentiate their product from competitors by creating incredible—and edible—goodwill with the customer. It's a winning formula, and the company before you is at present a huge winner.

Having gotten to know a little about this company, it's now time to match it up to our growth-stock selection criteria. "Is it worth adding this company to the list of stocks I follow?" you ask yourself. Well, you have the research material in front of you. Let's go through our eight-item checklist and see.

The Eight-Item Checklist
We Use to Pick Stocks

For the purpose of determining a given stock's suitability for our portfolio, we use a checklist of eight items, eight tests that any equity must pass before it makes our list. The point of this chapter, as stated above, is to help you generate this list of *potential* picks. The list itself does *not* comprise our final selections, but it is often from this list that we end up picking our eventual selections. Fortunately, each of the concepts below is so simple—in most cases, nonmathematical—that any novice can learn it without difficulty. And keep in mind, these measures are best used for finding *small* growth companies. Many of these measures do enjoy use outside of the search for small growth companies, but our list is tailored to small caps.

To that end, not all of what follows are qualitative judgments; the first four are mainly quantitative restrictions put in place to narrow the field, to keep our watch list from getting too big or unwieldy. We have no desire to follow seven hundred forty-eight different stocks, and we don't expect you do either. It's kind of like looking only for astronauts who are young, in top shape, don't have asthma, and don't suffer from any notable manias, phobias, or dependencies. Now, we *could* try to go to the moon with a team of fat old drunks, but our country—not to mention our investment portfolio—increases its odds of success through more demanding criteria.

Keep it simple.

1. The Company's Sales: $200 Million or Less

If we can agree that all stocks *can* be reasonably valued, then it follows that the least followed and least familiar ones have the greatest potential for not yet having been fully evaluated. It is among America's small companies that you're most likely to find an uncut gem—one that, as we've said before, institutions won't be able to buy yet. That is why we use limits on a *company's sales* to weed out the ones we want to follow from those we don't. Leave behind all the monster corporations for now, General Motors and Coca-Cola and all the rest, and set your sights on the lesser-knowns.

Scientific Technologies (NASDAQ:STIZ), the tiny maker of industrial safety equipment, was one of the first stocks we ever bought back in the days of Ye Olde Printed Foole, our erstwhile printed publication. Twelve months before we bought the stock, the shares stood at $1⅜. We bought them at $3⅞, and within 4 months they'd shot past $10. (It took another year and a half for them to surpass that height, but Scientific

Tech was most recently seen in the low $20s, a fifteen-bagger in 2 years.)

Now, has your celebrity stock market "gooroo" (the kind you see on television telling everyone where the market is going) ever heard of this company, even now? How about your dentist, Dr. Frequent? Or your sister-in-law Sally? We don't think so.

Please don't limit your investment prospects to companies with which you are immediately familiar. That you *are* familiar with them already suggests, in most cases, that a lot of other people are too, including a lot of institutions. While this doesn't mean that any company you already know won't sport a great stock, it does mean that we think you should instead focus on developing a small-cap growth list of lesser-known, upcoming companies—the ones that so often put up the greatest investment returns of all.

Fools prefer companies that did $200 million or less in sales in the past year. It's companies that have $200 million or less in sales that are mostly likely to double and triple in size over the next few years. And the nice thing about limiting yourself to $200 million in sales is that you can quickly eyeball an earnings report in your newspaper and see that a given company does or does not merit further scrutiny. Pass your eye down the earnings page of *Investor's Business Daily* or *The Wall Street Journal* and you'll typically encounter something like this:

GENCORP

Qtr. May 31:	1995
Sales	461,900,000

GENESEE CORP. CL B

12 mo Apr 30:	1995
Sales	131,367,000

HARTCO ENTERPRISES

Qtr. Apr 29:	1995
Sales	113,822,000

You can see right off that Gencorp's sheer size makes it one we would certainly not keep track of. Genesee, on the other hand, has sales of $131 million. Now, these numbers may be reported on a quarterly, multiple-quarterly, or annual basis, so you always need to make sure you know which. As it turns out in Genesee's case, its beer sales are $131 million for the year, so it passes our first checklist test: Its sales are under $200 million. Moving next to Hartco, the computer retailer appears to be all right with $113 million in sales, but then we notice that's only for the *quarter.* In this case, we assume that Hartco has had similar sales figures in its previous three quarters, so that we multiply the figure by 4. Arriving at a result that's more than double our $200 million limit, we see that Hartco obviously will not pass our test. (Note: Some operations have quarterly sales cycles with highly seasonal aberrations. Take a company involved in tax preparation, for example, which derives the lion's share of its revenues in the first 6 months of the year, and not much after that. We typically avoid these situations altogether, since investing in companies whose earnings show up just once or twice a year involves taking on extra risk. Only a couple of dates really matter, and they end up mattering too much. With so many "normal" industrial companies out there, why complicate matters by tracking hit-or-miss half-year wonders?)

Since Messages racked up sales of only $50 million over the past 12 months, it's certainly small enough for us. We move on.

2. Daily Dollar Volume: $3 Million or Less

Last chapter we discussed market capitalization, but capitalization is not the most useful measure for investors intent on classifying and generalizing about *the size of stocks.* In fact, once we've located a likely small-cap stock, we almost never use the capitalization figure. Much more important to us is the company's *daily dollar volume,* since that's our second Foolish requirement. The optimum range for daily dollar volume is between $50,000 and $3 million.

Whereas capitalization measures the total amount of value of a company's equity (remember the formula: *share price times number of shares*), our daily dollar volume figure tracks the total amount of money that trades in a given stock on an average day. This figure enables one to measure and follow a stock's "liquidity," which we consider far more meaningful than market cap. Particularly in the case of small- and micro-cap investing, the liquidity of stocks can greatly affect how they trade.

Like market capitalization, figuring the daily dollar volume is simple multiplication. To get the figure, just multiply a stock's share price by its *average daily trading volume.* You may already know a good source for average daily volume. But if you don't, the easiest place to find this information is probably, once again, *Investor's Business Daily,* which each day prints for every stock both the number of shares that traded in it, and the percentage change from the norm that that figure represents. Dipping open your *IBD,* you locate the following in the paper:

Stock	Vol. 100s	Vol. % Change
Messages	343	–65

From these figures, you'll need to deduce the average daily volume—a piece of cake. The "343" number is that day's volume, expressed in hundreds. In other words, 34,300 shares exchanged hands. The "–65" lets you know what percentage change that figure was from the average of the last 50 trading days. In this case, Messages' volume of 34,300 shares was actually 65 percent below recent norms. To calculate what is the normal figure, therefore, you simply take 34,300 and divide it by 1 minus .65, or .35. (You use 1 minus .65 because 1 represents 100 percent, or average daily volume, and in this case you were .65 below that, at just .35—or 35 percent—of daily volume.) Let's do the math: 34,300 divided by .35 equals 98,000 on the nose. In other words, we have just figured out that the average daily volume for Messages is 98,000 shares.

Now all that's left to do is to calculate the daily dollar volume in this stock. Let's take a more complete look at the listing:

Stock	Vol. 100s	Vol. % Change	Closing Price
Messages	343	–65	12⅝

We've already calculated the average daily volume: 98,000 shares. Multiplying by the closing price of $12⅝, we come away with an average daily dollar volume of $1,237,250. That means that a typical six-and-a-half-hour trading day sees more than $1 million of Messages stock change hands. Yowser.

Now, while the previous explanation took the better part of a page to explain, the actual time that it'll take you to do these calculations is minimal. Of course, if you are capable of setting up a spreadsheet to do this, even less time is required; you just type in (or import) the numbers and let your computer do the calculations.

A daily dollar volume of $1.2 million may sound like a fair amount, but it's peanuts compared to most stocks you've heard of. Apple Computer, for example, trades over $100 million a day. Microsoft, at last check, traded three times more than that. But $1.2 million is a very significant number to Fools, because it comes under our $3 million daily dollar volume maximum.

With few exceptions, we add only those stocks that trade $3 mil-

lion a day or less to our checklist. Messages, at $1.2 million, fulfills this criteria. Our reasoning, again, is to follow only those stocks that remain relatively "undiscovered" by institutions. We are intentionally seeking less "liquid" situations, situations in which institutions would have difficulty liquidating (cashing out). Institutions intentionally *avoid* these situations until stocks grow big enough to trade enough . . . it is at that point that institutions buy and stocks really begin to fly.

By limiting the amount of daily dollar volume to $3 million or less, you're using the advantage available to you as a small, private investor. You're scoring touchdowns against the big guys on *your* turf, turf too awkward for them to touch yet. That's not supposed to be the case. The popular press always seems to be emphasizing how *difficult* it is for the little guy to swim in institution-infested waters. But we're telling you that you can swim circles 'round the institutions, especially if you gain energy from feeding on the plankton.

Before we close this point, you may be wondering whether we're therefore recommending that you seek out penny stock situations featuring securities that trade $10,000 to $50,000 a day, or many days not at all? Never. Don't get too illiquid. Stick to higher-quality companies that trade over $50,000 a day and have NASDAQ listings.

3. Low Share Price: Between $5 and $20

The third Foolish requirement is also mainly in place to limit the field. It's simply a stock's *share price. We prefer stocks trading between $5 and $20 per share,* although we're not big sticklers on this point.

The reason that we don't take this one too seriously is because it is less consequential than our other seven criteria. The level of the share price is not nearly so meaningful as limiting the company's sales, daily dollar volume, or (as we'll show you shortly) net profit margins or positive cash flow. Then again, anyone familiar with Michael O'Higgins's version of the Dow Dividend Strategy knows that low price per share is used as the final criterion for stock selection, and it apparently *works.* (See chapter 10.) Over a long period of time, O'Higgins's lowest-priced five Beating the Dow stocks far outperform the list of ten from which they're selected. We cannot necessarily explain this in a highly scientific manner other than to suggest that, as explicated last chapter, small numbers multiply much more rapidly than large ones. All other things remaining equal, if you come across two compelling situations, one a stock priced at $10 and the other a stock priced at $50, you should buy the one sitting at $10. Low-priced undervalued stocks are, in our experience, far more likely "quick doubles" than their higher-priced twins. Theoretically they *should* move up to fair valuation at the same speed, regardless of share price. They *should*, but real-world experience shows that they don't.

Of course, we generally don't waste our time with illiquid junk under $5 per share.

4. Net Profit Margin: 10 Percent or More

The fourth Foolish requirement is also designed to limit the field. But whereas a company's sales and dollar volume and share price relate merely to size, a high *net profit margin* relates mostly to quality.

Let's learn just exactly what the net profit margin is by referring to Messages' financial statements. If you're right now looking at an income statement for the first time, you'll soon see how little you had to fear all those years:

STATEMENT OF INCOME —numbers in 000—	Messages Inc.
Revenue	**50,000**
Cost of sales	21,000
Gross profit	**29,000**
Operating expenses:	
Selling, general & admin.	12,000
Research & development	6,000
	18,000
Income from operations	**11,000**
Interest income	**50**
Income before taxes	**11,050**
Income taxes	3,650
Net income	**7,400**

All numbers in bold represent sales and profits; non-bold represents subtractions, or costs.

The income statement is an extremely simple and useful table. It simply shows a business's sales on the top line and its profits on the bottom. (Note that all numbers in the table—and in most financial tables—are expressed in thousands, as the "numbers in 000" indicates.) Between a company's top-line sales and its bottom-line profits are its costs of doing business, appearing on the income statement as deductions from the top line. In Messages' case, we see that it did $50 million in revenues for the year last year, almost all of it via TastiScroll proliferating like kudzu across Georgia. From this figure, we must deduct $21 million for the factory costs of manufacturing these products, also known as "cost of sales." The number we're left with is gross profit, or

$29 million. Some financial analysts like to use a measure of profitability called the "gross margin." This is simply gross profit—$29 million—taken as a percentage of (divided by) overall sales: $50 million. Messages' gross margin (29 divided by 50) is thus 58 percent.

The next deduction we'll take is in the so-called operating costs, comprising "selling, general, and administrative" costs (SG&A), and "research & development costs" (R&D). SG&A typically includes salaries, advertising and marketing expenses, office expenses, insurance, rent, and other miscellaneous fun stuff, like executive weekend trips to Kennebunkport or Taos. Messages racked up $12 million there. Research and development expenses represent the amount that a company pays to develop new products; in Messages' case, our psychologists are studying human behavior to determine which products will serve as the best vehicles for new messages by the year 2000. The psychologists' conclusions, mainly involving attempts at sticking messages wherever they'll best fit into mass transit, cost a total of $6 million last year in development expenses. Adding SG&A and R&D together, we reach our operating cost of $18 million.

Income from operations isn't too difficult to calculate next: $29 million in gross profits minus $18 million of total operating costs. Hmm. Looks like $11 million. (Can you believe accountants get paid so much to do this stuff?!)

Most small companies have little debt and not much cash, so that the line item that follows, interest income (or it could be expense), is usually small enough that it's relatively insignificant. Yep, that's pretty much the case with Messages.

Now it's time for income taxes . . . dreaded beast. Most corporations these days pay out about one third of their profits to income taxes. The corporation that we're subjecting to such extreme scrutiny isn't very different in this case. Messages paid almost exactly one third last year, or about $3.7 million. What is left over, as you already know, is the bottom line, profits, a.k.a. "net income," since it's income after having netted out everything else.

Congratulations! You just learned in about a page what takes a third of a term in a typical accounting course.

Back to the matter at hand, we're actually in search of "net profit margin." Above, we read about gross profit margin being simply gross profit taken as a percentage of overall sales. Net profit margin is simply *net income* (Messages' is $7.4 million) taken as a percentage of sales.

Thus, Messages' net profit margin is $7.4 divided by $50 . . . 14.8 percent. *Our Foolish requirement is that the companies we follow should show a minimum net profit margin of 10 percent.*

What does 14.8 percent—or our minimum of 10 percent—mean? And why do we bother making this our fourth Foolish requirement? Fools prefer this figure high because a high net profit margin indicates a company that is either soundly beating its competition or (Fool's choice) has no competition at all. In our capitalistic world, a high net profit margin is an achievement, a mark of excellence. That's because anybody who can manage to make 14.8 cents off every dollar of sales (as Messages is doing) must be doing something right. High margins automatically invite copycats, competitors who will be happy trying to run you out of business by selling the same product for profits of 10 or 12 cents off every dollar of sales. Again, it's called capitalism, darling of the consumer, bane of the complacent business. Now, a company that actually *maintains* a high net profit margin over the years gives clear numerical proof of its superiority.

A bit more context helps here. The typical net profit margin will vary from industry to industry, while in most cases remaining below 10 percent. Bargain-basement retailers and supermarkets typically sport margins of less than 3 percent, many closer to 1 percent. Why would that be? It's not hard to imagine. Retailers like Kmart have built billion-dollar businesses out of offering consumers the lowest price. In a cutthroat competitive world, it stands to reason these guys ain't taking too much to the bank. (You'll notice, for instance, that Kmart does "blue-light specials," as opposed to "red-carpet specials." Or red-carpet anything.)

Pop quiz: What margins are typical of airline companies?

If you answered "negative," you win the little white furry thing on the third shelf up. Airlines, almost as a rule, don't turn profits.

Technology companies are typically where you'll find the best profitability, the highest margins. That's because when a successful company carves out its own niche with a revolutionary product, it can get away with charging higher prices (taking in more profits) because no one else is making, say, cold-fusion automobile engines.

Reminds us of the situation in the pharmaceuticals industry, where new products have been creating lucrative niches for years. In fact, it was the impressively high net profit margins of drug manufacturers like Merck and Bristol-Myers Squibb that drew the attention of the Clinton administration in the first place, bringing about that administration's efforts to regulate the health care industry. (And creating, by the by, a wonderful place to jump into Merck stock, which the Fool Portfolio did at $30¼ in the summer of 1994, ripping off a 60 percent gain in less than a year.) Anyway, as Kipling may have written, "Ours not to reason why, ours but to make jokes about all the people who think that the government should run our health care system."

High margins aren't necessarily only for high-technology and drug companies, though. We've found some great small companies in a wide variety of industries over the years, everything from property and casualty insurance (GAINSCO—AMEX:GNA—a fine winner way back when) to plastic moldings for the light-truck market (Lund Industries—NASDAQ:LUND—which increased in value fourteen times over the course of 3 years, if you played it right . . . which we didn't quite exactly that well, but still caught a double).

(Hey, you think we talk only about our winners? Well, would you have it otherwise, having paid twenty bucks?)

Messages, at this point, has met all four of our Foolish criteria, being both small enough and profitable enough. Time to push on.

5. Relative Strength: 90 or Higher

Foolish requirement number five introduces one of our favorites: *relative strength*. Relative strength rates the performance of every stock listed on the three major exchanges (the New York Stock Exchange, the American Stock Exchange, and the NASDAQ). The rating system gives a numerical grade—just like the ones Mr. Spicer used to scrawl in bright red ink on your algebra quizzes—to the performance of a stock over the past 12 months. (The range is actually 1 to 99.) Thus, relative strength is a momentum indicator. A relative strength of 95, for example, indicates a wonderful stock, one that has outperformed 95 percent of all other American stocks over the past year.

Though the concept dates back a long time, we first read about relative strength in William O'Neil's book, the bluntly titled *How to Make Money in Stocks*. (O'Neil also happens to be the publisher of *Investor's Business Daily*, in which relative strength is printed for every stock, every weekday. Thank you, sir!) Mr. O'Neil favors purchasing stocks with high relative strengths, an approach that we have found very successful. O'Neil writes—somewhat Foolishly, we might add—"If . . . you buy equities that haven't yet moved or are down the most in price, because you feel safer with them and think you're getting a real bargain, you're probably buying . . . sleepy losers . . . .Why buy an equity whose relative performance is inferior and straggling drearily behind a larger number of other, better-acting securities in the market? Yet most investors do, and many do it without ever looking at a relative strength line or number."

Here we see the two fundamental mentalities one can take to purchasing securities on the stock market: that of the Pendulum, and that of the Horse Race. The Pendulum claims that what goes one way will, in time, go the other; buy stocks that are down and out, because they can swing only so far one way before you make money by going the other. On the other hand, the Horse Race mentality suggests that you should bet on the pony that's in first place coming down the stretch, because who else is going to win? The Foolish mentality on growth stocks runs much more toward the latter approach.

It really all comes down to physics, actually. Way back in the late seventeenth century Sir Isaac Newton penned the first law of motion: "Every body remains in a state of rest or in a state of uniform motion (constant speed in a straight line) unless it is compelled by impressed forces to change that state." This is the fundamental principle of relative strength, as well, that until "impressed forces" show up "to change that state" of a stock, your likelihood of turning a profit—maybe a quick, BIG profit (the best profit of all)—is very good. In other words, if it's already rising, chances are it will keep rising. Mere coincidence, by the way, that Newton was appointed master of the mint in 1699?

Tomorrow's strong companies and stock market heroes typically flock like geese in the high ranges of relative strength. This contrary notion confounds the Wise, who, when they see a stock with a 52-week high of $22 hitting new lows at $10, purchase the stock because it looks "cheap." The high-flying nature of turbocharged relative strength stocks, on the other hand, offends their staid sensibilities. They may even get blue in the face telling you, "The P/E is too high!" or "It's already had its run!" High-flying stocks, in fact, are the frequent targets of Wall Street journalists, who can always be depended upon to try to pick off the latest highflier in their *Barron's* or "Heard on the Street" columns.

Here's a typical example of a stock that you and I should've wanted in on, even if it rips at the establishment's cherished mores. When Glenayre Technologies (NASDAQ:GEMS) went from a pre–stock-split $11¾ per share to $24 early in 1993, its relative strength exceeded 90. Many traders no doubt saw the doubling of the share price and the high relative strength as reasons to avoid Glenayre. Having deeply regretted missing a buying opportunity below $12, they may have figured that a stock that had already done so well had more room below it than above. What must have *really* gotten their goats is that over the next few months Glenayre proceeded to run up over $110 a share! Thus, the stock quickly more than quadrupled *after the original double,* and it sported a relative strength of 99 all the way up. Only a Fool would dare hold that stock all the way up (though we never owned that one, shucks).

Preferring to bet on the winning horse, we limit our field to stocks that have a relative strength of 90 or more, taking Mr. O'Neil up on his idea. Messages, at $12⅝, happens to have a relative strength of 92, which not entirely coincidentally happens to meet our fifth Foolish requirement. Although the company's stock still sits a few points off its recent high after the *Times* piece, it's nevertheless up from a low of $3½ toward the end of last year, and has been a stellar market performer. Just the sort we like to welcome into Fool Stables.

6. Earnings and Sales Growth: 25 Percent or Greater

The aim of part V is to learn how to invest in dynamic small-cap growth stocks. It stands to reason, therefore, that we won't accept anything less than strong *earnings and sales growth* when we're scouring the investment world for new portfolio picks. Our sixth Foolish requirement dictates that in its most recent quarter, *any company we're following must demonstrate revenue and net income growth of at least 25 percent higher than the same period the year before.* We could lower this limitation to 15 percent or 20 percent, but then all we're doing is diluting the amount of growth that we consider worthy; we're not going to do that. We could also raise the limitation to 30 percent or 40 percent, but our experience suggests that 25 percent makes a better cutoff because it doesn't restrict the field too much.

Corporate financial statements are prepared and published four times a year, at three-month intervals ("quarters"). You should be following your stocks *at least* this often so that you're on top of your company's developing story. Additionally, the reports compiled by financial analysts typically make quarterly projections of sales and earnings, numbers that you should have fairly well committed to memory for the upcoming quarter.

Why is this important? Well, you've just checked in with your broker and heard that Forever Lightbulbs, your favorite stock, has lost $5 in morning trading. "Down five?!" you cry into the telephone receiver. "Any news?" Your broker informs you that Forever 'Bulbs reported its earnings that morning, showing sales and income leaped 100 percent in its most recent quarter, when compared to the like quarter the year before. Does this news anger you? That pretty much depends on how well informed an investor you are. In many situations, 100 percent growth looks wonderful. But here, the four analysts following Forever 'Bulbs had predicted 150 percent growth year to year. These quarterly numbers are therefore somewhat of a disappointing shock to the Street, but still perfectly explainable. Your job now is to plug in the new numbers and reevaluate the stock.

It is this act of reevaluating on a quarterly basis that should inspire you to keep a handle on the date when each of your companies expects to publish its next earnings report. If your broker can't furnish the date for you, you may obtain it by dialing your company directly and asking the representative in Investor Relations. (A mini-primer at the end of this chapter explains how to do so Foolishly.)

For those who don't know how to calculate growth rates, it's a very simple process involving obtaining the percentage difference between two numbers. In chapter 17, we'll have you calculating more growth rates than a dad who wants his kid to be an NBA star, so for now we'll restrain ourselves. It's enough to note in passing that Messages' sales and earnings are up more than 80 percent in its most recent published annual report. No significant competition, here, yet . . . the innovative company was first to market with its product and carved out a brand name, InfoCookie, that consumer awareness studies ranked even with Kentucky Fried Chicken. Messages easily passes our sixth test.

7. Insider Holdings: At Least 15 Percent

As we mentioned last chapter, a respectable amount of *insider holdings* is an attractive attribute in a stock, one that we actively seek out. *Fools typically prefer to see at least 15 percent of a small-cap growth company owned by management.* In many cases it's a good deal higher.

We've already gone over this point, so there's not much to add here other than that you should almost never be dissuaded by news of insiders selling their shares. As we mentioned last chapter, many insiders have most of their wealth tied up in their own company's stock. Just like you, they have loved ones to put through space camp, lots and lots of Ben and Jerry's ice cream to buy, and a fraudulent oil field or two to invest in (and later take a tax loss on). In other words, they too have costs that their salaries cannot always cover. Selling their stock is their way of getting rich, and in many cases they've worked hard as hell to earn it.

So next time someone points out to you that one of your stock's insiders are bailing left and right, ignore this person. Insider sales occur about ten times more often than insider buys, and are only in the very rarest situations cause for concern (e.g., multiple insiders sell out all or most of their positions in one pop, at about the same time).

What is Messages' management's stake in its own stock? Of the 10 million shares outstanding, fully 3.5 million sit in the coffers of Norman Vincent Steele, the founder and CEO of one of America's most talked about companies. Indeed, 35 percent is a high mark, well above that of most company managements. If Steele continues to think positively about holding his shares, and if over the next decade Messages can grow in line with some analysts' humongous expectations, our man may just become the Bill Gates of his own generation.

8. Cash Flow from Operations: A Positive Number

We've saved the figure that's hardest to explain to the very end. Number eight is *cash flow from operations.* Cash flow is a measure of the movement of money through a business. It is reported in the statement of cash flow that usually appears at the end of a company's financial statements. We want this number to be positive.

What does positive operational cash flow mean? It means that in the course of running its business, the company has managed to *generate* cash rather than consume it (which would be indicated by a negative number). You want your companies to crank out free cash from operations, making the necessary funds available for internal expansion, acquisitions, dividend payments, or whatever. A company that has negative cash flow has to borrow money in order to maintain and grow its business. For a small company, that's a discouraging indication that the company will either have to take on debt (borrow money for the short or long term) or issue more shares of stock (diluting the all important earnings per share; see chapters 16 and 17).

You might ask, "Doesn't *every* profitable business generate positive cash flow?" The answer is no. Messages is unfortunately one such example. Following the strong fiscal 2000 report that we've been looking at in this chapter, the company will go on to turn in a disappointing 2001, detailed next chapter. So that despite its obvious profitability, Messages goes "cash-flow negative," which is perhaps the only thing we don't like about MESS stock right now. Let's preview the situation (the brunt of the analysis of the company's finances for 2001 does appear next chapter).

In 2001 Messages does sales of $97 million in a further explosion of market penetration based both on brand-name expansion domestically *and* an unexpected swelling of international sales, as the "messages" concept suddenly seizes the imagination of the Far East. Unfortunately, foreign customers are notoriously slow in paying, taking several months. Further, in order to grow its sales so fast and generate publicity, Messages has extended extremely favorable payment terms to these foreign customers, allowing them to finance their purchases of Messages products at a low low low .5 percent annual interest charge, no money down. In other words, as it turns out, Messages has practically been giving the product away overseas. All of this has substantially bulked up the company's accounts receivable.

When you look hard at it (we'll talk about how to do this in the following chapter), you discover that Messages' customers are taking an average of more than 4 months to pay for their TastiScrolls. Meanwhile, Norman Vincent Steele has to pay salaries, advertising and marketing costs, Mr. Landlord, and his sugar suppliers, within *1 month* of services rendered. The predicament hurts Messages' finances pretty badly, though it simply represents a natural outgrowth of the company's business plan. Anyway, MESS now occupies the uncomfortable position of having to pay its costs three months before getting paid by its customers. Despite the impressive profitability we discovered in the income statement earlier this chapter, Messages is cash-flow negative; the act of growing its business consumes cash, rather than creates it. Unless the company can turn this situation around by making stricter payment demands of its customers, more business will only mean more short-term cash consumed, and an even greater need either to borrow money or to sell more shares in order to generate the cash on hand necessary to meet a 3-month cash shortfall.

A company with *positive* cash flow, on the other hand, signals a savvy management team and a strong business, the very sort of situation we like to buy and hold. (We'll read a lot more about cash-flow statements in the next chapter.)

Well, our darling stock met seven of our eight criteria, so we're left to ponder whether or not we should continue to pursue Messages. You don't think we'd write a whole chapter about the company behind this epoch-changing piece of technology and drop it flat just before the chapter on "Making Sense of Financial Info," do you? No way, Manet.

Let's thank our friend for turning us on to this one and for sharing his packet of financial info with us. It's time for us to procure our own set of statements. And maybe get a sample of the product, check out the quality of its breath mint . . . maybe try one or two of those TastiScroll stock tips.

Your Call to the Company Requesting Info

So, you have the phone number: 1-800-MESSAGE. Cute. Okay, time to call the company. But how do you reach the people you need to reach? And once you do, what should you say?

Well, first, let's list what you'll need to ask for. A full information packet contains the following, all of which you should request:

1. The annual report (most recent)
2. The 10-K financial statement (most recent)
3. The 10-Q financial statement (most recent)
4. Press releases (as many recent ones as you can get)
5. Analysts' reports (all available up-to-date ones)

Good news: ALL of this information will be furnished to you free of charge, no strings attached. Isn't America great?

Let's dial the number.

MESSAGES HQ: Hello, Messages Incorporated! How may I direct your call?

YOU: Hi, there! *[Never hurts to be friendly]* Um, Investor Relations, please?

> *[At this point, the receptionist will say either this:]*

RECEPTIONIST: Do you just want financial information sent out to you, or would you like to speak with someone?

> *[in which case you exchange:]*

YOU: Oh, I'd just like financial information.

RECEPTIONIST: Fine, I'll be happy to take your name and address, or you could leave it on Lucky Mintoro's voice mail. She's the director of Investor Relations.

> *[OR, the receptionist will say this:]*

RECEPTIONIST: One moment, please! I'm transferring you to our Investor Relations Department.

> *[Either way, you name the five pieces of literature you seek.]*
> *[Then, if you do end up talking directly with Lucky Mintoro . . .]*

YOU: Oh, and would you please include my name and address on your investor mailing list? I'd like to receive regular updates on the company.

LUCKY MINTORO: I'd be more than happy to do that. Yes.

YOU *[If you're really gung-ho and have the technology]*: Do you e-mail or fax out your press releases hot off the wire? Because in that case, I'd love to be on your list, as well.

LUCKY MINTORO: Sure.

> *[Or:]*

LUCKY MINTORO: No.

YOU *[just to be obnoxious]*: Really? *[Stunned.]* Wow. I can't believe that. *[Totally let down.]* Oh well . . . .*[If enough of us do this, we Fools will one day have every company in America e-mailing or faxing its press releases. Bear the torch. Keep the faith.]*

[And now it's time to draw the call to a close.]

YOU: Thanks for your time, and continued best of luck to Messages. I won a bake-sale raffle last week using the lucky number from my latest InfoCookie! Anyway, we invite your company to join us on America Online, at The Motley Fool, keyword FOOL. There, through the Inform America plan, your company can post all its press releases in Fooldom's Messages message folder. Shareholders love it.

And the call ends, as you're most likely hung up on. But hey, easy, isn't it? You've learned the eight things to look for when selecting a top growth stock. And now, when the stuff arrives a week later, it's time to learn all you can about Messages.

·16·

Making Sense
of Financial Info

· · · · ·

A Fool sees not the same tree that a Wise Man sees.
—*William Blake*

You've read about the company, you've checked it against our eight Foolish requirements, you've called up Messages' global headquarters, and you now have its full financial information in front of you. First time you've ever really looked at one of these packets, in fact.

The first thing you see upon opening the manila envelope is the colorful dossier containing the company's annual report, press releases, SEC documents, et cetera . . . and what else? A cinnamon-flavored message, of course! (It says, "Buy MESS below $20," showing you that Lucky Mintoro has a very good sense of humor.) Looking it over, you see that the folder has been artistically rendered with color photographs, expensive graphics, and the Messages logo plastered right smack in the center. Welcome to one of the first lessons learned about a company's financial information packet: It's as much a marketing device as anything else. As you read through the text portions of the annual report and press releases, you'll want to keep this observation foremost in mind. By sending you the darn financial info in the first place, the company is hoping to sell you on its stock.

Many different (and conflicting) inferences may be drawn from the presentation of a company's packet. Should an annual report look expensive or not? Every color photograph, every additional page of fine paper—these things cost money. When the company could be spending the money on its operation, do you really want an outfit in which *you're* invested to ring up a big expense on the annual report (a charge included on the selling, general, and administrative line item of the income statement, by the way, to review from last chapter)?

Then again, if you peel open a company's investor information packet and see grainy black-and-white pictures of drab people in a corporate headquarters sloppily appointed, do you want to invest your money there? Some financial commentators have said that's *exactly* the situation you want to invest in, but we're not so sure. If a company is that poor at "selling itself" in materials targeted at investors, how successful do you think its marketing campaigns will be? Can people who so fail to communicate their story in a compelling way to individual investors ever succeed in communicating that same story to the institutions who have the greatest power at moving the stock?

We'll unWisely leave this question alone, preferring instead merely to gaze bemusedly over the material, paying due attention to the cosmetic touches before digging in.

This chapter is about digging in, digging deep into a company's financial statements and departing with a firm understanding of how financial statements can help you make investment decisions for and against the companies whose reports you come across. But we're bringing more than just our pick axe to chapter 16; we also have crashed this party with our handheld weeder. That's because although it's all very well to break a sweat digging profitably through the numbers, you'll save yourself even more time if you know how to weed out the meaningless stuff and spend all your time examining what counts. Thus, please read this chapter free of delusion; we do not presume to cover financial statements exhaustively in all their intricacies, with all their manifold footnotes and exceptions. *Yuck!* If you're that much into this stuff, read some of the investment books that attempt to do this, then *write your own* with a conscious effort to crack a joke or two. You'll need your readers to be giggling along as they read about amortization, revenue recognition, nonstatutory stock option plans, and warranty reserves.

Below is what a perfect Fool should spend time investigating and pulling out of the standard available financial information.

The Income Statement

We've already seen the income statement once before, but in somewhat abbreviated form. Let's now look at the actual version as it appears in the company's annual report:

Statement of Income —numbers in 000—	Messages Inc.		
	2000	**1999**	**1998**
Revenue	**50,000**	**27,000**	**8,000**
Cost of sales	21,000	12,400	3,400
Gross profit	**29,000**	**14,600**	**4,600**
Operating expenses:			
Selling, general & admin.	12,000	5,250	2,200
Research & development	6,000	3,750	2,000
	18,000	9,000	4,200
Income from operations	**11,000**	**5,600**	**400**
Interest income	**50**	**50**	**50**
Income before taxes	**11,050**	**5,650**	**450**
Income taxes	3,650	1,875	0
Net income	**7,400**	**3,775**	**450**
Earnings per share	**$0.74**	**$0.38**	**$0.04**
Shares outstanding (000)	**10,000**	**10,000**	**10,000**

All numbers in bold represent sales and profits; non-bold represents subtractions, or costs.

The picture that emerges is of one of the nation's best-looking up-and-comers, the sort that should keep making next year's "200 Hottest Small Companies" lists. Sales and earnings growth is outstanding, profit margins improve with the passage of time, management is allotting a healthy amount to development of new products. Messages seems to epitomize what every small-cap growth company fan could possibly seek out.

And that's why it is so disturbing, to the savvier Messages shareholders, when the company posts the numbers below, for fiscal 2001:

Statement of Income —numbers in 000—	Messages Inc.	
	2001	**2000**
Revenue	**97,000**	**50,000**
Cost of sales	46,500	21,000
Gross profit	**50,500**	**29,000**
Operating expenses:		
Selling, general & admin.	27,500	12,000
Research & development	4,500	6,000
	32,000	18,000

Income from operations	18,500	11,000
Interest income	100	50
Income before taxes	18,600	11,050
Income taxes	6,000	3,650
Net income	12,600	7,400
Earnings per share	$1.05	$0.74
Shares outstanding (000)	12,000	10,000

All numbers in bold represent sales and profits; non-bold represents subtractions, or costs.

On the face of it, we still see tremendous growth. Revenues exceeded analysts' expectations, coming in up 94 percent to $97 million, while net income rose some 70 percent. But look deeper and you may change your mind about this report. Certainly the market didn't like it, dropping MESS stock from $18 (to which it had risen) to $14 in one day. Let's examine this income statement for the few Foolish indicators that we seek every statement of operations. It's another checklist. Take note!

1. Make sure margins remain at consistent levels if they're not actually rising.

A company's profitability directly affects its stock price, mainly through the vehicle of earnings per share (EPS). As we'd mentioned earlier, and as we'll explore much more deeply next chapter, earnings per share is the most important financial figure we use to value stocks. If a company's margins (a.k.a. level of profitability) decline, that decline translates directly to the "bottom line," or earnings per share. That decline will in turn dramatically affect the performance of a stock.

Messages' net profit margin in the year 2000 was an impressive 14.8 percent ($7.4 million divided by $50 million). But in 2001 the company followed up with only a 13.0 percent net margin (you already know how to do this: $12.6 million divided by $97 million). Still very high, but lower than the year before. A bad sign. Stocks often trade off of forward expectations, and forward expectations are deeply rooted in trends. Because the trend here is falling, even a Fool couldn't express much surprise in MESS stock's 22 percent decline the day that these numbers were released.

We prefer margins to remain at the same levels or (even better) rise slightly and consistently over time. This is the sign of good management and a healthy and competitive enterprise. This is the boxer who, light on his toes, can still shake and bake around the ring in round eleven.

It remains always to examine the cause of rising or falling margins; you should attempt to reach an understanding of the reasons behind any significant change in a company's financial statements, just as you would in your own bank account. In Messages' case, we find the primary problem relates to its cost of sales, which ate right into the company's gross margins. It appears that in the effort to ramp up production of new messages for innovative new inserts—particularly the construction of its scratch-'n'-eat mentholated series—the company couldn't achieve factory efficiency. Perhaps the company should never have introduced this new product at all. Or maybe the margin decline is a onetime event.

2. Make sure research and development (R&D) expenditures aren't getting shortchanged.

Perhaps the foremost financial trick that companies use to match or exceed their earnings estimates is to reduce their research and development (R&D) expenditures. What they are effectively doing is what the federal government has been getting accused of doing for years: jeopardizing the future by enhancing (or just preserving) the present. In an effort to save face today, companies that reduce R&D are imperiling themselves down the road.

Why would a company do this? Because unfortunately most companies feel tremendous pressure to meet or exceed the earnings estimates put forward by the analysts tracking them. In this day and age, if a company fails to meet estimates (as was the case with Messages) it can expect its stock to star in that day's "Market Losers" news segments. And it can sometimes take a long, long time for institutional confidence—and strong stock price performance—to reappear.

Having furnished the context that explains why companies feel the heat to hit estimates, we can now look down the income statement and see which of the costs deducted from sales is most under the company's control *and* least likely to exert any effect in the "now now now, earnings earnings earnings" atmosphere: research and development. R&D, as we mentioned last chapter, is simply the bucks you supply to a few mad scientists hidden away somewhere in the bowels of your corporate headquarters. Who's going to notice if you happen to shortchange these guys for a quarter or a year?

A Fool, that's who. Because we watch very carefully the amounts our companies are spending on R&D, particularly high-tech and medical companies, which rely so much on developing the superior technology that will put everyone else out of business. Look back at MESS's financial statement. Horrors! Messages just so happens to have spent *less* on research and development in 2001 (just $4.5 million) than it did in the year 2000 ($6 million). That's quite a bad sign, and it suggests that management may consciously have underfunded its development efforts in order to prop up its earnings per share. It is possible, of course, that a company's R&D needs can change, permanently reducing the amount spent. Quite unlikely for a small, high-growth situation, but possible. Anyway, your job will be to find out.

The traditional and best way to look at R&D is as a percentage of revenues for that year; doing so, we see that R&D accounted for 12.0 percent of revenues in 2000, and just 4.6 percent of revenues in 2001. This is a dramatic reduction; at your first convenience, you should be back on the phone to Investor Relations chewing them out and asking why. They may have managed to keep earnings per share up over $1.00 for the year, but how well will earnings fare in another year or two? The company has claimed plans to release its Virtual-Reality InfoCookie Experience modules in the first half of 2003—you still think it's going to make that schedule?

If Messages is not willing to maintain a consistent annual percentage for R&D costs, it'll only be that much more likely to get swept under the rug when Microsoft comes out with a better Virtual-Reality Info-Cookie Experience module.

Watch this figure carefully, dear reader.

3. Make sure the company is paying full income taxes.

Always look at your company's corporate tax rate. You can deduce this simply by taking the amount paid in income taxes as a percentage of income before taxes. Refreshing our memory in Messages' case, we see:

Messages	2001	2000
Income before taxes	**18,600**	**11,050**
Income taxes	6,000	3,650

So in 2000, the company paid 33 percent ($3,650 divided by $11,050), while MESS paid a slightly lower rate (32 percent) in 2001. This is fine, about what one would expect. Don't get hung up here on fine distinctions regarding a percentage point or two—that's for margins, where percentage points really count. No, in the case of taxes, you should never worry about slight changes between apparently high tax rates; who the heck can ever figure out tax returns anyway? The rules change slightly every year to keep accountants in business. Don't let this bog you down.

The reason that we do make a point of talking about income taxes here is because some companies record much lower income tax rates due to "tax-loss carryforwards." Our government gives money-losing enterprises credits against future taxes when (and if) they eventually turn a profit. Messages Inc., back in the prehistoric days of 1996 and 1997, lost a spot of money as a start-up. If you turn back a few pages, you'll see that the company's 1998 income statement shows it paying no income tax at all. The carryforward credits are the reason. (If a company lost lots and lots of money early on, in many cases the now-profitable company won't use up all its credits in one year. These are then "carried forward" even further, to be used over the coming years at management's discretion.)

In closing up this section, we simply caution you to make sure you're not using artificially high net income and earnings-per-share figures if the company was using an artificially low tax rate (in most cases, below 20 percent).

4. Keep an eye on growth in shares.

Companies issue more common shares when they need to create cash; with an investment bank serving as liaison, the public purchases the new shares, filling the corporate coffers. Reasons to issue new stock abound. Some companies are cash-flow negative, as we learned last chapter, and therefore need the bucks to fund expansion. Others might issue new shares or convertible warrants to pay off a new acquisition. Whatever the reason, whenever new stock is issued, the existing stock generally becomes devalued by the market. From a current shareholder's point of view, it's kind of like finally fulfilling your lifelong dream of purchasing the *Mona Lisa* and then finding out that there also happen to be three others in a dusty old backroom of the Louvre. Bummer.

As mentioned earlier, when we settle into the process of actually valuing stocks, earnings per share becomes the crucial figure for investors to watch. To review, earnings per share is simply the profits of the company (net income) divided by the total number of shares of common stock. So obviously when a company issues more shares, the earnings per share will decline (all other things remaining equal). Because many stocks trade mainly off a multiple of earnings per share, this is not a good thing.

In 2001 Messages issued 2 million new shares for no good reason we know of at present. (We may learn more later.) What that meant is that despite sales and profits gains of greater than 70 percent, earnings per share—the *most important* figure of all—rose only 42 percent. We've already discussed what that did to the stock.

Suffice it to point out now that you should scrutinize total shares outstanding. If you see significant increases, or hear of a new company share offering, always ask yourself *why*. Did your company need the money, or did it just want to cash in off a high share price following a great run in its stock? And if your company did need the money, did it need it for *good* reasons (like to launch a new subsidiary, or for development of a new product), or *bad* reasons (like to stay in business)? Oh, and by the way, no cause for complaint if total shares outstanding increase in bits and pieces from quarter to quarter, since extra shares are often rewarded to management as incentivized compensation. But if you see a large unexplained jump in the company's share total, or a consistent pattern over three to five years of significantly more and more and more shares, your guys are diluting the growth of their earnings per share. You can find better investments elsewhere.

The Balance Sheet

We've pretty much picked the income statement bare at this point. Time to move on to the second financial statement that we watch (see facing page): the balance sheet. Unlike the income statement, which reads like a top-down yearlong story of a business's progress, the balance sheet gives the reader a single snapshot of the company's books on the *last day* of the reporting period. The statement comprises two sections, assets and liabilities (which is grouped with shareholder's equity). The balance sheet is so called because these two sections "balance" each other out in terms of value. For every asset, there is a liability, and for every liability an asset. (Welcome to the wonderful world of financial accounting, where these guys make up their own definitions and their own rules and the rest of us just sit back and pay them to do our taxes.) (All right, that's probably enough cheap shots at accountants for one book. We'll stop now.) Both the assets and the liabilities sections are further divided between "current" and "noncurrent" items, where the "currentness" of the item in question refers to how quickly it could be recouped should the business be liquidated.

We're about to take up the balance sheet Foolishly, fixing on the items that matter to us. So again, we won't be laying out every term. You're paying us to take you to the stars' homes, not explain the history behind the street names that link them together.

Balance Sheet —numbers in 000—	Messages Inc.	
	2001	**2000**
Current Assets:		
Cash and cash equivalents	24,000	20,000
Accounts receivable	34,000	14,000
Inventory	20,000	10,000
Prepaid expenses	1,500	1,000
	79,500	45,000
Property & Equipment:		
Subtotal	12,000	6,000
Less accumulated depreciation	1,200	800
	10,800	5,200
	90,300	50,200
Current Liabilities:		
Accounts payable	6,500	3,200
Accrued expenses	18,000	10,000
	24,500	13,200
Long-Term Debt:	0	0
Stockholders' Equity:		
Common stock; $.01 par value	2,400	2,000
Additional paid-in capital	26,300	10,500
Retained earnings	37,100	24,500
	65,800	37,000
Total Liabilities and Stockholders' Equity	90,300	50,200

1. Cash: very, very likable.

The very first line of the balance sheet is always named, "Cash and cash equivalents," or some similar phrase. This is the amount of money a company has sitting in the bank. The "cash equivalents" part of the definition simply refers to the cash unnecessary for running a business that is currently earning a speck of short-term interest. (If a second line below it is labeled anything like "short-term investments," that line should be *combined* with the cash line; both serve similar functions and should always be grouped together, for our purposes.)

Our only real rule with company cash is that we like to see lots of it.

Companies build up cash for several reasons. The first one is the best of all: Good operations generate cash. To review, operational cash flow is simply the dough that is piling up in the course of the company running its business. We call businesses that take in more than they put out "cash generators," green machines cranking out seven- and eight-figure additions to this most-favored-status line of the balance sheet. Watching a cash generator do its thing can bring tears to a good capitalist's eyes, an emotional response to finance that can only be augmented by actually being *invested* in such situations. One of the great lines from Peter Lynch's book *Beating the Street* (1993) captures the feeling perfectly: "It's no accident that there's a snapshot of [his favorite company] Fannie Mae headquarters alongside the family photographs on the memento shelf in my office. It warms my heart to think of the place. The stock has been so great they ought to retire the symbol."

But there are other ways to come by cash as well. A common one is a share offering. We just ended last section mentioning companies that issue more shares of common stock in order to raise cash. When those offerings occur, the resultant cash comes right to this asset line.

Some analysts like to express the amount of cash a company has in per-share amounts. All you'd do is just divide the cash and cash equivalents figure by the total number of shares outstanding. For example, Messages has built up an impressive $24 million in cash by the last day of 2001. With 12 million shares out, Messages sports cash alone worth $2 per share. This means that no matter how many earthquakes shake the company's Reno, Nevada headquarters, ain't no way this stock is dropping below $2. (Stock prices *can* conceivably fall below a company's cash per share, but this extremely rare occurrence generally would happen only if the business's cash flow was so extremely negative that the cash on its balance sheet showed little likelihood of being there much longer.)

But cash means more than just a dependable rock-bottom stock price. It also represents the power to pay off debts, if a company has them. Or it could represent the potential to acquire complementary businesses, or buy out a competitor. The best growth companies on the planet create future growth with their own cash.

Additionally, having a lot of cash on hand lessens the requirement for a company to run a cash-flow-positive operation. That's not to say that any business should manage itself poorly, spending cash to make profits. But take a perfectly good stock like Boston Technology (NASDAQ:BSTN), which we added to the Fool Portfolio in early September 1994 at $13. The company had some $25 million sitting on the top line of its assets at that point but was consuming cash each quarter, an unfortunate model of cash-flow negativity. Why was this the case? Boston Tech, much like Messages, was making a huge push at the time to build its foreign sales. The company sold a lot of systems to Europe, South America, and the Far East and essentially said, "Pay us when you like, guys." So it was recording sales and profits well before it ever got paid for them. That's perfectly legitimate as an accounting standard, but it makes for murder on a company's statement of cash flows. However, with so much cash on the balance sheet, Boston Tech could afford to do this for many quarters more before creating a need for more financing; ideally, before that day came to pass, Boston Technology would build a foreign business so strong that it would no longer need to extend generous payment terms and would suddenly flip to cash-flow positive, further enhancing its attractiveness.

As it turned out, this stock had its ups and downs, but we eventually cashed it out at a 48 percent gain 10 months after purchase—a 48 percent gain we would have missed if we hadn't been willing to make an exception to our checklist requirements now and then.

Develop a bias toward stocks backed by cash-generating businesses that have a wad of bills sitting in the bank gathering interest (and ready to be deployed whenever a good opportunity presents itself!).

2. Avoid debt.

Very few successful small-cap companies have any debt to speak of. Thus, if you're using the stock selection criteria expounded last chapter, you generally won't have many run-ins with long-term debt of any kind. Keep it that way. The idea, after all, is to locate superior companies that wouldn't need to borrow from anyone in order to subsist and grow. You can afford to be choosy with your money; be a snob and invest it in only the best. Enough said.

Oh, "long-term debt" (if it exists) is an item found midway down the liability side of the balance sheet.

3. Make sure growth in accounts receivable and inventory approximates sales growth.

Accounts receivable and inventory both constitute assets, insofar as both represent money that the company would receive if it were liquidated. Accounts receivable measures the amount of money that a business is owed by its customers, not all of whom pay 100 percent cash up front for every product. Inventories are an asset because they represent finished or near-finished products that the company simply has not yet sold.

Both of these items are indeed considered assets because they have monetary value to the company, but from an investor's point of view they're more like liabilities. Gaze through a Foolish lens and you can well see that both accounts receivable and inventories represent momentary failures on a company's part to convert its business into cash. Accounts receivable are what your loan sharks have failed to collect so far, and inventories are what your unctuous salesmen have not yet managed to foist off on your unsuspecting customers.

Both these assets will always exist as inevitable components of running a business. What you as an investor need to track is how the *growth* in accounts receivable and inventory tracks against overall sales growth. You'd ideally like to see this growth rate decline in comparison to the sales growth rate. However, that's the ideal; a more realistic expectation is for the growth rates of accounts receivable, inventories, and sales to move roughly in sync. If that's the case, you have nothing to worry about.

When, on the other hand, accounts receivable and inventories for a company you hold are rising at a significantly higher rate than sales, or demonstrate a huge one-quarter jump, you need to consider very seriously whether you want to remain in that investment. Accounts receivable in particular are worthy of your scrutiny and respect as a financial indicator. We've seen many otherwise healthy small-cap stocks literally fall apart (lose 80 percent or more, quickly) because they failed over time to collect what they were supposedly owed, creating a *huge* cashflow drain. (We say "supposedly owed" because in some situations it may have been questionable whether a company really had made the sales it claimed in the first place.)

Classic case in point at Fool HQ was Styles on Video (AMEX:SOV), the manufacturer and marketer of "hair imaging systems." The Styles on Video product, essentially a computer hooked up to a video camera, enabled customers to see what they would look like with a selection of different hairstyles. The simulation was achieved with the video image by superimposing these other coifs in a seamless manner right over top of the customer's existing hair. This was a story that—so sue us—we bought.

We first acquired the stock in our personal accounts via an April 1993 spinoff from another company whose shares we owned. Styles on Video then proceeded to rise from our cost of $5 to over $15 by January 1994. As it was quite near its full valuation at that point, we actually cashed the stock at a very nice profit. We weren't about to hang a photo of the SOV corporate headquarters next to those of our loved ones, but we were seriously thinking of submitting to the humiliation of a Styles on Video photo session and printing up the results in Ye Olde Printed Foole.

That winter, we were invited to join a prestigious investment club in Washington, D.C., one that featured exclusively older men (mostly friends of our father). We proudly accepted, the youngest new members in years. What young rakes we were, and what pressure we felt to make a good stock pick or two.

We began our very first meeting with three words in our mouths, "Styles on Video."

We explained how much we'd regretted selling in the first place, now that we'd seen the latest earnings estimates from Thomas James, the regional brokerage firm that had SOV down for $1.35 per share for 1994, and $2.40 per share for 1995. We told the whole humorous story about the "hair imaging" and went on to discuss the company's R&D plans for (no joke) "eyewear imaging" and "weight-loss imaging." Our trusting fellow club members, of a generous spirit, agreed. Our club bought a fair amount of it.

Imagine our quiet disappointment when 2 months later our mailbox turned up a fresh copy of the company's brand-new annual report for the year ended December 31, 1993. We've cobbled together below the relevant figures from a few different statements, for your reading pleasure. Check out these numbers:

Styles on Video	1993	1992	
Sales	8,553,000	2,680,000	up 219%
Accounts receivable	3,594,000	505,000	up 611%
Net cash flow	(2,570,000)		
Cash and cash equivalents	2,107,000		

What you've just looked at was very bad news. Allow us to explain. First, you see the sales growth: up 219 percent! So far, so good. Now look at the growth in accounts receivable: up 611 percent. Bad. *Real* bad. The growth in receivables was way, way ahead of sales growth. In fact, the year-over-year receivables growth of $3 million-plus far outstripped the company's entire $2 million in net income. Glancing at cash flow from operations (a figure we went over last chapter), you see a big fat negative $2.6 million; cash and cash equivalents were *less*, reported at $2.1 million.

Take the time to incorporate what you've learned so far and then ask yourself what was going to happen to this company in 1994. Its sales were projected by analysts to leap from $8 million to $23 million. What might you expect that would do to Styles' accounts receivable? Does the term "explodamundo" in any way convey our meaning? And what would that receivables explosion create? A gigantic cash-flow problem. And how much cash did the company have in its coffers to solve the problem? Far too little.

Right about that time, a couple of things happened. The first is that despite these disgusting-looking numbers, CNBC financial television correspondent Dan Dorfman gave the stock a big plug, quoting an analyst who was very bullish on the company's "explosive" prospects. The second thing that happened is that we were stricken with acute and irreversible mental paralysis that prevented us from acting on what we knew for the benefit of our investment club. That we might actually announce to the club that we wanted out of this pick just a couple months after we made it was too intolerable a notion. How embarrassing! Plus, the stock had stayed propped up pretty high (in the $15 to $16 range), and staying the course was the way of least resistance.

We should've shorted the bejesus out of it.

You can only imagine our chagrin when Styles on Video declined from $15 to $10 to $5 in the course of a few months, and halted trading altogether less than a year later, after some of the company's management resigned to go to work for the firm that audited its statements! (We'd never heard of such a thing, and are now curious whether that auditor is publicly traded so that we might short it instead.) Meanwhile, our Washington Investors Club was left with worthless shares thanks to our first-ever stock pick. Could we have made a more striking first impression? (Fortunately, we can laugh about this, since most of the rest of the members of the club set the example by laughing it off in the first place.)

Styles on Video is our definitive accounts receivable story, though as we mentioned earlier, numerous examples of similar demises exist. Unless they have a lot of cash, small businesses have to maintain a tight control on growth in receivables and inventories; the imperativeness of this simply cannot be overstated. Don't even bother considering investing in any companies that are having problems in this arena. You can find too many better ones that aren't.

Incidentally, beyond just looking at the growth rates in accounts receivable, we also watch to see what percentage of overall sales that receivables make up. This is a useful measurement to track quarter by quarter because you can see what portion of sales are getting paid for right away. In the case of Messages, we see 2001 receivables at $34 million, with 2001's sales being $97 million. That means that receivables are running at 35 percent of sales ($34 divided by $97), or, expressed in calendar terms, receivables take about 4.2 months (35 percent of a year) to pay off. Messages fans, 35 percent is a discouragingly high figure. It gets even worse when put in the context of the previous year, in which sales were $50 million and receivables were $14 million. That's 28 percent, meaning our receivables-to-sales ratio is already high and trending higher. It appears that bakers are welching on their InfoCookie fees. A strong, well-managed business won't permit this to happen.

Finally, please note that the reverse equivalent of accounts receivable and inventories is accounts payable and accrued expenses, which are liabilities that a company *owes* but which (paradoxically, again) a company should do its best to increase. That's because the longer a company can string out its suppliers and creditors, the more use the company will get out of the cash it keeps on hand (for operations or interest). It's called smart cash management. However, in most strong small-cap growth companies, accounts receivable and inventories will still far exceed accounts payable and accrued expenses, making these latter balance sheet items less meaningful.

4. Do whatever ratios catch your fancy.

Some people spend a lot of time poring over various ratios calculable from the data in a balance sheet. We don't find this terribly meaningful, but we'll share with you a couple of things you can learn.

The most common ratio associated with balance sheets is probably the *current ratio*. The current ratio provides an investor with a basic test of short-term liquidity, since it simply takes the current assets (cash, receivables, inventories, et cetera) and divides them by the current liabilities (accounts payable, accrued expenses, et cetera). Ideally, this figure will fall somewhere in the range from 2-to-1 to 7-to-1 for the typical American industrial company, tending toward higher ratios for small caps. What the current ratio tells you is how nimbly a company can act to take advantage of an unforeseen circumstance. If, for example, TastiScrolls were found to cause mild increases in the libidos of laboratory rats, Messages would be far better prepared to deal with this potential crisis with a current ratio of 5 than with a ratio of 1.

As it is, Messages' current ratio for 2001 was 3.2 ($79.5 divided by $24.5), which is certainly acceptable. Note that this is *down* from the previous year's mark of 3.4 ($45 divided by $13.2).

You can apply the current ratio to any annual report you look at, though we've never let it make or break an investment decision for us. We like to see the ratio remain even or trend slightly higher, but you won't find us getting emotional on the subject.

Still, a survey of the current ratio can be a useful way to discover potential new investment ideas among financially healthy mid caps. Just flip through the *S&P Stock Guide,* going down the current assets and current liabilities columns (conveniently located next to each other in that august publication). The ones with high ratios are the businesses that generally offer the best investment opportunity. A second ratio, very similar to the current ratio, is the *quick ratio.* The quick ratio is more "cashcentric" (to coin an abominable-looking term); it is simply the cash and cash equivalents divided by the current liabilities. It gives you an even better read on how prepared a company might be to encounter unforeseen difficulties or opportunities, or just to meet current short-term debt obligations. Messages' quick ratio declined from a powerful 1.5 in 2000 ($20 divided by $13.2) down to a still-impressive 1.0 in 2001 ($24 divided by $24.5). Still, the magnitude of this drop may portend ill.

Another fairly common ratio is the *debt-to-equity ratio.* As you know, companies issue bonds or shares of stock in order to raise money. One of the fundamental differences between debt (bank borrowings or bonds) and equity (stock) is that debt has to be repaid. From a stockholder's point of view, therefore, the less debt the better. Indeed, if a company maintains little debt, it retains the ability to go out to the capital markets and float a bond or convertible in order to raise cash, should the need arise. We rarely use this ratio because, as has already been noted, we avoid long-term debt; almost none of the companies that we look at has any debt at all.

To calculate the simple version of this ratio, you simply need to locate a company's long-term debt and its equity. Long-term debt sits in the liability portion (noncurrent) of the balance sheet. Equity may be culled from the stockholders' equity section of the balance sheet, below liabilities. Take the values for "common stock" and "capital surplus" (also known as "additional paid-in capital") and add them together. Then you just divide the debt figure by the equity figure. You want this figure to be as low as possible, with zero being the preference, in most cases. Messages, because it has no debt, has a 0 debt-to-equity ratio.

A final ratio we'll mention is perhaps the most important, but again not one upon which we found any investment decisions. It's called the *return on equity ratio,* one additional measure of corporate profitability. For this one, you divide the net income by the total stockholders' equity from the balance sheet (the bottom line). By so doing, you are measuring the amount of profit a business generates relative to the amount of money shareholders have put into it. A respectable figure is 15 percent; a strong figure runs over 20 percent. As with most of these ratios, you want to see a high number that remains high over time either by standing pat or increasing slightly. For outstandingly profitable emerging-growth companies, this number may start out ridiculously high (50 percent or even greater, in some cases) and trend down as the company grows. This should not be counted against a stock.

Messages produced net income of $7.4 million in 2000, and a check of the balance sheet reveals total shareholders' equity at $37.0 million that year. Thus, the return on equity was 20.0 percent ($7.4 divided by

$37.0). The next year, as you might expect by now, was a tad worse: Return on equity for 2001 came in at (you now know enough to calculate this yourself) 19.1 percent.

◆   ◆   ◆

Having drawn to an end of our Foolish discussion of the balance sheet, you've now plotted enough points on your map that you can safely navigate the crucial parts of the terrain while still leaving yourself room to explore the out-of-the-way places, should you so desire. We close our discussion of making sense of the financial info by turning to the cash-flow statement.

The Statement of Cash Flows

By now, you've already heard a fair amount about cash flow; we've stressed the importance of positive operational cash flow again and again. Last chapter, we learned that positive cash flow is one of our eight Foolish criteria for selecting growth stocks. And this chapter, we told the sorry tale of Styles on Video, the company that was sunk by its own negative cash flow. Many financial analysts value stocks off of cash flow, not earnings. We're not in that camp, preferring to use earnings multiples, but we still ascribe profound importance to a business's ability to spin off—not consume—cash. Your own small-cap portfolio should be replete with, if not totally dominated by, "cash generators."

Novices sometimes have difficulty conceiving of the cash-flow statement. If it's measuring income and expenses, how is it any different from the income statement? The answer is that the cash-flow statement simply provides you a different way of looking at income and expenses. The statement of cash flows is most akin, in fact, to your monthly bank statement. If you view your own personal or family bank statement as a business, you'll notice that the various income and expense items that show up there are all accounted for *when paid*. On the other hand, the corporate income statement—*unlike* your bank statement—contains items (like sales, for instance) that have been recorded but not yet paid for. This is perfectly legitimate accounting but not the most useful way to focus on the guts of a business. The guts of a business reveal exactly when and what money is going out, and when and what money is coming in. That's exactly what a cash-flow statement shows, and why we watch this report so carefully.

Now the cash-flow statement is actually three statements in one, because accountants organize all inflows and outflows in three categories:

1. operating activities (the most important one), or the company's businesses,
2. investing activities, generally expenditures on "hard assets" such as property and equipment, and
3. financing activities, typically inflows like common-share offerings and outflows like repayment of debt.

The cash-flow adjustments coming out of these three separate categories are cumulative, and the bottom-line result of this statement is usually called "increase [or decrease] in cash and cash equivalents." As you may recall, that's the very same top line item in the asset side of the balance sheet. Here we have yet another example of how the income statement, balance sheet, and statement of cash flows hang together; the reason that financiers often link these things into a single spreadsheet is because when you change one figure on one statement you'll often affect at least one other figure on one of the other statements. As investors, we like to see the "cash and cash equivalents" line increase with the passage of time; it's to the statement of cash flows that you go to understand why (or why not) a company's cash is increasing.

We typically don't spend much time looking at anything but the first section on operating cash flow. With that in mind, let's end this chapter with a look at the operational portion of Messages' cash-flow statement:

Statement of Cash Flow —numbers in 000—	Messages Inc.	
	2001	**2000**
Cash flows from operating activities:		
Net income	12,600	7,400
Adjustments to reconcile net income to net cash provided by operating activities:		
Depreciation	1,200	800
Effects of change in operating assets and liabilities:		
Accounts receivable	(20,000)	(5,000)
Inventory	(10,000)	(4,000)
Accounts payable	3,300	2,000
Accrued expenses	8,000	4,000
Net cash provided by operating activities	**(4,900)**	**5,200**

1. Determine the driving reasons behind a company's cash flow (or lack thereof).

In many cases, the top section of the statement of cash flow makes for the single most enlightening reading in a business's financial reports. You should always scrutinize this section with the intention of coming away with a pretty clear picture of just exactly how a company is managing or botching its finances.

The top line of "cash flows from operating activities," and generally the biggest cash-flow source, is net income. Just below that appears an addition in the form of "depreciation," a technical term that you really don't have to know for our purposes. (But for readers who want a taste, here goes. "Depreciation" is basically the amount a company's accountants annually reduce the value of its fixed assets [plant and equipment] to represent the general wear and tear on these objects. Because a company is still getting use out of its "depreciated assets," however, the amount of the depreciation is added back in to cash flow.)

Adding together net income and depreciation gives you a figure that some analysts refer to as "cash flow." In Messages' case, this would equal $14.9 million for 2001. But we're just mentioning this by the by . . . we don't use this definition. We prefer instead to make the normal adjustments of balance-sheet items to reach the operational cash flow.

We've already learned about the balance sheet, having featured several items on it (like accounts receivable). The bottom section of "cash flows from operating activities" simply presents the changes of these items from the previous year to the current one, making each an adjustment to cash flow. So, for example, if you go back and review Messages' balance sheet, you'll see that the company reported accounts receivable at $34 million and $14 million for 2001 and 2000, respectively. The difference between these figures is obviously $20 million. That very figure, $20 million, appears as the 2001 change in receivables on the cash-flow statement. The number is reported in parentheses, meaning it is accounted for as a deduction from cash flow. This makes sense, given that the company is now owed by its customers $20 million more than last year, a cash drag.

One can thus go on to fill out the rest of the bottom section by making similar adjustments for all other significant operating assets and liabilities. Of course, this isn't necessary, since the company's accountant has already done it for you. The resulting sum is then deducted from net income and depreciation to obtain the operational cash flow.

For the first time, we can now see how clearly Messages screwed up its 2001 cash situation. After showing a positive flow of $5.2 million in 2000, the company went cash-flow negative to the tune of $4.9 million in 2001. This partly explains floating another 2 million MESS shares in 2001; foreseeing the business going cash-flow-negative, perhaps management wanted more working capital on hand to start the new millennium.

Our review of the cash-flow statement helps us see the main reason behind Messages' problems: a gigantic leap in accounts receivable from $5 million to $20 million, indicating the company is having trouble collecting money owed by its customers. As an investor, you would want to focus on this primary issue going forward.

The cash-flow statement gives you the opportunity to see what's going on in a company's bank account. Take advantage of this by poring over the statement and formulating a notion of what's working financially and what isn't.

2. Read the management discussion of "liquidity and capital resources"!

Required by law to appear in annual reports and 10-Ks, this write-up makes for the best few paragraphs of substantive reading you'll get anywhere in a company's information packet. We're mentioning it in this section because the "liquidity and capital resources" text relates directly to the business's cash flow, to which you'll often read several overt references. Here you have the opportunity to hear straight from management how it will manage its cash and finances in the next year. You'll learn the size of any credit lines that your company has established at banks, and how far (if any) it has drawn off those lines. You'll sometimes get estimates of a company's capital expenditures over the next year, and explanations of how the company will fund those expenditures ("from operating cash flows" is the best explanation). In short, this section provides you a nice read on a company's immediate financial future, in no-fluff talk.

◆　◆　◆

Okay, that's it . . . a list of ten separate items. You now know most of what we look for in financial statements. Oh, sure, an occasional eleventh or twelfth thing will catch your eye—and should—but what that particular thing is will emerge out of your own experience and expertise. For now, by learning how to digest and understand the most important parts of financial statements, you're prepared to invest Foolishly.

Except, oops, we haven't talked about where to buy and sell!

·17·

The Fool Ratio

* * * * *

Any fool can make a rule
And every fool will mind it.
—*Henry David Thoreau*

Having learned how to find promising growth stocks, how to request information about them, and how to scan that information for the meaningful numbers, it remains now actually to *value* the stocks.

There are many ways to value stocks. In our Dow Dividend section (part III), we wrote about a highly effective way to value certain stocks off of dividend yields. More commonly, investors use earnings or cash-flow multiples, the return-on-equity ratio (discussed last chapter), and sometimes "book value per share" (the measure of a company's net worth: total assets minus total liabilities divided by total number of shares). Others use little more than momentum indicators, like relative strength. And finally, let us not forget those wily types who have arrogated to themselves the name "technician" for the purpose, perhaps, of legitimizing the reading of tea leaves. We'll touch upon that subject in part VIII, "Here Be Dragons."

At Fool HQ, we use a pleasingly simple ratio that we developed several years ago and have been using ever since: the Fool Ratio. (We have since seen it used by some few money managers and financial analysts as well, but as we developed it independently and now use it to evaluate almost every stock we hold, we've taken to attaching our unWise moniker to this most unWise device.) The Fool Ratio, easy both to understand and to use, remains our primary technique of figuring out where to buy *and* sell a stock.

You wouldn't buy a truck for *any* price just because it had great balls of fire painted down the sides, rocketlike acceleration, the loudest stereo system on wheels, and a dozen accessories pumping up the body. (If you're like us, you might not even want this truck for free.) It might be the best truck on earth, but everything has a right price. The goal of investing is, after all, to make money, and if you pay too much for the stock of even the best company on earth, it may take you a *long* time for it to yield a profit, if ever. And it will certainly make it more difficult for you to beat our 25.5 percent Foolish Four returns. Some people say that when investing in stocks, you should just buy good companies, or good products, and then be patient. We're here to tell you that whatever you do buy, your most important consideration should be getting it for a good price! Conversely, even if you buy shares in the lamest possible excuse for a modern American corporation, if you pay the right price, you'll make money.

So it's time to learn how to value growth stocks.

Our Foolish investment approach is predicated on the relationship between the *price-to-earnings ratio* and the company *growth rate*. Below, we'll define and explain these two simple concepts, then yoke them together into our beloved Fool Ratio that effectively estimates the fair, full value of the stock price. Looked at in light of the stock-picking information provided in the preceding chapters, the Fool Ratio forms a final piece to the puzzle, as well as just serving generally as a very nifty tool . . . so nifty, you might even find a way to fix a broken alternator with it.

The P/E Ratio: The Market's Price Tag

Before you can play with the Fool Ratio, you have to work through some other numbers. The first of these is the P/E ratio. The price-to-earnings ratio ("P/E ratio") equals the price of a stock divided by its company's earnings per share over the past 12 months. A simple, widely known device for valuing stocks, the P/E is reported in the stock tables of many daily newspapers.

Let's take two examples:

> *Yuckie Yogurt Corp.* (NASDAQ: YUCK), the retailer of exotically flavored frozen yogurt, has earnings per share of $0.50 and a stock price of $5. **Its P/E ratio is 10.** ($5 divided by $0.50 = 10.)

> *Doors Incorporated "C"* (NASDAQ:REMAC), the software conglomerate whose operating software—Doors—has suddenly cracked a competing brand's seemingly unshakable hold on the PC market,

has earnings per share of $0.50 and now trades at $30. **Its P/E ratio is 60.** ($30 divided by $0.50 = 60.)

The P/E for a given stock varies based on changes in price (which happen every day) and changes in earnings (which happen once a quarter). Think of it as the price tag that the market has put on the shares. The market is saying, in effect, "If you want to buy stock in Doors, you're going to have to pay sixty times the company's earnings." Buying stocks like Doors Inc. that trade at thirty-five times earnings or higher (as do many of the best growth stocks) is akin to shopping at Tiffany—high prices for desired goods. Purchasers of stocks at ten times earnings or less have opted to shed their discretionary income on the equity equivalent of a blue-light special.

The less you pay up to buy a stock, the lower your risk. Would you prefer to buy our ingenious developer of the Windows ripoff at forty times earnings rather than its current sixty times earnings? We think so. You should, anyway, just as you'd rather pay $1.00 instead of $4.00 for the exact same half-gallon of jalapeño-flavored Yuckie Yogurt! Likewise, the more you pay up for a company's stock, the more risk you're accepting. The company better produce the gigantic earnings growth for which you're paying such a premium, or you're in *big* trouble.

Looking closely at the examples, notice the extreme disparity. Both companies, after all, have trailing 12-month earnings of $0.50 per share, but YUCK is trading at $5 per share and there's REMAC at $30. This seems just too good a deal to pass up—one in a lifetime—so you stake half of last year's salary on Yuckie Yogurt. For the same amount of earnings, you have only had to pay $5 per share . . . quite impressive in comparison to the Fools who are paying six times that for Doors. Darned clever of you; you've outsmarted the market. Yuckie's share price, you convince your in-laws, should probably race to $30 sometime soon . . . a cool 500 percent profit. You're seeing big things: a week in Paris, then a leisurely yacht cruise along the Côte d'Azur. Not that you wouldn't stand for 200 percent and a *weekend* in Paris—lose the yacht—just the same. No need to be greedy.

What a desperate and woeful state you'll be in when, a year later, Doors Incorporated has run to $52 a share, even as YUCK's management has dismantled and sold its seventy-third Yuckie Hut year-to-date, inducing a decline in the stock price to $1¼ per share. Well, you can still take your in-laws to Hardee's . . . if they'll treat.

The lesson: The P/E need not (and often does not) correspond between stocks; some stocks may be considered underpriced at fifty times earnings, whereas others may be grossly overpriced when their P/E rises to 12. This is because the market's price tag is based on past history, present circumstance, and future projections, all of which vary from company to company. Think of the P/E as representing the present circumstance (stock price) divided by past history (trailing 12-month earnings per share). Finally, the future projections (or growth rate) made by analysts have a great effect on how high a stock's P/E gets. The term "analysts" refers to those fearless Wall Street professionals who research companies and their stocks with an eye toward predicting their future performance, numbers, valuation, and current attractiveness as an investment. We can find no more accurate future earnings estimates than those arrived at by analysts, on whom we rely for one of the building blocks for our valuations.

So now you see why you didn't have to pay up much to buy Yuckie Yogurt. The market remained unconvinced that the company's Froz-Gurt Cubes™ would ever sell.

And Now That *You* Know What a P/E Is . . .

Having learned what the price-to-earnings ratio is all about, you've now entered a select minority of the U.S. population. Congratulations. Was the concept difficult? *No!* Are *any* of the concepts in this book difficult? No. Which is what makes the illuminating and completely true story below such an exercise in Folly:

"Is this The Motley Fool? Great! Hi there, my name is Mark Etless [name changed to protect the guilty] and I'm an editor at Big Company Magazines [same again]. We're going to be launching a new financial magazine targeted at people in their twenties and thirties. We've read your stuff, and we're big fans. We'd love to get you involved writing an article for our first issue. Whadda ya say?"

So began the effort to incorporate a bit of our Foolish stuff in *The Gen X Rag* (our phrase). We scribbled up a short thing that essentially said: (1) avoid mutual funds and choose stocks, but (2) don't take stupid risks in an effort to get rich quick, so (3) to help you out, here's the basic way that we pick stocks. It was about the Fool Ratio.

The article came back aggressively edited. By "aggressively," we mean that Copy Editor had rewritten the article, had effectively written us out. Gone was our criticism of mutual funds. Gone was our simple explanation of the beauties of the Fool Ratio. Gone, in fact, was any remnant of the Foolish tone.

We ignored Copy Editor and went right to the top. "Mark Etless, please?"

"This is he."

"You cut out the part about the Fool Ratio! That's our primary simple way of valuing stocks. It's the way we do what we do, the foundation of our investment approach!"

"Sorry, guys, but market research says that our readers will not understand 'price-to-earnings ratios.' Market research simply won't allow us to include that phrase or that concept in the article. It'll fall on our readers' deaf ears . . . ."

We told Etless that whatever his market research dictated, we'd never paid attention to market research when planning our investment approach (or our business, for that matter). We believed in just going with what you believed in, and that if what you believed in was true and you conveyed the truth of it to your readers, that you'd build your own market. Etless told us this was a point he couldn't budge on, and so our article never made the pages of *The Gen X Rag*.

We consider that an achievement.

If the P/E ratio is far too difficult for the next generation to understand, and if "market research" is going to curb any serious teaching, then the coming decades look to be a juicy time for Fools to invest!

The Growth Rate: Gentlemen, Start Your Calculators!

We've done P/E. The next thing is the growth rate. Fixing on an accurate estimate of the growth rate is the single most important challenge for the small-stock investor. The speed at which these small companies grow will be mirrored in their share prices. The careful investor must therefore devise a means of determining just how much growth to expect. Such a design must reflect revenues, net income, and earnings per share.

A fundamental mistake some people make is to look at only one of these numbers, for example, just sales. Messages (NASDAQ:MESS) had sales of $97 million in 2001, and analysts estimate $155 million for 2002. Is the company's growth rate, therefore, fairly reckoned at 60 percent? ($155 − $97 = $58; $58 divided by $97 = .597, or, rounded, 60 percent.)

No. Sales alone is not the way to arrive at a company's growth rate. If operational costs are already high and growing higher, profitability (the most important thing of all) will be jeopardized, rendering the company's sales growth less significant. Again, selling 600 million macadamia nut cookies for a nickel each will generate you a lot of sales. But if every cookie costs you ten cents to produce, you'll be out of business in no time. As you can see, then, sales growth on its own should not serve as a basis for calculating a growth rate.

You'll need to look at net income, too. Messages had $12.6 million in profits from 2001, and a scan of our research reports shows that analysts are projecting $20.8 million for 2002. Carefully punching those numbers into our official $5 Motley Fool calculator, we arrive at a growth rate of 65 percent. ($20.8 − $12.6 = $8.2; $8.2 divided by $12.6 = .65, or 65 percent.) *Voilà!* Let's move on, right?

Wrong. Net income is certainly important, since our valuation approach is based on earnings, not sales. Thus, at this point in your estimation of the growth rate, you'd tend to give extra weight to MESS's profit growth of 65 percent, rather than its 60 percent sales growth.

But we need to account for a third and final factor, *earnings per share* (EPS), which means we'll need to account for the total number of shares outstanding. Remember, while we search out emerging-growth companies with great potential, we can't ever let ourselves forget that we're valuing their *stock,* not their business. And we value the stock based on earnings per share.

Again, the annual earnings per share is calculated simply by dividing net income by total shares. Thus, with 12 million shares outstanding in 2001, and $12.6 million in net income, MESS made $1.05 EPS. Analysts are calling for 2002 totals of $20.8 million in net income, 14 million shares outstanding, and thus $1.49 EPS. So what's the growth rate of earnings per share? Right, just 42 percent. ($1.49 − $1.05 = $0.44; $0.44 divided by $1.05 = .42, or 42 percent.)

So at this point, we've found sales growing at 60 percent, net income at 65 percent, and earnings per share at just 42 percent. We're trying to figure out the company's growth rate. Which is the most important of the above numbers? Earnings per share. So our tendency is to go with 42 percent as the company growth rate. In some situations, we might take the average of these numbers and go with that (about 56 percent here); those would particularly include when earnings per share fall somewhere in between sales and net income (i.e., with sales growing at 20 percent, net income at 30 percent, and earnings per share at 22 percent due to new shares issued, we'd tend to take the average of 24 percent). But in this unusual situation, Messages keeps offering more new shares and therefore diluting EPS, to the point that EPS is growing slowest of all. We ask ourselves: Will this condition persist? We think so. The company is cash-flow negative, as we learned last chapter. And the year 2002 proves once again that there's no short-term solution for this problem; we'll have to assume that the company will keep having to bum greenbacks off its shareholders to fund growth. Thus, the 1-year growth rate for the company we'll estimate at 42 percent. Still not done, however. (It's not a simple process, is it? We told you it was the most important, difficult, and subjective thing you'd do as an investor.)

You see, the best growth-rate estimates look ahead more than just 1 year. Sure, Messages is supposed to grow 42 percent in 2002, but if 2003 projections show sales and earnings rising only 20 percent, we don't want to set the company's growth rate at 42 percent right now! As an investor, you should always try to look ahead. The market does; the market *always* looks ahead. We think a 2- or 3-year horizon works best, neither too short nor too long a time. And as it turns out, for 2003 analysts see Messages earning a whopping $2.36.

So now we're calculating a 2-year growth rate. The method is to find the total percentage growth from $1.05 (2001 EPS) to $2.36 (2003 EPS). You then take the square root of that figure, since this is the proper way to show the annual average growth over the 2 years. (We hope your eyes don't cloud over upon seeing the phrase "square root." Square root's about as difficult as it gets in here, which means this stuff's easy! Note to the innumerate: The reason you take square root is that you're trying to average out 2 1-year growth rates that have already been multiplied together to calculate total growth. When two items have been multiplied together, mathematics tells us always to take the root to determine their average.) To find the percentage growth in this instance, just take $2.36 and divide it by $1.05. You wind up with 2.24761905—for those who like to take their fractions out to eight digits—demonstrating that total growth over the 2 years is estimated at 125 percent. (A second note to the innumerate: From the 2.247 figure, you subtract 1, since that 1 represents the equality of two figures. For instance, if we divided 12 by 12, we'd get 1.00, telling us that the first number is 100 percent of the second. But we want growth rates; is there any growth from 12 to 12? No, there's 0 percent growth. We need to subtract out the 1 from 1.00 to remove the equality, leaving us with 0.00, which shows us the true growth rate. It's just the same above with 2.247—subtract out the 1 to get 1.247, and then round to 1.25 to arrive at 125 percent growth.) Now we'll take the square root of that nine-digit number and what we end up with—having rounded it off—is 1.50.

Thus, we've ended up with a 2-year annualized EPS growth rate of 50 percent. And that's the average annual growth rate we'll use. It's *higher* than the 42 percent single-year growth rate because, of course, growth in 2003 is expected to accelerate.

To keep on top of your stocks, you should rerun the growth-rate numbers on your companies every time they issue a new earnings report, which is quarterly. (Also, if you're apprised of a change in earnings estimates, that's another time to rerun the numbers.) This can be done in the following steps:

1. determine the new trailing 12-month amounts for sales, net income, and EPS,
2. note the current earnings projections of the more farsighted analysts, if any (most companies will enclose analyst reports in the financial information packets that you learned how to request at the end of chapter 15),
3. figure the amount of EPS growth by dividing the expected future earnings by trailing earnings (as done in the example above), and
4. calculate the *average annual growth rate* by taking the proper root based on the number of years from present value to future value. To reiterate, the proper root to take corresponds to the number of years from present to future value, because each year is a multiplicand, and to take an average of them you'll need to take the root corresponding to the number of multiplicands.

What's above may sound elaborate, but it isn't. Reviewing the numbers, we found the future value to be $2.36 and the present value to be $1.05. Step 3 tells us to figure the amount of growth, which we did: 125 percent. Step 4 informs us that we must take the proper root of 2.245 based on the amount of time from present to future value. That amount was *2 years,* so we took the *square root.* If the amount had been 3 years, you'd have taken the cube root; 4 years, the fourth root. Was that a "quad root"? We certainly can't remember. And so on. You'll need a better machine than our top-o'-the-line $5 Motley Fool calculator to take any root besides the square root of something; most business and scientific calculators can do the work in a snap.

If the amount of time from present to future value is not a round number, like 2 or 3 years, your root will *also* not be a round number. The rule is that you take fractional roots for fractional years. Thus, for 1½ years, you'd take the 1.5 root. And if your estimates were 9 quarters away, you'd take a 2.25 root.

Just to be difficult then, and in order to give you a chance to test out what you've learned, let's complicate things in as realistic a manner as possible, and assume that Messages is now beyond 2001, already midway through 2002. So we must first update our numbers to reflect the company's *trailing 12 months* of operations. We'll need to combine EPS from the first 6 months of 2002 (which appears in the June 10-Q, or quarterly report) with the last 6 months of earnings from 2001 to complete the task.

Note: The closing 6 months of a year can often be extracted from the back of a company's annual report, where a section sometimes appears listing quarterly financial results for the most recent 2 years.

Let's assume, then, that quarterly earnings for our company go like this:

	1Q	2Q	3Q	4Q
2001	.22	.25	**.28**	**.30**
2002	**.32**	**.36**		

As we're now halfway through 2002, trailing 12-month earnings (printed in bold) come to $1.26 per share. To estimate the growth, we need to annualize the rate of growth from $1.26 to the endpoint of $2.36 by the end of 2003. Total growth from the first number to the second is 1.873, or 87.3 percent. Now we need to take the proper root of this number to calculate growth. How many years from present to future value? One and a half. Thus we take the 1.5 root (reflecting the distance of 6 quarters) of 1.873, which comes to 1.519, or 51.9 percent. Thus, 52 percent is our new estimated growth rate.

The best way to become comfortable with calculating your own growth rates is to get the financial information of some companies in which you're interested and start running the numbers yourself. Test your results against your friends', and come join us online to double-check that you're doing it all correctly.

The Fool Ratio: Read Carefully and Carry a Big Stick

All right. We know the P/E now, and we can calculate growth rates. Here comes the fun, putting the two together.

A fundamental Wall Street axiom is that a stock's P/E should equal the company growth rate. Convenient, huh? Thus, if a company is growing at 20 percent, the P/E should be 20 for a fair, full value. The technical underpinnings of the theory have something to do with anticipated cash flows looking years ahead, but the actual principle itself has melted away over the years. It's now become a generally accepted investment principle. It's actually kind of like the NFL's quarterback rating; nobody really knows the formula but everyone takes it for granted.

The important issue here is how well we've found this gadget really works. Let's take an example. Let's say HeadComm Corporation, the maker of implantable cerebral chips designed as communications solutions for people on the go, is growing at 20 percent a year. Let's also say that the company's trailing 12-month earnings are $1.00 per share, and let us finally assume that the stock is currently trading at $15. All right, we know the growth rate (20 percent); what's the P/E? Right, dividing the share price by the earnings makes 15. Now, our rule of thumb says, *The P/E should equal the percentage of the growth rate for a fairly and fully valued stock.* Thus, were HeadComm fairly and fully valued, its P/E would be equal to the percentage of its growth rate (20 percent). Is it? No. At $15 per share, it's trading at a P/E of only 15. The stock looks like it could certainly rise to a P/E of 20 (and thus a share price of $20) in the short-to-intermediate term—if the market comes to agree that the company's growth rate is a dependable 20 percent, which is largely dependent on the company's new full-featured Head-Fax chip going over well.

Given the numbers above, where would you like to buy HeadComm? You'd like to buy it as low as you can. If you buy the stock at $10 per share, and its fair, full value is $20, then you have room for a quick double—the goal for almost every growth-stock recommendation issued from Fool HQ. Now, where would you *not* want to buy the stock? You would probably not want to buy it much above $10, since a double would be more difficult and less likely. Interestingly, you'll often see Wall Street brokerage reports advising people to buy HeadComm when the stock's already at $20! The so-called professionals make a lot of strange calls, as they should be the first to tell you. And in general, the Wise are not as aggressive as we Fools, and don't as a matter of habit look to double their money in a stock in 12 to 18 months. It's often enough for them merely to toss their clients into "a good name," regardless of price or valuation.

A wonderful way exists to measure a stock's current price against its fair, full value price: the Fool Ratio. You calculate "The Fool" by taking a stock's current P/E ratio as a percentage of its growth rate. (For this reason some analysts call it the "Price-to-Earnings-to-Growth Ratio," or "PEG.") It's that easy.

So what's the Fool for HeadComm, trading at $15? Well, the stock's P/E is 15, and we've estimated the company growth rate at 20 percent. Thus, 15 divided by 20 makes .75, which is HeadComm's Fool Ratio. Expressed differently, ".75" means that the stock is trading at 75 percent of its full, Foolish value. The full value is $20, which we find out simply by multiplying the earnings per share ($1.00) by the growth rate (20 percent). So our conception of the stock is that in the near term it could appreciate $5, from $15 to $20, giving you a 33 percent return ($5 divided by $15). That sounds pretty good . . . but not good enough for a Fool. We're neutral on HeadComm because we like to purchase small-cap growth stocks whose potential for rapid appreciation is much greater. We can find many better Fool Ratio prospects than the company that is coming soon to a skull near you.

We typically purchase stocks when their Fool Ratio is .50 or less.

That's another way of saying that (1) we purchase stocks whose P/E is half their growth rate, or (2) we purchase stocks whose current price is half their fair, full value price. They're one and the same thing.

So, to review: (1) determine the P/E, then (2) calculate the growth rate, and finally (3) take the P/E as a percentage of the growth rate.

If it's .50 or less, and you like everything else about a company (after a thorough review of the financial info, press packet, and analyst reports), consider buying it. This is what we spend most of our time looking for. These stocks aren't a dime a dozen, certainly, but the ones you find can often wind up your biggest winners.

If it's between .50 and .65, hold off unless you're convinced this is *the* next big thing. It may be, in which case we permit ourselves to buy above .50. But the company must demonstrate excellence top to bottom and should have soundly beaten its previous earnings estimates. Don't be in a hurry to pay up for the typical stock in this range; there are literally thousands of other investment opportunities, and you can generally do better if you sniff around a bit. Patience.

If it's between .65 and 1.00, the stock is in its "muckaround range." Most stocks trade at these Fool Ratio values, and we generally call them "holds." At these prices, we just sit tight and root our shares higher. We rarely make an initial purchase of anything in this range.

If it's at or slightly over 1.00, the stock is ripe for a sell. Your chances of making much more here anytime soon aren't great, and you can find other places to put the money. Now, you may be taking a very long-term view of the stock (looking ahead years and decades, not months), in which case you may make the right decision holding on. If you think you have a good thing going, we're not here to tell you you don't. Otherwise, though, you have a fully valued stock on your hands, most likely one that has appreciated more than 50 percent. This is what you were waiting for! With most of the short-to-intermediate-term appreciation probably now behind you, better prospects will present themselves. Think about taking your profit.

If it's up in the range of 1.40 or higher, you are looking at one of the more richly valued public properties in the United States. It's time you read part VI, "Shorting Stocks."

◆ ◆ ◆

Finally let's take a look at Messages, the company with the amazingly edible paper products that have proven so lucrative to so many. We've now spent a fair amount of space learning about the company: its story, its numbers, its past, present, and future. But our aim—the aim for every investor—eventually has to be to put a price on the stock. It's not enough to know a company or to like its products or prospects. The idea of investing is to put values on stocks so you can buy the right ones, those expected to make you the most money. Do we buy Messages?

Earlier, we learned that Messages was midway through 2002 with trailing earnings of $1.26 and an estimated annualized growth rate of 52 percent. Checking our paper, we now see that MESS has put up some rippingly good investment returns over the past several months, more than doubling to $35. Wow! So what's the P/E ratio? This stuff is now so easy for you we're tempted to let you respond completely on your own, without our ever printing the answer. For those who paid for our book, however, we owe you an answer. (If you borrowed your copy of the book, or are browsing in a bookstore or library, we absolutely insist you avert your gaze and turn ahead to the next section.) The answer is 27.8, or just 28. ($35 divided by $1.26 equals 27.78.)

The Fool Ratio? It's .54 (28 divided by 52). Where would you like to buy this stock? When its P/E is half its growth rate—when its P/E, in this case, is 26. That would mean at a share price of $32¾ or less. It's very near already, so you may be tempted to pick up some Messages right now. But the cash-flow negativity, among other factors, may warrant patience. Do you really want to pay up for a cash eater? That will ultimately have to be *your* decision.

You see, investing isn't about black-and-white, sure-thing situations. It's about judgment, the continual use of discretion following periods of examination and scrutiny. You'll be able to figure out whether you were *truly* right or wrong only after the fact, when that information is least necessary or useful. Until then, you have the thrill of making decisions that will affect your future. Some people consider that terrifying or paralyzing, as if it were preferable *not* to be making decisions that will affect your future. We're not among them. The investor's mentality is one that relishes taking responsibility for one's own decisions. But further, the investor actually puts money on the line in doing so.

As mentioned earlier, superior companies whose P/E ratios are just half their growth rate are not always easy to find, but they exist. There are many places to look for them: in clipping earnings reports, in checking out that new store that just opened across town, in mixing with other enthusiastic investors online. The place you're most likely to *find* them is among smaller, lesser-known companies, the very sort of small-cap growth stocks that part V features. Finally, the place to figure out *where to buy and sell* them is, for us, ultimately centered on the Fool Ratio.

When you buy a stock at a Fool Ratio of .50, you're getting it on the cheap. Your risk is lowered, since a stock is less likely to decline significantly when it's already trading at a low multiple of earnings. And you're more likely to double your money very quickly, because the fair, full value of the stock is generally more than twice the price at which you'll be buying it right then. You just need some people to sit up and take notice. Be patient. They usually do.

Limitations of the Fool Ratio

Some people, seeking a simplistic "one-number" investment approach, will err if they try to make the Fool Ratio do too much. The beauty of the figure is indeed that it suddenly provides a frame of reference for buy and sell points for individual growth stocks. For many novice investors, no such points currently exist at all. The Fool Ratio has a tremendous amount to offer them as a way of providing a context in which to understand a stock's value and trading ranges.

But don't pin all your hopes on our ratio, as the blindfolded try to pin tails on donkeys. Love is blind; don't fall in love with the Fool Ratio. You must always make sure that you thoroughly understand a company's financial statements, its planned new products in the pipeline, and a profile of its competition. These are essential elements to any investment decision that shouldn't be glossed over, let alone ignored!

And in some cases, the Fool Ratio may not work at all. For instance, some industries trade off P/E multiples that will never come anywhere near to their companies' growth rates. You should not apply the Fool Ratio to financial companies (banks, S&Ls, brokerage firms, leasing companies, et cetera), airlines, oil drillers, utilities, precious metals, and others. (To generalize about them, they're the more cyclical industries, as opposed to the "straight-growth" industries we favor, like high technology.) Experience will teach you for which industries the ratio works best. As a rule, if you find a company with a Fool Ratio of .15, you should be more cautious than optimistic.

A second situation in which the ratio is less helpful is with large-cap companies. These companies tend to be more cyclical and also tend to get valued as much off of assets as anything else. Smaller companies tend to be valued off the earnings power that can be generated from a given service, or product line. The Fool Ratio obviously spends no time at all looking at property, plant, and equipment items, goodwill values associated with powerful brand names, and so on, much of which critically factors into big-company valuations. This isn't to say you shouldn't use the Fool Ratio for putting price tags on behemoths, just that you should recognize the limitations of the tool. It's a little bit like trying to mow a football field with a Swiss Army knife.

You'll do best when you confine your Fool Ratio explorations to small-cap and mid-cap manufacturing and retail operations in straight-line growth industries. Where does that leave all the other stocks, like banks, and power companies, and airlines, and whatnot? Nowhere, in Foolish terms. We just don't bother investing in those companies. Even without those, we still have several thousand more choices than we'll *ever* need.

•18•

Selling Strategy

• • • • •

[Exit, pursued by a bear.]
—William Shakespeare

66 **I** have no problem knowing when to buy a stock, but if I just knew when to sell, I'd be a great investor!"

The line above expresses the single frustration felt by more investors than any other. If we *all* just knew *when* to sell. Heck, if we all knew when to sell, when to buy wouldn't matter! Ay, there's the rub. Because every time you sell, you're effectively predicting the future. You're effectively saying, "This stock will no longer do well (or well enough)." Foolishly, most of us don't invest under the presumption that we can predict the market; what the heck are we doing presuming to predict an individual stock?

To be sure, some investors avoid this problem altogether. Warren Buffett, for example, almost never sells at all. His investment approach is predicated on locating outstanding companies, buying their shares, and holding them for decades. In fact, the only typical situation that might cause Buffett to shed his shares would be something like a management change. (Ironically, because of the power that he wields over the companies in which he's invested—owning chunks of their stock—and because of his reputation, none of his companies would change management without at least his tacit approval.) So what Buffett's created is a situation in which he just buys stocks and never sells them. He feels very little of the angst about selling strategy from which most of us suffer.

Well, it has all worked very well for Buffett, but the rest of us don't typically enjoy close enough relationships with management that we can help call the shots. And we simply can't get close enough to know the intelligence and character of most of our companies' leaders either, which is so integral to a strategy based on locating "can't miss" long-term properties. In other words, most of us aren't Buffett: We need to sell. In this chapter, we'll confront head on the investor's *bête noire*.

Pick a Selling Strategy, Any Selling Strategy

Before we discuss our own sell rule, we think it's useful to imitate stout Cortez and, silent upon a peak in Darien, stare with eagle eyes over the Pacific of selling strategies. In other words, let's recognize the ocean of possibilities; there are lots and lots of ways to navigate the market. In fact, the many different ways to invest are really what *make* the market in the first place.

If everyone had the same opinion about a certain stock being under-valued, what would happen? The stock would get bought and would quickly rise in price until some portion of the crowd dissented, no longer believing the stock to be undervalued; additional points of view would automatically come into existence. For instance, the investment approach that we expound in this book is just *one* point of view. If everyone read and agreed with our book—*everyone*—well . . . first off, we would achieve total domination over the solar system (due to the subliminal messages contained herein). But en route to our achieving that total domination, what would happen to the markets? They'd quickly reflect all the tenets of the Foolish approach, raising stocks with .50 Fool Ratios and lowering those over 1.40, most likely creating a soup of 1.00 valuations. Dow Dividend stocks would probably lose their charm as the range of dividend yields "equalized," congregating en masse around some specific yield. What would effectively happen is that investors would have trouble drawing significant distinctions between "undervalued," "fairly valued," and "overvalued." We at Fool HQ would then begin writing a sequel propounding theories exactly the opposite of our existing ones, and in so doing create a newly profitable investment approach. And right about then we would come to rule all life in our galaxy as we know it .

Fortunately for you (and us), everyone will *not* read our book, and some of those who do will call it utter poppycock. Perfect. Many other investment approaches are out there, and they help make the market. They make it possible for us all to capitalize off of other people's ignorance.

We've already referred to one such *other* investment technique: War-ren Buffett's. Completely opposite Buffett is the day trader, perpetrat-ing another investment strategy altogether. The day trader's the guy who buys in the morning and sells in the afternoon, perhaps even multiple trades in and out of the same stock in a given day. (This approach may work for institutions; on the other hand, it's murder for individuals, due to the "friction costs" of trading.) And between these two extremes lie many intermediate spots.

Those who lean more toward Buffett typically look to hold their stocks for a few years. These are patient people who believe in the American stock market and certain, select companies over the long term, don't have a tremendous amount of time or inclination to monitor their investments, and won't exit their investment unless they perceive a significant change in a company's fortunes, its management strategy, vision, competitive field, something like that. We may have just described you. If we have, please notice how your sell rule colors your investment approach. If you're going to aim to hold your stocks for several years, you'll be far more likely to buy bigger-cap, more dependable brand-name sorts of companies. That means stocks like The Gap, Intel, McDonald's, Microsoft, Reebok, et al. You are *not* going to dicker around too much with small caps, Fool Ratios, and the like.

Those who lean more toward the day trader extreme have their own (generally more elaborate) sell rules. Experience suggests that these rules tend to be more systematic, on the whole, than those of long-term investors. Some short-termers automatically sell out any stock that exceeds a certain percentage gain, or percentage loss. The idea in the latter case is never to lose more than, say, 10 percent; in the former case, the idea is that once you've made, say, 30 percent, you've gotten enough "pop" out of that investment and you should probably look elsewhere to find the next thing ready to "pop." Other systematic rules are of a more technical nature, involving trading volume, reference to stock charts, and other dubious techniques. Obviously, these trading styles involve a much more active, hands-on brand of investing. And as with the patient, brand-name player, this sell rule colors the quick-time trader's investment approach. If you're operating off of shorter-term trading rules, you're less likely to care much about what companies you're investing in. The quality of a company's finances, its future prospects, and all those other numbers may not even matter at all. Many active traders don't know much more about a given stock than its ticker symbol and a graph of its recent share price performance.

So we've now learned that your selling strategy profoundly affects your investment approach in terms of what you'll buy and what you'll be expecting out of it. (In fact, taking this even further, your selling strategy ultimately has important effects on your quality of life!) But we can turn that around to say the following: Your personality, your way of living, your risk tolerance all should probably *determine* your selling strategy. *Make your selling strategy reflect your personality.* Many different personality types exist. So can—and should—many sell strategies. Don't get put in the position where your sell rule doesn't jibe with who you are. If you're a patient person who has little time for investing and you have a broker frequently trading you in and out of a large number of stocks, you need a new sell rule (probably a new broker, too). If you're a more restless type who has primarily adopted the Dow Dividend approach, and you find yourself constantly wanting to tinker around with it to see if you can improve the returns, you may be better suited to more active management (and trading) of your account.

"When You Find a Better Place . . ."

At the beginning of the book, we pointed out the opposite extremes of investor error: Greed and Fear. Greedy investors go wrong when they take too much risk; fearful investors go wrong because they don't take enough. Fools aim to find the happy medium, taking "just the right amount" of risk and maximizing returns.

It's really quite the same, once again, with regard to selling. We won't "do Buffett" because we can't be Buffett . . . we can never enjoy the advantages that Buffett has, and therefore won't adopt a no-sell approach. But we also think that automatic "loss-cutting" sell rules are ridiculous. We hear many people advocate selling out anything that's down 5 percent. "If you can limit all your losses on average to about 5 percent this way," they begin. But we find that once you've had to pay a commission and factored in the bid-ask spread you're just about *already* down 5 percent from where you were a couple minutes beforehand. Is that good investing?

Here's another bad way to sell: devising a strategy of sell rules based on your own experience with one or another specific investment. More often than not, such rules are like maxims that seem entirely plausible until you encounter other maxims that *also* seem plausible but directly contradict them. You can do this with any maxims, investment-related or otherwise. "Absence makes the heart grow fonder," we hear Robb say. But then the next day he muses, "Out of sight, out of mind." "If you find something that works, stick with it," we are told, but "Variety is the spice of life." It's quite the same with investing. Let's say you buy a certain stock that does nothing for three years through a very strong bull market. What a waste; you eventually sell it. But further, you decide that from now on, if an investment doesn't move appreciably after 3 months, you're automatically going to sell it to reinvest in a better stock. Your next three buys all do nothing for a few months, and so you sell them. Ah . . . but two of those just happen to explode right after you sell them, rising more than 100 percent in a matter of a few weeks. What's going to be your next new rule?

Don't mimic bad football coaches after they lose a game because their defense gave up too many rushing yards. For the next game, they'll decide to pack it down underneath with additional players guarding against the run, only to be outsmarted by an opposing coach who throws long passes over their defense instead. Our natural human instinct is to overcompensate for the reason behind our most *recent* failure. In so doing, we open ourselves up to completely new failures from unexpected sources. If we constantly redesign our selling strategy based on only the most recent lesson learned, we'll lose money on the market.

Fortunately, the motley-clad have a rich valuation technique off of which to work, the Fool Ratio. That 1.00 sell mark constitutes a handy ruler for measuring investment value. However, the Fool Ratio best suits the analysis of individual stocks. As an investor, you have a bigger picture to look at—that of your overall portfolio. In acknowledgment of this crucial bit of information, our single sell rule says the following (trumpets, please):

When you find a better place for your money, put it there.

That's it, the entire simple thing. Profoundly simple, though. You see, investors too often fixate on kicking out individual stocks based on particularly good or bad recent performance, as if these events have suddenly enabled them to foretell the future. Why make things so difficult? If you have a ten-stock portfolio, don't look at it as a series of ten separate, difficult decisions about when to sell. No! Look at it as a single investment portfolio to which you'll want to *add* new stocks when the time arises. *When the time arises, you can make room for that exciting new opportunity by shedding whichever of your holdings looks to be the most fully valued (i.e., appears to have the least room for more near-term appreciation).*

The Fool's selling strategy has you concentrated on keeping your money *in* the stock market, where we think it should be. And it also concentrates you on managing a portfolio—one of the themes of this book—as opposed to managing a bunch of individual stocks.

Now, the experienced investor might ask, "Hey, shouldn't you guys be recommending that investors get out of their dogs, though? You should never let *anyone* go down more than 20 percent in anything!" Our response to that is simply, "Do they have a better place to put the money?" If you have a tragic stock that has lost half of its value, and you can't find a better place to put the money, leave it there. In certain market periods, big losers that are still dependable companies own a higher probability for short-term gains than your typical momentum investor's darling.

Before closing out this brief section on our sell rule, we must add one related note about loser stocks in general. Namely, we almost never, ever add to them. There's one old maxim with which we do agree *strongly:* "Don't throw good money after bad!" Too many people get excited when their latest buy drops from its original purchase price of $20 to $15. They work up a lather in their attempt to get more money into the stock, when their reaction should be just the opposite. When the stock goes to $10, they get depressed. Then it goes to $6, and they're so bummed out they lose their heads and put down half of everything they have left in the world on it. They figure they can make it all back by loading up on it right there, for once and for all. It can't possibly go any lower . . .

Then it never reaches as high as $6 again.

This is a Wall Street commonplace, about as common as really, really bad *Saturday Night Live* skits after the show's first half hour. Don't get trapped by the shortcomings of human nature. When one of your investments begins to take on water, resist the urge to pile even more goodies aboard. Only one *Titanic* ever sailed the ocean blue, but *Titanics* play the blues every day on our nation's stock markets . . . mostly because of boneheaded investment practices.

The Sell Game: Don't Look *Now*!

When we sell a stock, we try to avoid becoming infatuated with how that stock does in the days and weeks after our sell. You can beat yourself up forever about how you could've gotten that half point if you'd only just waited half an hour, or that extra point if you'd only just waited 8 days. Yeah, right. In only a tiny minority of your trades will you ever pick the *exact* primo exit price, selling out a whole position just before the stock (or the overall market) tanks. The majority of the time, your stock will uptick over your sell price at least once in the ensuing few months after selling. Experienced investors should know this and not worry about it, but to a certain extent none of us can help looking over our shoulder to see if some old stock might be gaining on us.

This isn't to say that you're wrong to keep an eye on your selling decisions. Holding yourself accountable by tracking your "sell-side" performance is admirable. For many people, however, the tendency to dwell on what might have been makes this time not well spent. They can't hear enough the old line about "letting bygones be bygones."

To address this situation, we invented "Don't Look *Now!*" It's such a simple little game that it doesn't deserve any more ostentatious a title than that. The idea is to go back at a sufficiently distant date and figure out just exactly how your erstwhile holding ended up doing. We typically make it a period of 3 months. You start off on the day you sell by noting the price at which you sold the stock *and* the closing price of the S&P 500 index. Three months from that date, you go back and check (1) where the stock is now, and (2) what the overall return for the S&P 500 index has been over that time. Very simple.

And here's how the game is scored:

If the sold stock has risen 20 percent or more over your exit price, give yourself a "Total Defeat." If the stock has failed to rise 20 percent but is currently outperforming the S&P 500, take a "Marginal Defeat."

If, on the other hand, the stock has dropped more than 20 percent below your sales price, serve yourself up a "Total Victory"! If the stock hasn't dropped that far but is underperforming the S&P 500, claim a "Marginal Victory."

Just to share some of our game's rationale, notice how we treat *this* interesting scenario: You sell a stock that then happens to rise 30 percent in the *1 week* right after you sell it, but after 3 months it closes 22 percent *below* your exit price. How's that scored in our Foolish sell game? It's a "Total Victory." And you deserve it! You would've been kicking yourself during that 30 percent week, of course, but if the stock did zoom up that quickly, getting out right there would've been very lucky, given the dramatic decline soon to follow. And after 3 months, you now have the luxury of looking back a fair distance and discovering that you made a very fine sell. Total Victory.

It will take you a matter of a minute or two every so often to update a file on your computer (or a series of notebook entries) with your latest "Don't Look *Now!*" result. But the statistics you obtain will help you immensely in evaluating what is for everyone the most difficult aspect of investing. Let's say that after 2 years your sell game results look like this:

Total Victory	4
Marginal Victory	10
Marginal Defeat	2
Total Defeat	2

Beautiful! Keep working your magic; don't change a thing.

Then again, your game results may look more like this:

Total Victory	0
Marginal Victory	5
Marginal Defeat	4
Total Defeat	9

. . . a performance that speaks for itself. Of course, there are different ways to slice and dice the numbers, and you can certainly tweak the game's parameters if doing so helps you tailor the analysis better to your own particular situation. For instance, maybe you're a shorter-term trader and would prefer to look back after only 1 month (or 1 week, God forbid), since that time frame better applies to your style. Or maybe you prefer a different "Total Victory/Defeat" percentage than 20 percent. The idea is just to keep the game simple and the results meaningful.

Notice, in closing, that "Don't Look *Now!*" has nothing to say about your *overall* investment performance or ability. You can get a "Total Defeat" for a stock that you carried to a four-bagger . . . all of us would rather have a totally defeated four-bagger than a totally victorious dog. Our sell game is just that: a game that focuses completely on one aspect of investing, your selling ability.

◆ ◆ ◆

Selling *never* will be easy. Don't try to make it so. But in this chapter we've at least attempted to give you both a way to think about selling and a way to track your selling decisions.

Our Foolish sell rule discourages you from ever thinking about selling as a fearful, isolated predicament that you must face with each of your stocks. No! From now on, you'll think of selling simply as a prelude to smart buying, a necessary step in the betterment of one's portfolio. You dispense with the stock or stocks at fullest value in order to buy a new stock or stocks markedly undervalued.

"Don't Look *Now!*" encourages you to track your selling performance. That puts you well ahead of most investors, who never even think about it. It also puts you way ahead of those investors who think *too much* about it. Those are the people who intensely scrutinize the performance of a stock for 1 week after they've sold it and then never look back again. Overrating the significance of a few days, they may come away with a highly distorted view (whether better or worse) of their selling fortunes. With your Foolish game results handy, you, on the other hand, will have a document you can use as a guide to understanding your strengths and weaknesses on the back-end of investments.

PART VI

SHORTING

STOCKS

·19·

Shorting Stocks

· · · · ·

In short, I deny nothing, but doubt everything.
—*Byron*

I f you've ever swaggered up to a craps table, cleared away the necessary elbow room, and slapped down a few candy-colored chips on the Pass Line, you were doing what most of the people at a craps table do. You were betting with the crowd.

Adjacent to the Pass Line, however, is a cheaper strip of real estate (usually a vacant lot) known as the "Don't Pass Bar." It's virtually the opposite bet; you win when the Pass Line crowd loses, and lose when it wins. The odds for Don't Pass are no worse than the Pass Line. But because you're betting *against* the roller and most of the rest of the table, betting Don't Pass is considered bad form. Craps jargon for people like you is "wrong bettor." Many other bettors will actually dislike you for doing it, a feeling which will be reinforced whenever you smile at dice rolls that make them frown.

It's quite the same for those who habitually sell stock short.

A Short Lesson: How It Works

We've already mentioned selling short in part IV, "Building a Foolish Investment Portfolio." Shorting stocks is the third and final component of our investment approach. When you short stocks, you profit not when they rise but when they *fall;* it's a neat idea that not everyone realizes is even possible. And of those who do, most won't consider it. Some think it's un-American to profit off the failure of corporations and other investors, giving "hedge investors" a Don't-Pass-Bar reputation. Many others have rightly heard that the stock market has been the best place to put your money in the twentieth century. These people don't want to short stocks, because they fear that the market's tendency to rise will pull their short up with it.

But prior to an intelligent consideration of the pros and cons, let's make like engineers and first learn how the thing works.

For starters, to short stocks you'll need a margin account. To obtain one, deposit $2,000 or more at a brokerage firm and sign a form saying you wish it to be a *margin,* not a *cash,* account. The distinction between the two is simply that with a margin account you do not have to pay full price for every investment you make. In other words, you can borrow additional money (paying interest on it) to buy stocks in a margin account. Current margin requirements necessitate your having enough cash to pay for at least 50 percent of a new transaction. If you, for instance, put $5,000 into a brokerage account, you could buy $10,000 worth of stock ($5,000 is 50 percent of the overall investment). This is called *buying on margin.*

Your margin account also entitles you to short stocks, which you initiate by first borrowing shares from a current shareholder. This may sound difficult, but it isn't. In fact, you'll never notice it happening, because your broker does this for you automatically. In the very next breath, you *sell* these borrowed shares at the current market price. Then in the coming days and weeks you sit and wait, rooting for the stock to spiral downward. When you're ready to cash out of your investment—whether for profit or for loss—you close out the position by buying the stock back, so that you can return your borrowed shares to the lender—another thing your broker does for you automatically. That's it.

Let's look at a couple of examples.

You decide clandestinely to short 100 shares of the corporation you work for, Overrated Technologies (NASDAQ: FALL), at $56½. You just call up your broker and say, "Judy, I want to sell short 100 shares of Overrated." Judy will borrow 100 shares for you and then sell them immediately at $56½. Three months later, when the stock has dropped to $46½, you want to cash out. You'll place an order to buy 100 shares of FALL at the market price ($46½), enabling Judy to return these newly bought shares to the lender.

So what have you made? Well, you sold 100 shares in the first place at $56½, meaning your sale came to $5,650. Then, to close out, you bought 100 shares back at $46½, or $4,650. Your profit was $1,000. Off the initial investment of $5,650 you've made $1,000, a 3-month return of 18 percent. Snazzy.

Now let's reshuffle the cards and pretend things get ugly. You've sold your Overrated Tech shares short at $56½ and alas, the stock begins to go up—$60, $65, $70. You keep holding, thinking, "My company is *so* overvalued now!" A year later, it has surpassed $75, and you can't stand it any longer. You want out. With the price at $76½, you call your broker. "Judy," you wheeze into the pay phone, "I've got to get outta this thing. Buy it back and get rid of it. And don't bother returning my call to confirm the trade; Ma Bell has cut me off for a couple of months. Just return those damned borrowed shares!"

So what have you lost? Tally up the damage and you see you sold 100 shares short at $56½ ($5,650). You eventually bought back those shares at $76½, for which you had to come up with $7,650. You lost $2,000, or 35 percent.

Now on the face of it, the technique would seem to require no cash at all. You're borrowing shares and selling them, right? That *creates* cash, adds bucks to your account. When you then decide to buy back, you're just paying out of your cash to reacquire the borrowed shares. However, if you're buying the stock back at a *higher* price than that at which you sold (the second example, above), you'll pay more than you initially received. In other words, you'll need additional money to cover your losing short position. It's for this reason that brokers require you to have enough cash and stocks on deposit to meet the margin requirements. You should always check with your broker first and make sure you understand the firm's policies for margin requirements and shorting. Of course, we have helpful people who hang out in our area online answering questions on the subject, some of whom know more than you might ever *want* to know about the abstruse details of the subject.

A tidy way to summarize shorting is simply that the normal order of trading stocks is reversed: You sell first, *then* buy. Selling short is really no more difficult than that.

Why Bother Shorting?

In fine old Foolish style, we're first going to examine why *not* to short. After all, you really don't have to short. Stocks do go up over time, and you already know that the Dow Dividend strategy can net you market-doubling gains if history continues to repeat itself. Heck, you may not want to spend any more time with your investing than that. In fact, if you don't follow the market closely (i.e., quote your stocks at least once a week), then you definitely should *not* short at all. Shorting requires an almost daily attentiveness to the stock market and should not be attempted by those unwilling or unable to pay the requisite attention.

Then there is the specter of the rising short. When a stock you short goes up, you have to fork up extra dollars to bail yourself out. It's the nature of the investment. You have what some people refer to as "unlimited upside risk." That sounds scary. Maybe even real scary.

If this makes you uncomfortable, or if you are at all uncomfortable about anything you read in this chapter, stay well away. We did, in the 1995 bull market for technology stocks, which sent the NASDAQ ripping to 30 percent-plus gains in a matter of months. Tech stocks could do no wrong, sometimes rising multiple points *more* than one day a week. We cashed out the two shorts in our ten-stock portfolio in March and, fortunately, stayed away from shorting all summer long. You can take this approach, too, moving in and out of shorting as it suits your whim. Or you can ignore the strategy altogether. Whatever. BUT, do at least familiarize yourself with it in this chapter. We're almost the only ones in the financial world who are going to teach it to you. The concept is anathema to the establishment—the very reason they won't teach it to you, the *very* reason we will.

Short People Do, in Point of Fact, Have Reasons to Live

Picking up right there, let's talk a bit more about why the shorting of stocks is vastly underpracticed by the "professional" investment community at large. First of all, from a purely Foolish point of view, this makes shorting stock even more compelling. As you well know by now, Fools relish a good swim against the tide. When most investors are trying to figure out how many more half-point gains they can squeeze out of their equities, you're looking the other way. You're regarding these same securities from the top down, assessing how far each might fall. The seldom-taken contrary view can be lucrative.

But let's fix on why exactly the establishment is so uninterested in shorting, why in some cases it is openly hostile to shorting. Not many brokers suggest short selling to their clients. Only a tiny fraction of mutual funds do any shorting. Probably an even smaller percentage of banks and pension funds short. Further, we live in a world in which Wall Street firms cannot even safely issue sell recommendations. How peculiar!

Not really, actually. Investment firms make millions by helping companies raise money to finance their growth, in addition to their reliance on access to corporate insiders for equity research. So let's say you own a company, and you take a Wall Street analyst out to a cushy lunch to share your whole business outlook with her: all about next year's growth prospects for hot dogs, how misunderstood hot dogs are by the conventional dietary press, how resilient the hot dog is as a traditional player at deli stands. She then goes back to New York and 2 weeks later issues a sell recommendation on your stock, dropping it several points in the process. How would you react? The answer is not only would you skip sharing a hot dog with her next time, but you'd probably never talk to her again. You wouldn't share your business plan with her firm, and you also wouldn't consider employing her to help you raise capital or float a bond.

That's why Wall Street never says, "Sell." It only says "Buy" and "Hold." "Buy" means a recommendation to buy your stock. "Hold" means a recommendation to sell your stock. What an unpleasant work environment! Deceit in the form of euphemism, institutionalized.

Given what you've just read, you can now clearly understand why the establishment may *never* say, "Short." So pity Wall Street. In fact, do it one better: Take advantage of its constraints. Short stocks.

We're constantly coming across establishment ideologues on CNBC or in *The Wall Street Journal* who make shorting stocks out to be incredibly risky. They love to play up this idea of "unlimited upside risk." The idea, again, is that if you short a stock and it goes up, and just keeps going up, you'll *have* to cover one day. The stock could theoretically cause you to have to cover at infinity—a very high price. That's right, you just shorted Etter's Ermines at $27 and whadda ya know, the fur retailer went to $infinity. You're out of luck. In fact, you're in jail, bankrupt. You've now felt the sting of "unlimited upside risk."

Hmm. Is the concept of "unlimited upside risk" reasonable? Does anything go to infinity tomorrow? Do you spend long sleepless nights worrying about the potential threat of our planet getting clocked by a gigantic uncharted iceball?

In the brief twenty-some years we've spent on this steadfast little rock in its unremarkable corner of the Milky Way, we have yet to meet the bloke who got victimized by "unlimited upside risk." Oh sure, we've met people who've lost money shorting . . . in some cases, *lots* of money. We've also met people who've lost lots of money investing in all sorts of things: options, stocks, options, real estate, options, precious metals, and their own businesses. And options. (See part VIII, "Here Be Dragons.") The world presents us hundreds of opportunities to lose money every day. But find us the guy who suffered the ultimate indignity of "unlimited upside risk" and we'll mail you back the cereal box-tops you submitted to receive your copy of this book.

In fact, we consider shorting stocks a *low-risk* investment approach.

The way we play it, anyway. You see, we set a "quitting price" whenever we short a stock. The quitting price is typically 20 percent above the price at which we shorted. If our short sale rises to its quitting price, we throw up our hands, wave the white hanky, and make like a tree; we're outta there. Now, do we do this when we *buy* a small cap? Nope. We have *no* downside sell rule with our purchases, and have been known to lose more than 20 percent on many a small-stock investment. We have lost more money, historically, on our losing longs than on our losing shorts. (We have also made more money on our winning longs than on our winning shorts, for obvious reasons. That's what we mean by low-risk.)

If you, dear reader, concur with what you've just read, you now see how silly we find the pratings of the Wise, those who would have us avoid shorting altogether because it's so "dangerous." If you don't have time for shorting, we well understand—a perfectly acceptable excuse. But if you're only letting fear hold you back, you're playing wallflower at your own wedding. (Okay, that's a little overstated, but these days you nearly have to shout obscenities if you want anyone to read your stuff.)

If we believe we can identify undervalued stocks, it stands to reason that we can locate overvalued stocks as well. And once you've learned how to short, you can take advantage of these very situations to augment your bottom line.

We include shorting stocks in our Foolish investment approach primarily as a hedge. You're taking compensatory measures to counterbalance a potentially plummeting stock market. As it is a hedge, we short in moderation (no more than 20 percent of our portfolio), because although a good short seller will make consistent money on his shorts, he does well to keep the majority of his funds invested traditionally—long. The primary direction of the stock market is up. Accordingly, most of the short positions you take should last only a few months. (It should be easy to remember that "shorting" stock is best used as a "short-term" strategy.)

You can make money selling stocks short in almost any market environment, though. Ultimately, therefore, you should short stocks not because you think the market is going to crash, but simply because selling stocks short can lead to consistent profit. The whole idea is to make money both ways, simultaneously—long, as your small stocks and the general market rise, *and* short, as the stocks you've identified as overpriced wither. When it works right, it's a gas! In fact, before we turned Foolish enough to short stocks, we didn't know just how much fun we were missing.

The Real Issue: What and What Not to Short

At The Motley Fool, we look for shorts among small-cap highfliers that have, in our Foolish estimation, risen out of control. Way out of control. "Momentum investors"—those who buy certain stocks primarily because they're hot—drive up some prices to stratospheric levels, which is easier to do to small-cap companies. The slightest failure to fulfill such grand expectations can send their shares crashing lower.

So the first reason we like to short these companies is that they have to perform perfectly to justify their share price. And as any Fool will tell you, "every . . . thing that grows / Holds in perfection but a little moment" (Shakespeare, "Sonnet 15").

The second reason we like to short big winners is that in most instances, their Big Short-Term Move is behind them. Even if the market keeps rising, a drastically overpriced stock will at best rise maybe another 10 to 20 percent. If the market goes flat, you can often expect overvalued highfliers to decline 20 percent. And if the market turns down, look out.

What?! Short big winners? The very sorts of stocks that we often look to buy and hold? Short the stocks of some of the best young companies in the world, mini-powerhouses? Sure. Sometimes. Any experienced investor knows that stocks sometimes perform drastically differently from the companies behind them. Archer Daniels Midland (NYSE:ADM) declined steadily throughout the first half of 1995 despite record earnings; it had the specter of a government investigation into price fixing overhanging it. After a blowout first quarter in 1995, Motorola (NYSE:MOT) gave back a quick 18 percent after announcing some inventory problems. Conversely, Sybase (NASDAQ:SYBS) reported *horrible* earnings for its first half of 1995, but with the second horrible report bounced up 10 points off its lows due to takeover speculation.

When you buy stock, you're not buying a company. You're buying shares of stock in that company. This may seem like a tautology, but we've found that some people need reminding about this. In the short-to-intermediate term, a stock can go the opposite direction of its company. Keeping in mind the independence of the two entities, we never harbor any ill feelings for companies whose stocks we short. We have no gripe with the business; we just think its stock is overvalued. (In fact, when we're short we'll often publicly root the company onto success, confident that our valuation of its stock is accurate and impregnable.) This distinction between the two is at the heart of Foolishness, and illustrates the Byron epigraph: "In short, I deny nothing. . . ."

We use three primary tests to determine which stocks to short:

1. Short stocks with a Fool Ratio of 1.40 or greater.

The first yardstick we bring to bear in picking short sales is one with which you're already familiar. It's the Fool Ratio, featured in chapter 17. We won't waste much space here summarizing that work. Suffice to say that the number shows the ratio between a stock's price-to-earnings ratio (P/E) and its company's growth rate. The premise is that a stock becomes fairly and fully valued when its P/E (reported daily in many business sections and financial papers) equals the percentage of the company growth rate.

Here's our key to shorting: When a stock's P/E ratio exceeds the company growth rate by 40 percent or more, consider selling it short. For Fool Ratio fans, that would be 1.40 or more.

As you can see, then, we're not aiming to short every stock that's quadrupled over the past year; some of those may quadruple again in the next one. But we are shorting some of those quadruplers—and triplers, and doublers—those whose stock has run up 40 percent or more beyond what we consider the fair, full value. And as you might expect, the chances of those highfliers moving up much more when they're already so overvalued is small.

2. Short "closed" situations; avoid "open" ones.

We actually like to draw a distinction among overvalued highfliers between "open" and "closed" situations. "Open" (or open-ended) situations are those we never short. They're the companies that have the capacity to create a humongous surprise by crushing all earnings estimates in sight. Often, these companies have just introduced revolutionary products, have hit the groove of a tremendous growth period, or have industry peers who have recently reported consistently stellar earnings. Avoid shorting these companies, because they have the capacity to blow away the estimates on which you've based your Fool Ratio valuation. A good example of this was America Online (NASDAQ:AMER), a consistently popular and *killing* short all through its 1992–95 rise from $2¾ to the mid-$70s. The company demonstrated the capacity to beat every earnings estimate tossed its way, became the top online franchise over that period, and sat squarely at the center of the Internet craze that invaded the market in 1995, sending everything remotely linked to the Internet skyward. AMER was a classic "open situation" and carried with it the strong possibility all along that it might be acquired by a much larger suitor. You'd have had to be an imbecile to short it.

"Closed situations" are just the opposite, overvalued highfliers that have no real compelling product and little likelihood of dramatically surprising market expectations. They're typically in nothing-special industries, probably moving toward the end of their maximum growth phases. A good example here was Bed Bath & Beyond (NASDAQ:BBBY), a fine company whose stock happened to be beyond—way beyond—its full, fair valuation for much of 1993-94. (The company's motto, "Beyond any store of its kind," gave rise to many a wisecrack in the halls of Fool HQ.) Bed Bath operates national superstores that sell at bargain prices every color of household item imaginable. When we found it at $30 in mid-1993, the stock was changing hands at forty times earnings. Now, you simply couldn't find an estimate on the Street that would credit the company with anything higher than a 27 percent forward growth rate. Was this a compelling industry? Nope. Was Bed Bath's "product" unique, life-changing, and capable of seizing the imagination of an entire generation? No. Was Bed Bath blowing away all its earnings estimates? Not really; it was hitting its targets or exceeding them by a penny or two. Having shorted it right about $30, we had to wait more than a year for the stock to drop to our target price below $24. When it did, after an unimpressive earnings comparison, BBBY dropped hard, moving from $25 to $18 in the first 3 weeks of April 1995. Over the next few months BBBY recovered on stronger earnings and improved prospects, but they always go down faster than they go up.

3. Short stocks with low short interest; definitely avoid those with high short interest.

Having now explained that you should short only high-flying "closed-situation" stocks with Fool Ratios of 1.40 or higher, we have one more test left to apply before deciding to short. It's time to check the short interest.

Short interest is simply the total number of shares of a given security that have already been sold short. This figure is reported monthly in *The Wall Street Journal* and *Investor's Business Daily*. Why do we bother checking it? Well, let's think for a second about what short interest represents.

On the one hand, it represents the amount of bearish sentiment in a stock. Let's take a Foolish example. *Investor's Business Daily* prints short interest of 4 million shares for Lunar Development Technologies (NASDAQ:NEVR). The company has only 16 million shares overall, meaning that 25 percent of its total shares outstanding have been borrowed and ditched. Hordes of bears are obviously skeptical about the company's efforts to terraform our satellite neighbor.

On the other hand, however, short interest represents latent buying power. That's because in the short-to-intermediate term almost every single share already sold short will be bought back. The irony is clear: While high short interest *looks* like a bearish sign, it's actually a bullish indicator.

Knowing this, you should *avoid* Lunar Development Tech as a short because too many others have already shorted before you. If the stock has resided at $18 to $19 per share for months, what's going to happen if it drops to $16½ suddenly? *"Finally,"* many short sellers will say to themselves. And a fair number of those holders of 4 million in short interest will buy back impatiently to earn the long-awaited small profit. Result? Stock goes right back to $18 to $19 again. You'll have a hard time ever earning the 20 percent profit you're shooting for.

Now, if Lunar Dev Tech happens to announce surprisingly good news—say, early indications that it has maintained plant life for more than 4 weeks in an airless atmosphere under a geodesic dome—*look out!* The stock suddenly jumps to $22 on the news and creates a panic among stunned short sellers. They start covering. The stock rises to $24 on volume of a million shares more, driven by fearful bears. That rise creates even more fear—wow, the thing's up over 30 percent in 2 days!—and so even more short sellers buy back at these higher prices, creating further upward spiraling in the share price. We have before us, ladies, gentlemen, and Fools, a "short squeeze."

As we've just demonstrated, stocks with high short interest are bad to short because (1) they're less likely to drop significantly due to short sellers impatient to take profits, and (2) they're ripe for the dreaded short squeeze. Conversely, stocks with a *low* short interest are just fine to short. Little short-selling has taken place so far, with the likelihood of more occurring if the stock remains overvalued. When your fellow investors move in and begin to short this unshorted stock, they'll create downward pressure, increasing your returns.

The best way to measure short interest is actually the "short-interest ratio." Above, we looked at the percentage of a company's total shares outstanding that are short. That's one sort of short-interest ratio and it's not bad. But we can go one better by comparing the stock's short interest to its *average daily volume*. This figure will reveal the number of days of normal trading volume that it would take short sellers to cover their positions completely. Blasting back off into outer space again, we find that NEVR shareholders are trading 200,000 shares of this stock on an average day. So let's take short interest (4 million) and divide it by the average daily volume (200,000), giving us a short-interest ratio of 20 days to cover. That is, as you may have expected, very high. We almost never, ever short any stock with more than 10 days to cover.

We prefer to short stocks whose short-interest ratios are 5 days or less. You should too. Chances are you've found a good one, and you're *not* going to get squeezed.

As a follow-up example, over the period that America Online scored its twenty-five-bagger, a consistent 20 percent of its total shares outstanding remained short, making for a short-interest ratio of 10 days or more almost all the way along. This was further confirmation of just how bad a short-side pick AMER was. Many a short squeeze occurred. Oomph.

Setting Goals and the Five Annoying Little Things

You know why to short, you know how to short, and you now know what and what not to short. It remains to examine the trading strategy you'll want to adopt for shorting stocks.

First off, before placing your trade, you should formulate some idea ahead of time for what your target and quitting prices will be. You may also wish to consider the length of time you want to maintain your position; odds are that the longer you hold the short, the more likely it is to follow the overall market's long-term uptrend.

At Fool HQ, we set target and quitting prices 20 percent below and 20 percent above our short, respectively. And we generally hope to cash out at a 20 percent profit within 2 to 3 months. We've held some short positions as long as a year (like Bed, Bath & Beyond), but we don't necessarily recommend the practice. After all, if you've had to hold a whole year in order to earn only a 20 percent return, you could've just sat in high-yielding Dow stocks instead and done as well. Still, even if you have to hold your short for a full 12 months and only earn 15 percent on it, you'll have posted a market-beating performance most years. (We do need to maintain that perspective, in the face of so much ambition.)

All right, you're ready to take the dive, ready to root for something that will, you hope, take the dive with you. Before doing so, we need to catalog five annoying little things that can work against you, as a short seller. Just so you'll be prepared.

First, you call up your broker, and you're told that the shares *aren't* available. What?! Hmm. Well, that may be the case. It does happen sometimes with stocks that are either small caps, or recently popular shorts, or both. In these situations, about all you can do is to ask your broker to put you on the waiting list, then call him back each day and plead. Seems like a raw deal, since no waiting list exists for those who want to buy. But that's one of the limitations to shorting stocks, and we all live with it. Fortunately, it doesn't occur too often.

You also may be tripped up by a second minor annoyance, the need to get an "uptick" before your trade goes through. In creating this rule, the exchanges have effectively said, "If you want to short a stock at $34, you'll have to wait for a trade at $34⅛ before we can carry out your order." This really is a raw deal, because it's a completely artificial stumbling block put in place to prevent short sellers from piling onto a losing stock and sinking it. If a stock you want to short goes into sudden free fall after reporting bad earnings, you can't hop on the shorting bandwagon until some brave soul pushes the stock up. Does any rule prevent buyers from piling into an issue that is suddenly rising? No way, Josiah. Short sellers are hosed on this count.

Third, once in a blue moon your broker may be forced to "return" your shorted shares to the anonymous lender, usually because the lender wants to sell them and your broker can find no other shares to borrow. Forced into doing so, you may have to buy back the shares prematurely—whether you've made money or not. This happens only with very small stocks that have few shares outstanding (the sort that you probably shouldn't have shorted in the first place). In fact, despite having sold dozens of small caps short over the past several years, and having received "warning calls" from our broker letting us know we may have to return the shares early, we've never once had to do it. Should the incident ever take place, however, we wouldn't sweat it. We'd just put the money somewhere else.

A fourth niggling little detail involves no additional interest on your short-sale-inflated account balance. To review, when you sell a stock short, your account's cash balance rises (as it does with any sale) to reflect the liquidation of the stock. However, what you'll find is that most brokers won't pay you *any* interest on this additional money. This compares with the close-to-100-percent interest that institutional investors typically receive on money raised by short sales. This is yet another minor drawback to the small-time short seller, who can now number the government, Wall Street, and his broker as hostile parties to his short sales. Fighting back, our online readership joined together to poll a slew of deep-discount brokers to determine whether any would be willing to offer individual investors interest paid on short sales. As it turned out, we discovered that K. Aufhauser & Co., the Manhattan-based deep discounter, *did* pay this interest. (Some new accounts were opened at Aufhauser that day.) Meanwhile, a top-ranking officer of National Discount Brokerage, another deep-discount firm in New York City, stopped by our online area to make a special offer to pay interest to our readers for their short sales. All they had to do was to say they were from "The Fool." The transforming powers of cyberspace . . .

Here's a fifth bee in your bonnet: If a stock you've sold short pays a dividend, *you* pay that dividend. No way around it. This is, in a way, a form of recompense for your borrowing these shares from your anonymous unsuspecting fellow investor. In most cases, however, the dividend amounts to less than 3 percent annually.

Despite this list of five lesser irritations, we still love selling short. None of them is terribly consequential, and even all five taken together give us no pause. We just wanted you to know about them.

We'll close this section with an exhortation to follow your shorts carefully, and respect the goals you set for them. If you're using our Foolish 20 percent upside/downside goals and your stock dips 20 percent without any clear announcement of horrible news, don't get greedy. Take that profit! If your stock instead rises 20 percent, you're going to think, "Now, more than ever, it's *really* overvalued!" The last thing on earth you're ever going to want to do is to have to buy the damn thing back. But you should. You've timed your investment ill-fatedly, whether your valuation work was good or bad. Just admit you've been wrong and move on. Fact is, some really great short-busting news could be abrewin', and the stock's run-up may presage superlative (and unexpected) developments at the company.

A Short Conclusion

Is the Foolish way to short the *only* way to short? Of course not. Where we short some of America's best operations when we think their stocks have gotten overvalued, some people do quite the opposite, focusing on companies that are going down the tubes. Others play sectors, concentrating their short selling in specific industries that they believe are either overloved or in trouble. Others short with everything they have, eschewing the Foolish notion that only a minority of one's portfolio should ever be short. Their records aren't too good, but they do represent another alternative and must make *some* money from time to time.

One alternative model for shorting that does seem to show promise is "momentum shorting." That's where you pile onto the worst stocks on the exchanges, riding them further downward. Online, we've run a few small (that is, unscientific due to limited sample size) studies that took baskets of five stocks, each of which had a relative strength of 5 or below, with a share price of $5 or above. The 5 or lower relative strength focused us on some of the very worst stocks you could find in

America; the $5 or higher share price is required by most brokers for shorting stocks (i.e., you're not allowed to short stocks below $5). We then followed how these stocks did over the following month. Each of the several times we did this, the basket dramatically underperformed the market. Often, four of the stocks would sit around and do nothing, but one would fall from $6 to $2. That would still give a short seller a 13 percent total monthly return.

We include that example not to suggest that you adopt this strategy, but rather to illustrate how some other approaches to shorting can and do work. The additional point is that the more you bring your imagination, intelligence, and experience to bear on your own investing, the better you'll do.

Shorting stock is one approach that separates the sophisticated investor from the novice, even though it's not terribly difficult to do or to understand. Believing that selling shares short is difficult and highly dangerous, some people pay oodles of money to enter "hedge funds," mutual fund partnerships whose managers short stock. Having read this far, you already know most of what these "pros" know, and you can do it yourself.

Having now graduated from The Fool's School on shorting, you've reached a fork in the road. Your choice. You may either seek to share with others the joy and happiness that comes of learning, living up more truly than ever before to the words of Oliver Goldsmith:

> *Cheerful at morn, he wakes from short repose,*
> *Breasts the keen air, and carols as he goes.*

Or you can play it the other way. Once your "Pass Line" friends find out you're shorting stocks, they may start to regard you as Darth Vader. That's the impression most people have of short sellers. So what the heck? Divest yourself of your motley, put on some dark clothes, sport a low visor, breathe loud, and milk it.

PART VII

PUTTING IT ALL TOGETHER

·20·

Why Invest?

· · · · ·

No! I am not Prince Hamlet, nor was meant to be:
Am an attendant lord, one that will do
To swell a progress, start a scene or two, advise the prince.
—*T. S. Eliot*

Actually, if you sat down at your desk and looked at the hard numbers based on any average 1-year investment performance, you'd
have to conclude that there's no reason to put your money into the
stock market. Consider this: If you have $10,000 to put away in stocks,
the average market year (10.5 percent) will reward you with profits of
$1,050, nearly one third of which you'll shell out to the federal govern-
ment in taxes. The hassle of pulling together the funds, transferring
them to a discount broker, moving them into an index fund, monitoring
your monthly statements, and sending the documentation over to your
accountant at year's end—all that effort and what do you get? Profits in
the neighborhood of $700 a year. Divided out, in an oversimplified fash-
ion, that would be about $58 a month, $1.93 per day, or 24¢ per business hour.

Less than two bits an hour just ain't inspiring. Take that same amount
and run it out ten years and you'll have made a mere $7,000 on your ini-
tial $10,000 investment. Seventy percent growth per decade should
have you asking yourself why you paid anything for this useless book.
There simply must be better ways to put your savings to work for you.

How true all of the above would be if there wasn't one great flaw to
the analysis. Can you locate it? If your portfolio grows at a rate after
taxes of 7 percent per year, you don't actually make $58 a month. The
percentage growth might remain the same, but the dollar growth will
increase each month. After all, 7 percent of $10,000 is less than 7 per-
cent of $11,000. And in those numbers lies the simple beauty of com-

pounded growth. Time builds wealth. You'll make more in the second month than in the first, and you'll make more still in month twelve. By the tenth year, you'll be realizing over $100 in pure aftertax profit per month, and this assumes that you don't put away any additional money between now and then, an assumption that we hope will prove misguided.

But maybe $100 a month on a $10,000 investment 10 years later doesn't inspire you either. That's equivalent to $1,000 a month pure profit off a $100,000 starting kitty, and $10,000 a month off a $1 million personal bank. Maybe those numbers don't move you, given what you think could be achieved by, for example, investing the capital in your own business. If you're, say, an architect, you probably believe that those monies put toward new projects and staff would reap far greater rewards over the decade. Oddly enough, given the focus of this manuscript, you'll find a Fool agreeing with you. In the short to intermediate term, the stock market pales in comparison to intelligent investments in your own small business.

But let's not oversimplify here. Let's not make life all about a commitment to short- and intermediate-term profit. When you make fast money on your own, you usually work long, hard hours for it—building more homes, teaching more classes, fixing more engines, manufacturing more semiconductor wafers, selling more Foolcaps, whatever your business. This business of "more" takes a lot of effort. And since technology hasn't yet found a way to lengthen the twenty-four-hour day, there's only so much you can do professionally before your spouse and kids don't remember what it's like to hear your voice, can't recollect the last time you all went biking together on the weekend, don't recall whether you like blueberry or buckwheat pancakes.

The very opposite is true when you build a Foolish investment portfolio, letting compounded growth carry your savings forward generationally by investing in other people's efforts. Your capital grows without any herculean effort on your part, particularly as—in the least challenging strategy—you'll just be loading it into an index fund. Let the scientists at Johnson & Johnson, the salespeople at The Gap, the reporters at *The Chicago Tribune*, the technologists at Hewlett-Packard, and the bankers at Citicorp turn profits for you, as they will if you invest in an S&P 500 index fund. By letting others build up your savings, you'll free up the hours for recreation that every Fool needs to live a spirited life.

With the seeds of market-average growth and compounded returns planted, watered, and flowering, we introduced Dow Dividend investing, an approach that, when fashioned Foolishly, has compounded 25.5

percent annual growth. Only a handful of investors on the planet wouldn't be satisfied with compounded growth that has more than doubled the U.S. market average for two decades running. Jaws have been dropping all year as we've presented and scrutinized these numbers in our forum; 25.5 percent annual growth with zero research commitment is well-nigh unfathomable. Put your money into an index fund and $10,000 will turn into $19,700 at the end of a decade. Take that same ten grand and use the Dow approach, and history shows that ten years down the road it will have swelled into over $51,600. And all of those numbers suppose that you won't be putting any savings away between now and then, a move that is très Wise.

You can see that the initial dollar amounts don't mean much compared to the basic principle of compounded growth: You'll generate greater and greater returns with time. Investors who focus on that longer-term perspective, who can hammer together a vision of what their life will be like ten, fifteen, twenty years hence, and who recognize how much sweeter it'll be to have a larger and larger portfolio generating higher and higher dollar profits, these are the people who will successfully guide U.S. and global markets into the twenty-first century. Save, invest the dollars intelligently in stocks, and watch the portfolio grow.

Mixing in Small-Cap Growth

It is precisely this awesome potential for long-term profitability in low-risk vehicles that encourages a Fool to seek compounded returns in excess of 25 percent per year from financially strong small-capitalization growth stocks. When you've cobbled together an awesome frontline in football, it's time to collect a couple flashy running backs. In the last decade, investors have seen sprinters like America Online, Microsoft, Dell Computer, Starbucks, Broderbund Software, Cisco Systems, Williams-Sonoma, and dozens of other small and midcaps burst forward to all-star status in their respective industries. All of these companies have made their long-term shareholders extraordinarily happy, and all of them were sitting there right under our noses, waiting to be plucked up and added to an already thriving Dow portfolio.

Of course, while you'll hear all sorts of talk about how great small-cap stocks are—quite a bit of it in these pages, since growth stocks have given us our greatest investment successes—you need to understand how to value them. The volatility of small caps will sometimes be your bane, not your boon. And please don't buy a piece of ownership in a company simply because you like its products. We hope our chapters explaining how to select and value growth stocks, and how to read their financial statements, went a long way toward dissuading you from the ever popular "Buy What You Like" approach. You wouldn't, for example, buy a bicycle for $2,000 just because the training wheels looked cool. Believe it or not, comparable sorts of gross overvaluation exist out on the stock market, and it doesn't take a terribly well trained eye to spy them. Thriving companies can be overpriced and suffering ones can be had on the cheap. The challenge is to properly value the ones you plan to invest in by creatively applying, to each situation and with every new quarterly earnings report, the basic yardsticks outlined in our chapters on investing in growth stocks.

Whenever you think, "Ahh, I really like this one, I'll skip running the numbers this time," just recall our presentation on Styles on Video (AMEX:SOV), the company that burned a hole in our investment club portfolio. Everything looked terrific: tremendous growth, a compelling story, a stock on the rise. But sitting right there in full view on the balance sheet was the tale of an accounts-receivable disaster. Apparently, they weren't much bothering to collect the monies owed them for their glamour systems. And the stock, six months later, was worthless.

One of the beauties of the U.S. market is that by law companies have to lay out their performance for all to see four times a year. That makes the mission of seeking and finding less onerous. And even though there are plenty of examples of creative bookkeeping out there, far more often than not, the cheap pages in the back of each annual report tell a clear story to investors willing to look in and listen. How much of a time commitment would it take to review the quarterly financials? We don't think there's any reason to spend more than a handful of hours each year on any one of your small-cap growth stocks. As we've noted, you'll want to run The Fool Ratio, our P/E-to-growth-rate model, you'll want to examine the cash situation, understand the products, and have some sense of management's philosophy. Also, you'll want to consider the company in the context of its industry, comparing it to the competition, and determining very broadly why its sector will or will not outperform in the years ahead.

Picking market-beating stocks isn't a great mystery; it isn't a random-walk process, and it isn't something only M.B.A. graduates can do—quite the opposite, actually. If you're going to invest in small caps, your aim must be to outperform the Foolish Four Dow High Yielders and their 25 percent annual growth. If you can pull it off, twenty years from now you won't be worrying much about your financial position, no matter how much money you have put away for investing today.

The fully Foolish portfolio contains 50 to 60 percent of its money in small- and midcap growth stocks. However, given that we spend so much of our time focusing on the long-term ramifications of investing in the stock market, be advised that we think your entry into small-cap stocks ought to be a cautious one. There's no rush. Why not enter into the Dow heavies exclusively in your first year, while merely simulating growth-stock investing? Then balance some of your savings on this, the second pillar of Folly, only when you've convinced yourself you can outdo dividend-yield investing. It doesn't seem like a bad plan.

Shorts

The third pillar of Foolish Portfolio theory is the shorting of stocks, an approach badly misunderstood by the vast majority of individual and institutional investors. Shorting stocks poses comparable risk to going long, makes for an excellent contrary play, and when applied selectively, should outperform 25 percent in annual returns. As we said before, the fully Foolish portfolio will have up to 20 percent of its money short.

Just as with growth stock investing, shorting should not be done casually, recklessly, or qualitatively. If you conceive of overvaluation simply as bad products, publicity bordering on hype, new competition entering the market, even a high Fool Ratio alone, you're apt to do greater harm than good to your market-smashing Dow and growth portfolio. Don't wreck it with simplistic thinking. When you find yourself saying, "This thing just can't go up any higher," while neither understanding the business nor the relationship between earnings growth and price appreciation, look out. Prince and princess have been paupered thus.

The clustering of a high PEG, a low short-interest ratio, an unimpressive balance sheet, and a "closed" situation make for a great possible short. Let's review those four factors. Fools should not short highfliers with a Fool Ratio sitting anywhere below 1.40; nor should they borrow and sell shares of a stock with any more than ten days of short interest outstanding; nor should they bet against a stock with fiery cash flows, plenty of cash on the balance sheet, and negligible long-term debt; nor lastly should Fools bet against wide-open markets, like the Internet, computer networking, new patented technology, biotechnology outfits with a hot new product, et cetera, all of which often present premium-price buyout potential.

Your ideal short might be a retailing growth stock (closed situation, duplicable business) with a current ratio under 3.0, a bit of debt on the balance sheet, cash and equivalents on par with current liabilities (neutral cash position), 5 days of shorts to cover, and a Fool of 2.00. (Mercy!) Now that one looks like a candidate—the sort of stock that sits in the company of Bed Bath & Beyond, Bombay, and Men's Wearhouse at the end of 1994, the three retailers that all fell more than 40 percent within a year of our naming them overpriced in Ye Olde Printed Foole.

In keeping with our broader philosophy, don't rush into shorting; it's better to wait things out a bit at the outset. Play some of your hunches on paper, and figure what was and wasn't accurate in your valuation before plunging in with the spinach. And once you are shorting stocks in your portfolio, stay on top of them; this is a much shorter term approach to the stock market. When your shorted stock has fallen off 15 to 20 percent, celebrate and reevaluate. Does the issue still meet the four requirements above? Does it still look badly overpriced? Might it free fall lower than you thought? Demand answers to these questions. And when your stock goes the other way, as Paychex (NASDAQ:PAYX) did on us Fools in 1995, reconsider your investment when it has moved 20 percent against you. We were slow to get out of Paychex, and lost money by expecting it to be less profitable with each quarterly report. It doesn't pay to sit around hoping against hope when your shorts have moved 20 percent against you. Accept that the market has spoken, and move on.

The Foolish Accounting Standard

Once you have the three Foolish approaches in place, the most important addition—and really the most meaningful thing that could be taken away from this tract, and something The Motley Fool pushes at every turn—is the application of proper accounting standards to your portfolio. If you don't know how you've been doing relative to the market over the past five years, how can you be certain that you shouldn't hold shares of an index fund? Paying out no commissions, matching market average, saving a little bit of money each month to put away, and getting on with the rest of your life, index fund investing sounds somewhat Foolish to us.

If you've made the bright decision to use financial software like Quicken to track your investments, you'll not find it difficult to compare the bottom-line returns of your portfolio to the market's average performance. Take advantage of the fact that McGraw-Hill's subsidiary, Standard & Poor's, has compiled an index of five hundred of the most widely held common stocks, which represent 80 percent of the market value of the entire New York Stock Exchange. The S&P 500 is the best measure of overall market growth. Track your portfolio against it, and base your future investment decisions on your performance relative to it.

Then raise the bar. What about Dow Dividend investing, which asks no research of you and rewards handsomely? Are the high-yielding giants of the Dow beating you to the profits? You need to know at all times how your portfolio is doing compared to our Foolish Four Dow stocks. If it's losing out, your next decision is a pretty clear one: beat the Dow by loading up on the high yielders.

Typing these numbers every week won't take more than ten minutes, and it'll open your eyes to how the market works and how the growth in your savings compares to the norm. Gauging your returns against market-average growth also protects you from the investment sharks surfing through every community in the nation. No money manager or broker, no matter how friendly, ought to get paid much (if anything) for underperforming the S&P 500. So if you're committed to having someone manage your savings over more than 3 years, ask them to agree that they get paid only if they outperform the Vanguard Index fund, a commission-less vehicle, risk-free over the long haul. If they balk, find another adviser, or turn Foolish and manage your own money. Again, no one has your long-term interests closer to heart than you.

Looking out for yourself by accounting professionally for your portfolio and stacking it against the market also steers you clear of the Wise bunko artists who mail or fax out their stock picks every month for hundreds of dollars without properly accounting for their recommendations. No stock market newsletter that we know of reports commissions in its profit statement, which is absolutely outrageous. That means that they can advise trading one hundred times a year without ever reporting a single expense. Oh, that the same were only true for the rest of us! Furthermore, no newsletters that we know of account for the bid-ask spread, the price at which a stock is bought and sold, respectively. The absence of these two—commissions and spreads—can inflate returns enough that all reported portfolio growth is rendered meaningless for those of us living in the real world investing real money. If you can't see the bottom line, don't buy it.

Finally, don't forget that mutual funds are in business to make money for *the fund* first and you second. To this end they do a number of things to feather the fund's nest, including a host of creative expenses, among them the dreaded 12b-1 fee. After all costs are deducted from the bottom line, the majority of mutual funds will lose to the S&P 500 year after year. If your funds to date have underperformed market average, you've blundered. But it's not an error that can't and shouldn't be fixed quickly. Learn from your mistakes rather than harping on them;

begin accounting for the medley of your investments alongside market-index growth. That popular line, "I've had some winners, and I've had some losers," is no longer allowable in the company of Fools. You simply have to know how you've done versus the S&P 500. And if you're not beating it handily, it's time to reconsider how your money's being invested and by whom.

Doing Good Business with the Right People

When Fools look around the financial world, spying dubious investment-product sales practices, hyped initial public offerings that only institutional investors can get their hands on, the steady spate of high-priced newsletters, and the burst of thousands of mutual funds onto an already overcrowded financial stage, we note a lot of bluster amidst an abundance of conveniently medieval, self-serving accounting. It's just the sort of bookkeeping that theater owners employed to beat up playwrights like our liege Shakespeare four hundred years past. Now we know well enough to hold strictly accountable anyone indirectly or directly tied to the management of our finances.

No doubt Fools for centuries have learned a lot of these lessons the hard way, but at least there's great strength in being a witness. As much as anything, belled-cap investors now are singing loud praises to Warren Buffett in our online forum. As you'll recall, it was Buffett who proclaimed: "You can't do good business with bad people." That's just a very simple, very plain, very Foolish fact. When someone's putting the heat on you in any business scenario, whether it's stocks, real estate, your own business, whatever, you can be certain that you're in the wrong conversation. Don't waste time on bad business, of which there are so many examples, they could fill the Library of Congress. We'll take one example here: If you spend enough time floating around the business world, you're bound to hear something like this: "So, we convinced him to pay X dollars when what we we're selling was only worth Y dollars. Just awesome, it was brilliant." That's bad business because it's a short-term win with no long-term viability. Creates bad blood, too. And it's the very sort of quote too frequently echoing through the halls of America's money managers, brokers, and financial advisers.

The key for you is to be so thorough in your accounting, and so clear on your long-term expectations for growth, that any meetings designed around the management of your money are studies in composure, patience, and logic. And anyone intent on creating a win-lose investment partnership, with you left holding the shorter stick, is merely fodder for a couple good jokes among good friends.

Losing sight of your bottom-line expectations can create havoc in your portfolio; don't open the door on your own personal Barings or Orange County disaster, where some rogue trader you don't much know goes nuts leveraging your savings, trading options, dabbling in $3 stocks, playing the commodities game, and gracing you each month with an unreadably incomprehensible account statement. Remember that when you're investing *your* money, you're running *your* own business. Act like it. Keep as much of the control in your own hands as possible. It makes the future much clearer.

Sharing Information

The dark ages for the individual investor are, blessedly, coming to an end as we enter into the digital world. With tens of thousands of investors linked by modem, never again will you have to make tough investment decisions without guidance. We've spent the last two years listening to countless tales of cold-calling brokers pressuring customers into buying the next great biotechnology company trading under $4 a share, or some such wonder. Access to capital has never been so easy for companies like our own disaster scenario, the hypothetical Huge Fruits. But just as the regulatory pressure is easing and private investors are becoming more vulnerable, the Information Age is building momentum. Immediate distribution of accurate information is going to make the Huge-Fruiting of individual investors less and less likely. Amen to that.

You should never find yourself denied access to the information necessary to making a levelheaded, well-informed decision about an investment. When a salesman is pushing an investment product on you and you don't have it in yourself to just walk away, at least take down the company name, ticker symbol, and stock price. Then post them all in our online financial forum, and you should get a prompt flow of analyses. Of course, we've heard of telephone salesmen pushing Dell Computer (NASDAQ:DELL) before its fantastic run in 1995 was over, so there are some fine investment opportunities presented. But unfortunately, more often than not it's $3 stocks with few prospects that telemarketers are hawking—just the ones that can devour your savings.

What you need to do is to get yourself into a research team of sorts with other investors where you'll be able to patiently sort through stocks and their valuations together. Year after year, investment clubs have outperformed the market, as private investors in groups have focused on keeping commissions down, building long-term wealth, and outperforming the market. The strengths of the club format are the sharing of research responsibilities and the broader range of expertise, bringing together individuals with experience in a variety of industries. If you're just starting out, the Fool thinks you ought to find other investors in your community with whom to compare notes.

Not surprisingly, we're also huge proponents of the online world. We welcome tens of thousands of entries into our forum each day of the week. As you can imagine, the accumulation of information and analysis is unmatched in the financial industry. If you have questions about 401(K) plans, tax strategies, dividend reinvestment plans, individual companies, industry analyses, Dow-stock investing, shorting stocks, you name it, the financial questions that float around in your head have been and are being addressed in our forum. The Motley Fool Online is, in essence, a national investment club and research firm with tens of thousands of daily participants. And in this context, it's not a surprise to us that in its first year, our Fool Portfolio posted year-end returns of 59 percent versus S&P 500 growth of 22 percent. With research on thousands of stocks, with the Dow approach in place, and the Foolish valuation and portfolio-management strategies operative, we expect to continue to outperform the market averages. Collaboration, good business, and clearheadedness all packaged together have drubbed the market, and we expect that to continue in our forum in the decades ahead.

Avoid Bad Investment Approaches

It certainly can be tempting to free up some of your capital for more active trading, trying to speed the compounding of growth. After all, decades—that's a long time! Day traders get more involved in the stock market than Fools do, and they may even, on occasion, have more fun. Active trading makes money management more of a sporting challenge, serving up greater highs and lows, making the whole experience far more volatile and far more emotional. It can be more addictive than nicotine soup or heroin soufflé, and it can teach you a lot about market psychology, not to mention human psychology. No wonder so many investors become "traders" at some point in their lives.

But short-term trading features two punishing attributes often ignored by its proponents. The first, commissions, has dealt death blows to many an individual investor. Imagine making two trades a day for the entire year at the bargain-basement rate of $30 a trade. With approximately 300 trading days gone by, you're looking at $18,000 in commission payments waved off into space.

At what point is it reasonable to partake in such active trading? Out of the kindness of our hearts, let's just say that the active trader can compound 30 percent in pretax, precommission growth per year over a matter of decades. We've never seen anything scientific that proves such returns attainable, but we'll run with it for the sake of this analysis. With $18,000 eaten up in commissions, a $50,000 portfolio with the most generous accounting standard (commissions deducted only at year end) would become worthless, would put you in *debt* by the seventh year. Now *that's* investing! A $100,000 portfolio afforded the same returns at the same bargain commission rate would compound 17.6 percent in annual growth, more than 7 percent short of our sleepy Dow Stock portfolio. A comparable $150,000 portfolio would compound 22.6 percent, still a few percentage points below the Dow Yield performance. Anyone tackling the market this actively with anything less than $210,000 would do better to load the denarii into the Dow heavies and call it a day.

The second powerful objection to active trading revolves around quality-of-life matters. Can you actually imagine day trading stocks for two decades? Computers flashing charts at you, the phone on your shoulder, a handheld quoting device Scotch-taped to your forehead, ticker symbols flooding the unconscious, closed office windows, dusty books, dimly lit rooms, a moldy half-eaten bologna sandwich on the chair beside you. Day trading pretty much demands total dedication, and as noted above, it takes just an awful lot of capital to make it worthwhile down on the bottom line.

Consider also that you're not the only one who'll suffer through dank rooms and reams of information; imagine your poor tax accountant, hunched over the record of trades for the year, sorting through cost bases and capital gains (you hope), and wincing. That work ain't going to come cheap! Factor in as well that when the tax estimates do come back, they'll reflect the higher short-term capital-gains rates, ouch! Trading doesn't come dollar cheap, nor does it come inexpensive to the mind and spirit.

Oh, and did you just hear a Fool use the word "accountant"? Accounting is taboo in the circles of short-term traders. Our experience of the world may still reflect a youthful insufficiency, but we have yet to see a single active trader properly account for his bottom-line returns. Not one. It's to the point where Fools listen to short-term-trader victory stories with levels of enthusiasm and credulity they reserve for Vegas gamblers who always at least break even and scratch golfers who don't actually putt out.

Stack it all together: the high commissions, the low quality of life, and the difficulty in accounting, and you'll understand why Fools eschew active trading. We hold in low regard the strategy of entering the stock market looking for a quick buck, watching stock prices lift and fall, and trying to capitalize on that short-term volatility. It ain't worth it.

Measure More Than Twice

To end our recapitulation, we simply remind you that future profits aren't going to run and hide. If this book is your first foray into stock market investing, delay, Fool, delay. You needn't plunge your savings in before sorting back through this guide, building your own Foolish portfolio on paper, tracking it in a spreadsheet as if you were actually invested, and entering with real money only when you're comfortable.

Too many individual investors jump in before understanding what they've gotten themselves into and what they ought to expect. In our minds, no one should invest money without understanding the concepts of market-average performance, dividend-yield investing, and earnings-growth analyses. Astonishingly, this limitation, imposed broadly, might put a large number of "professional" investors on the sidelines. The entry bar is still that low on the institutional side.

To repeat: The stock market isn't going anywhere. Your entry point isn't nearly so important as your commitment to invest for the long haul when you do enter, to save and invest portions of your future earnings, and to think in terms of decades, not days, weeks, or quarters. The market will rumble at times, and you should certainly expect cracks of thunder, bolts of lightning, and powerful corrections in the years ahead. But a portfolio bolstered by Dow stocks, spread thick with well-chosen growth stocks, and shored up with some shorts should survive the bad weather quite winningly. Your aim at all times, dear Fool, is to outperform the market. And if the S&P 500 drops 15 percent and you fall a punishing 10 percent, drink a toast to perseverance, gong the celebratory bell, jangle the belled cap, and take even a few more vacation days than you did when the market and your portfolio both rose 30 percent in a year.

Putting It All Together

Just as with any business, higher returns open up new worlds for investors, whether that means a new career, extended travel abroad, a chance to buy some time for more creative, less profitable ventures, more hours to spend with the family, the opportunity to pursue charitable works, or just a chance to blow a lot of money buying up merchandise offered on late-night TV. Prosperity leads to opportunity, and opportunity, prosperity.

Just to prove that we believe it can't be overemphasized, we'll close the section by stating once *again* the importance of compounding long-term growth on your savings through investments in well-chosen stocks. The stock market, while volatile, has provided and will continue to provide the best annual returns of any investment vehicle, by a large margin. That's because it will always offer investors the best, most liquid opportunities at capitalizing on the greatest business growth opportunities available in the known galaxy. Taking advantage of these situations and committing yourself to long-term prosperity, come hell or high water in the near term—all of these will contribute to the great financial and emotional rewards associated with forsaking Wisdom.

PART VIII

HERE BE DRAGONS: INVESTMENT APPROACHES TO AVOID

·21·

The Carnival of
Freak Delights

. . . . .

Abandon all hope, you who enter here!
—*Dante*

Some people do subsist on an intellectual diet of just the facts, ma'am, the sand-and-sawdust, hammer-and-nails reality of a situation. They can glance at the numbers and hear the story they tell. They understand that here be the dragons of fiscal demise while over there lie the Elysian Fields of profit and prosperity. Others, particularly newcomers, tend to want a peek at the meat and marvels of a situation before deciding to stay or flee. So, rather than simply post a series of WATCH OUT FOR FALLING ROCKS signs to caution you against the most dangerous ways a Fool can be parted from his money, we much prefer to invite you to a carnival, The Carnival of Freak Delights.

Welcome to the Carnival of Freak Delights

Please, please, take your seat, have a little cotton candy, and relax. The ringleader will take the spotlight in a minute or two. We're here to entertain you! You're going to have lots and lots of fun. Lots of fun. For a while.

Hey, you! Yeah, you. You gotta pay to enter this establishment, Mac. And of course, we hasten to add that this entertainment won't come cheap. You think carnivals just show up in your hometown and let you ogle the bearded lady for free? Forget it. In fact, you'll find that our Delights may cost you more than you'd ever have imagined. Sorry if you misunderstood before you walked in.

Well our Delights are now waiting in the wings, and our ringleader is ready, so we'll keep our fingers crossed that you'll *love* the show. The popcorn is, of course, free.

◆ ◆ ◆

Ladieeeeeeeees and gentlemen, welcome to our carnival! My name is Malbowges, I am indeed the ringleader—note my bright suit and my gold cane—and I have the pleasure of welcoming you to the most dangerous show on earth. Now, let us begin.

Your State Lottery

Bring in the Fat Man! Oops, I mean *roll* in the Fat Man, please! Roll him in.

Ah yes, here he is. The Fat Man, ladies and gentlemen. The Fattest Man in the World! Right here in our carnival, playing right now in your home state—in almost *all* your home states, ladies and gents. What a load! Give him a hand.

Okay, I'll need a volunteer. Preferably, if I may, someone not very well educated. You, sir! Thank you. Very good. Now, come right down here, and if you would please, sir, extract a dollar bill from your wallet. Yes, that's right. *Very* good. Okay, now if you would just insert it in the Fat Man's mouth. Right in there, if you will. Oh no, I'm quite serious. Right in his mouth. Thank you! And . . . well, of *course* he's eating it! Yes, that's his act. Oh, don't worry, there's something in it for you. Don't you see, sir, what he's holding out in his pudgy paw? Indeed yes, a ticket. *Your* ticket, sir. Please accept it with the Fat Man's compliments.

Yes. Yes it is. A very pretty ticket, sir . . . glossy as can be. I see you're very happy with it. Feeding the Fat Man does have its little pleasures, doesn't it?

Oh no! No, you can't return to your seat yet, sir. The very next thing you need to do is to extract another dollar bill from your wallet. Well of *course* you'll get another ticket, sir . . . we wouldn't *shortchange* you. But first you must feed the Fat Man. Good. And now there's another nice shiny ticket for you.

My, ladies and gentlemen, just look at that Fat Man eat! His appetite knows no bounds; don't worry about him. Yes sir, another dollar bill gets you another wonderfully glossy ticket! And another. Another dollar bill, sir. Yes, sir. And another ticket. A bill, a ticket. Why, of course you *must* empty your wallet of one-dollar bills! Yes, just exhaust the supply but please do make *sure* you get all your tickets, sir.

You say you'd now like to redeem your tickets? Actually cash them in, eh? Okay, sure. Alecto, if you would please present this nice man with 44 *cents* per ticket. Yes, indeed, ladies and gentlemen . . . say hello to my beautiful assistant Alecto!

Why of course, that's exactly the way it works. Every single one of them: 44 cents. Well, 44 cents is 44 cents, sir . . . not a penny more and *not* a penny less. Why, you're quite welcome! And we hope you enjoyed it! Yes, it's a very simple little act. . . .

And for the rest of the show, the Fat Man will be right here so that all others who'd like to get their own pretty tickets may do so at their discretion . . . I'm sorry, madam? Ho-ho, bite your tongue, madam! Of course it's all legal!

Okay, now, back to you sir. All out of one-dollar bills, yes, I see. Would you happen to have a twenty or a hundred?

Vegas

Next, ladies and gentlemen, I'd simply like to reintroduce my lovely assistant, Alecto. Wave hello, Alecto! We met her briefly during the Fat Man act, but now I'm introducing her more formally. As you can see, Alecto is beautiful and looks great in a bunny suit, but you may not have known that she is also an inexhaustible source of free drinks for customers. Needless to say, we have no problems filling the seats every night. Which is really what this business is all about.

But above all, Alecto is a killer card player who plays for money. And she plays with a few advantages. For one, she won't let you count cards . . . that's illegal. And if your score ties hers in blackjack, she always wins by default. Additionally, some people think she stacks the deck, but I must confide to the audience my own belief that she does not. Every game she plays offers her opponents worse-than-even odds, so why bother?

Alecto is eager to play cards with you and will be circulating through the crowd throughout our carnival.

Finally, before we move on to our next act, a brief lesson for the budding entrepreneurs among the young members of our audience. Note if you will, kids, the importance of both filling our seats every night *and* fixing all the odds against our gracious guests. With a combo like that, you'll do some very good business in life. The whole key here is that we've created a very attractive *environment* in which to lose money, and I can see that despite my admission that that's what it's all about, many of you are *still* itching to lose money to Alecto tonight. A further sign of our success is our ability to attract out-of-town visitors in huge numbers who come to us for the very same purpose. This mingling of glamour with inevitable failure appears to be somehow seductive, and uncannily successful . . . a freakish delight in its own right. That's my assistant, ladies and gentlemen: Alecto. She's in a major growth industry, and we're looking to hire more of her.

Day Trading

Now, if the house manager will kindly dim the lights, we can bid a proud welcome to the many-veiled, mysterious fortune teller Commissionia. For thirty dollars she'll tell your fortune. Thirty dollars for a fortune, anyone? If you're interested in the stock market—and who isn't—for a mere thirty dollars our soothsayer will gaze deep into her crystal ball and tell you exactly where the market will go tomorrow or an hour from now or even sixty seconds in the future.

She's even right some of the time.

Thirty dollars, here!

Of course, right or wrong doesn't matter that much . . . what matters is the conviction on *your* part, my friends, that with Commissionia's help—for a measly thirty dollars a consultation—you too can figure it all out. Every stock in your portfolio . . . thirty dollars will tell you your destiny! Where will your high-flying telecommunications stock be at 11:00 A.M. tomorrow morning? Commissionia—a wealthy woman in her own right—may know. Should you discard that dog you bought yesterday, now that it's off half a point? If you have thirty dollars, why not indulge yourself in a freakish delight?

Let us transport ourselves back to ancient Greece briefly, where we meet Cassandra, Commissionia's illustrious direct ancestor. Daughter of the king of Troy, Cassandra was blessed with the gift of prophecy but cursed by the god Apollo never to be believed. A somber plight. Ladies and gentlemen, in yet another ironic instance suggesting that history is out to have a bit of fun with us all, a hundred generations later our own Commissionia possesses virtually the *opposite* gift: She'll never ever make consistently accurate short-term predictions, but she's still fated to be believed by too many.

Thirty dollars, my friends!

Perish all thoughts of accountability. When you spend this much money and energy on making your picks every day, you can't afford to look backward. In fact, you can't afford to do anything else, period. Forethought is too dear a luxury; tallying, valuing, and accounting are out of the question.

Before concluding, boys and girls, please indulge your ringleader once more for a brief lesson in accounting so that we may learn a finer appreciation of Commissionia's superb business sense. At $30 a weekday for her predictions, her active clients will pay some $9,000 per annum for the privilege of playing the trading game. Any client with less than $180,000 to invest is therefore spending more than 5 percent of his entire nest egg on Commissionia alone! Small wonder that cynics have called her the Prophetess of the Profitless.

But thirty dollars, dear audience, thirty dollars is all for every single consultation!

Options and Futures

I'd like to take this opportunity now to mention a feature of our carnival that is simply too big to fit underneath our tent. What might I be referring to? The Ferris wheel! I want to draw your attention to it because of its uncommon relevance to our Carnival of Freak Delights, as it's just another way that we can induce *you* to support *us*. Hope you good people will give the wheel a try.

A few things you should know first, of course. The first is that this wheel costs lots. You have to buy a package of expensive tickets for the ride, though the actual number of tickets you wind up with will be well below the number you paid for. Before an attack of sudden outrage overcomes you, my friends, let me explain! The difference is pocketed by a middleman, and in the case of our Ferris wheel, the middleman just takes a lot.

Let me make this amply clear with an apt analogy. Um, how about the financial markets? Every stock has two prices, as most of you probably know by now: the bid and the ask. When you buy a stock, you pay the asking price; as soon as your buy order has been filled, your investment is now valued at the bid price (the lower price), because it is the bid price that investors receive when they eventually sell. The reason for having two prices rather than just one is that the "market maker," the middleman who's matching buy and sell orders, needs to get paid for his work. So he sets two different prices and pockets the difference for every trade.

The more "liquid" an investment, the more people are trading it (and the more easily it is disposed of). Liquid investments typically feature narrower spreads than illiquid ones. The huge volume of shares traded in a stock like IBM, my friends, means that the spread will be very low; there is little "penalty" involved in purchasing that stock. When you take a separate sort of investment like, say, options for example, you're dealing with a very illiquid investment. The amount an investor might pay in spreads can be 10 percent or *higher* for some options. It goes without saying that spreads of that magnitude will kill *most* investors' returns.

Purely coincidentally, I suppose, the spread on ticket sales for our Ferris wheel are right about at that level. "Why?!" you ask. Simple, because we have only one person selling the tickets and not many more than that buying them. It's not because our Ferris wheel isn't any good! On the contrary, our Ferris wheel is extremely *exciting* . . . too exciting, it seems, for most people. It probably has something to do with the "jump-off point," which I haven't told you about yet. Anyway, suffice it to say that riding our wheel is an expensive proposition.

Okay, it is now high time that we spoke of this jump-off point. Our Ferris wheel, you see, never stops running. It spins and spins, and you rise and fall and rise and fall with it in a most volatile manner. Don't think, good people, that our wheel runs at a predictable, rhythmic speed. On the contrary! Our wheel operates in an unpredictable herky-jerky motion designed for thrills. (Creates a lot of spills, too, but to maintain our gay carnival atmosphere, we instinctively accentuate the positive!)

So when you want to stop riding, you must jump off. If you jump off too early, we will of course have succeeded in ripping you off on the ticket purchase. But if you jump off too late, you'll lose it all . . . as in "kill yourself." Again, I refuse to get into the negative, nitty-gritty details here, so, dear friends, suffice it to say that when riding our wheel you'll need to time your jump *expertly.* Very little room for error if you want your investment to pay off.

When I think about it, that's probably why few people ride our wheel for very long. They either grow discouraged because they keep jumping off early, or they jump off late . . . and it generally only takes once. Of course, we'll always have a steady flow of new customers looking for a thrill, and there's nothing quite like the excitement of going up the wheel—*way* up—your first time.

Anyway, I hope you'll all ride our Carnival of Freak Delights' Ferris wheel before you go! I haven't ridden myself, of course—never would—but I definitely think that once is *not* enough.

Technical Analysis

Next, put your hands together for the *amazing* Phyrum—magician to princes, wizard of the North, prestidigitator extraordinaire! Observe the sleight of hand, the sheer hocus-pocus, the hypnotic influence that this master of mummery exerts over millions. . . .

If I may just interrupt Phyrum for a few moments, I'd like to mention that I have spent no small time observing the sorcerer at practice, and right now, right here, I will *share* with you the secrets of his art. Yep, folks, let us start with an example.

Let us say you, my investor friends, come across a stock at $17. That stock rises to $21 in the course of a month, then loses four points back to $17 over some indefinite time period. From there, it rockets back to $21 in 3 days, only to fall back again.

Presto!

Did you not see it? The magic?! Did you not see Phyrum waving his diamond wand, seemingly enslaving the stock, bending it to his will? When Phyrum pronounced "Support!" the stock magically levitates just *before* dropping below the $17 level, while when he intones, "Hssst! Resistance!" the stock instantly retreats from $21.

Resistance and Support are Phyrum's twin towers of delusion, the foundations of his legerdemain. And while I admire a great magician as much as any man, my admiration doesn't prevent me from revealing his tricks. You see, in the example you just saw before your very eyes, Phyrum looks at a graph of the stock and notices that recent history shows that twice the line rose above $17 without going below, and twice the line fell from $21 without rising above. Phyrum's sorcery is completely predicated on the notion that those magical "price levels" will hold power over the future. The stock will not drop below $17 because of Support; the stock will not rise above $21 because of Resistance.

In your utter mundaneness you, my dear audience of investors, probably study financial reports, plod through long write-ups about company products, and calculate numbers until your eyes glaze over . . . *all* in the quest for value, I presume. How Phyrum's followers would shake their heads, bemoaning this sorry waste of time! You see, technowizards like Phyrum can make money hand over fist without ever referring to a company's financial statements. Promise! (Can we brighten the spotlight on him, Vinny?) Yes, indeed, a good sorcerer need not even know a company's *product,* or in fact the company name at all! Give the astounding Phyrum a ticker symbol and a stock chart, and he *shall* make gold appear.

We cannot, of course, return your money if he's wrong.

Phyrum scorns the tedious reality to which you are bound, inventing instead entirely artificial schemes of perception. A most precarious craft but highly profitable to him who manages to induce others to go along with it! And that, in the end, may be his greatest magic of all . . . the mass hypnosis that mighty Phyrum has practiced upon his minions.

One more thing I'll say about Phyrum before we whisk the great man off the stage. Ah, but listen closely, because this is the most important thing, the deepest secret of all: You *must* believe in Phyrum for his magic to work. And I don't mean just *you* sir, or *you* madam, no . . . I mean *all* of you. *Everyone* must believe in Resistance and Support for them to work.

Some Fool once said, "I never met a 'resistance' or 'support' level that wasn't broken." Scoundrel! We have no room or patience for dissenters. Another writes, "It rained two Fridays ago, and last Friday. And in both cases, it cleared up on Saturday. Should I therefore conclude it will rain *this* Friday and clear up on Saturday?" What bad faith. If there are any skeptics in our midst, do not spoil the Delights for the rest of us. Begone, Fools!

Meantime, I ask the rest of you now to continue to suspend your disbelief and view the mighty Phyrum with awe and wonder. Close your eyes, ladies and gentlemen, boys and girls. Close them! Now, picture yourself throwing away all your financial reports, your ratios and your cash flows, your calculators, and your common sense, and believe only in Support and Resistance, Resistance and Support. And now repeat after me, "The stock hit $17 twice and bounced back. Resistance is at $17, so it can't go below. . . ."

Penny Stocks

Ladies and gentlemen, we have a special guest in attendance this very night. Introducing Mister . . . Joey . . . ROMAN!

Software That Makes Investment Decisions

Ladies and gentlemen, if you will please, a *first* at our hallowed carnival, and a moment of great private satisfaction: I'm about to activate a robotic replacement for myself! Allow me a minute or so to explain the rationale behind, and advantages of, this grand development.

The robot that will soon take my place is reputed to be able to perform in the role of ringleader *better* than I do on my own. The robot will operate completely independent of me, using a neural–network artificial intelligence, much of which was designed by our friend the *amazing* Phyrum. The machine has been programmed by a score of brilliant techies to match my every gesticulation, my every speech pattern, my instincts, my emotions, my intellect . . . all of it ingeniously synchronized.

The advantages are obvious. In opting to use the robot, I free myself from the burden of decision making, turning over my performance and reputation to a highly competent, highly skilled machine. Meanwhile, I'll be able to take advantage of the "body double" to spend more leisure time doing the things I really enjoy doing: going to Club Med perhaps, or reading Ayn Rand. The replacement will take care of everything!

And from your point of view, my friends, there should be no noticeable difference. Just the same charming emcee you're used to.

Technology has come so far! Its ability now to relieve us of the burdens of duty and personal challenge is truly wondrous; we live in an incredible age. I just hope I don't get addicted to using this thing. Just think: Soon you can do the same—turn your money or your life over to your very own robot.

Okay, friends . . . I hope you have enjoyed our show tonight, and if any of you are still at the carnival next week, I think I'll be back from vacation then.

Robot—*activate!*

Ladies and gentlemen, welcome to the Carnival of Freak Delightss! My name is Malbowges, and Ill be your ringleder this evenig . . . evenig or morng???????? System resrouces checking . . . 5:17 reporting incorrecting date terminalerror 3.14169 Beware the Jub-Jub bird and the Bandersnatch terminalerror system. Shuttttttttdowwwnn.

•22•

The Leibniz Pre-Harmonic
Oscillator

· · · · ·

Fools are my theme, let satire be my song.
—*Byron*

We've already written of our affection for technical analysis, that catchall term for investment approaches founded on the collective suspension of disbelief in superstition, pseudohistory, and the "insights" afforded by price-performance graphs. Drawing on such fundamentally misleading concepts as Resistance and Support, technical analysis is for many the way to "play the market." It also represents almost everything anathema to Foolishness, which we hope our dear Carnival made amply clear.

But it isn't enough just to sit back and criticize. That's too easy. We have to have some fun parodying, as well. What better time, therefore, to introduce you to the one technical analysis tool that we *do* advocate?

It's time for the Leibniz Pre-Harmonic Oscillator (LPHO).

The first thing to notice about this most ingenious device is that its name denies even the discerning reader any possibility of comprehending its function or meaning. How terribly technical! Like the McClellan Oscillator, the Elliott Wave Theory, the Chaotic Energy Flow Indicator, Bollinger Bands, and a hundred other techie gimcracks, the name "Leibniz Pre-Harmonic Oscillator" stingily refuses to provide any real clues as to what it's all about. All the better to impress your unsuspecting listeners!

Take a moment to chant these choice words a few times. Anyone who can pronounce "Leibniz Pre-Harmonic Oscillator" quickly and confidently will be sure to win over admirers, readers, subscribers, you name it. Instantly.

Leibniz (correctly pronounced LIPE-nits, and the speaker should always affect a faint, generic European lilt) was, of course, the eighteenth-century German philosopher who proposed the metaphysical theory that we live in "the best of all possible worlds." The good baron's views were resoundingly mocked by Voltaire in his superb work of 1759, *Candide*. Little did either of them know that two hundred twenty-seven years later "the best of all possible worlds" would dramatically return to the world's stage, right here in *The Motley Fool Investment Guide*.

Leibniz used his concept of "pre-harmony" to describe the perfect state of existence preceding the Creation. (In other words, our world was perfect even before you and I got here to make it so. Go figure.) Leibniz also created the notion of "monads," which he described as the units that make up all living matter. Monads were alive, in contrast to atoms, which were dead. Infinite in number and variety, monads have no material form. The particular description of monad we're using here appears in the current edition of *The American Heritage Dictionary* as definition numero uno. Without Baron Gottfried Wilhelm von Leibniz, that is, "monad" might today refer only to single-celled microorganisms.

Naturally, none of this has the faintest application to the matter of analyzing finances and valuing stocks. But neither has technical analysis had anything to do with analyzing finances and valuing stocks, so we're working in the best spirit of the tradition, here. And a concept like "monads" could not be more perfect for our new technical device.

Okay, you've met Leibniz. And now you have some vague fleeting sense of what the "Pre-Harmonic" part might mean. Time to look at "Oscillator."

Here again, we've latched onto a term that means very little to most people. In the case of "oscillator," of course, it's also a term whose use is rampant among tech talkers. That's not surprising given that "to oscillate" means to swing back and forth. Because many technical indicators are focused on the *ignis fatuus* of predicting short-term price movements, "oscillate" is a perfect choice, with its suggestion of prices twitching spasmodically higher and lower. We couldn't resist, therefore, making our own technical indicator an oscillator.

By now, we hope our motive is becoming clearer. You see, we believe that technical investing has rendered unto the world a useless noise. Lots of them, in fact. (Anything from, "So, John, what are your Bollinger Bands telling you?" to, "We expect some overhead resistance at the $30¼ level due to an overbought condition combined with a breakdown in the 30-week moving average," to the simpler, equally useless, "Where's the market headed next week?") And so what better way to fight it than to create our own indicator based on the same premises: gaudiness, pretension, uselessness, obscurity, and lack of accountability?

And by propagating the Leibniz, you too can join the revolution. In our crusade against blather, help us fight it all with *more* blather. Perhaps we can even drown out the old noise.

Here's how this works. The next time someone at a cocktail party asks you where you think the market is headed, and you're bored of stating (Foolishly) that you don't care, that it doesn't matter to your long-term investment approach, answer instead: "Well, of course the Leibniz Pre-Harmonic Oscillator is showing very strong sentiment readings—"(Pause lengthily at this point to let that sink in, hoping to elicit some vague gesture of affirmation from your listener. Then switch gears . . .)

"—which is, of course, bearish as usual, since it's a classic contrarian indicator." (This to be accompanied by a very, very knowing look, something like the chess master executing a checkmate.)

You'll get one of three responses at this point. In many cases, you'll earn a pseudonod, a smile, or some other gesticulation intended to imply that your listener understood and agreed with you, even though in actuality he hasn't the faintest idea what your little speech means. Our recommended reaction here is just to go start another conversation with someone less superficial. You've accomplished your mission: One more piece of techie misinformation has been loosed on the world and seems likely to spread. The other two responses are the honest one (a blank stare) or the inquisitive one (asking what the LPHO actually is). In these situations, you now have the amusing opportunity of elaborating further upon a technical investing concept that, like its forebears, has nothing real behind it:

"Well, have you heard of monads?" you'll begin, and then launch into a brief, digressive biography of Leibniz. (A few notes: He wrote *Monadology* in 1714, he was an ardent opponent of Locke's notion of *tabula rasa,* and he is now considered—FYI—the founder of symbolic logic.) Completing your tour of Leibniz, you'll return to a discussion of monads—a subject by which you'll appear to be unduly fascinated, though without ever offering any genuinely useful or educated knowledge about it—and you'll suggest, vaguely again (vaguely, always vaguely), that the oscillator relies on counting the swinging to and fro of monads as a way of gauging market sentiment. "It's all about whether we're in the best of all possible market environments," you'll allow, reiterating, "and it's contrarian too, of course, so that a high degree of monadic oscillation means sure trouble, as usual." At this point, it's probably appropriate to leave it all go with the simple signoff line that our marketers dreamt up: "Well, have you read *The Motley Fool Investment Guide?* You can read all about this in there!"

Actually, although we said above that you'll encounter three separate responses to your cocktail-party explication of the Leibniz, a fourth response is possible: Complete understanding from your conversation mate, who's in on the game. Congrats, you just discovered an attractive new friend! To indicate that she is in on the joke, she should give the standard response: "Well, I've always favored Voltaire over Leibniz, but then I'm a sucker for irony."

Readers detecting similarities between *Candide*'s Pangloss and our modern-day technicians, as regards the vacuous optimism of their philosophical systems, may do so at their own risk, and may not necessarily *not* be hounds on the right scent.

We'll end this section exhorting all true Fools everywhere to join us, join the revolution, and talk Leibniz! We particularly need you on our side if you're a well-placed Fool, one of the "higher-ups" with access to airtime on a financial television show. *You need to introduce the LPHO.* As always, a quick and oblique reference will suffice: "We're hitting some seasonal highs now—the advance/decline line makes that obvious—and the Leibniz confirms it." That's all we ask . . . we get enough people doing this and financial television will suddenly become fun to watch!

Of course, if you're feeling cocksure, we invite you to consider something more elaborate. If you pull it off, expect rave reviews online; you'll be the toast of an entire Foolish world. "Where do *I* think the market is going?!" you might ask, greeting the interviewer with an irrepressible grin. "Oh, well, I just keep my ear pressed to the Leibniz Pre-Harmonic Oscillator, a dandy little device that perfectly epitomizes market-timing gadgets. And the Leibniz is of course bearish right now, since everyone thinks this is the best of all possible markets." Your gaze must positively shine with good humor, but without *ever* giving anything away, as you trail on, ". . . the Leibniz being, of course, a contrarian sentiment indicator, measured in monads . . ."

PART IX

CONCLUSION

A Foolish Farewell

• • • • •

Even bad books are books and therefore sacred.
—*Günter Grass*

The Motley Fool Investment Guide has, from start to finish, shared the same aim of all our online financial undertakings: to inform, to amuse, and to help you make good money. It is our earnest hope that our guide has smashingly exceeded these goals, making it at least as influential as Mrs. Susswein, the kindergarten teacher who taught you how to read. (Failing that, we'll settle for matching the fifth-grade phys ed instructor who taught you to jump rope without breaking your nose.) If, saddest of all, you've read all the way to here and you still don't see how to make your money make more money, we hope you at least liked a few of our jokes. And, say, did you ever hear the one about the ingrate and the spontaneous human combustion?

We spent the better part of the last decade designing our investment approach and several months' worth of late nights to stuff it into this clothbound book. So as long as we have you here, we're going to run the Absolute Essentials at you one more time. The Absolute Essentials are simple because Foolishness is, and they work.

Manage Your Own Money

No one on the institutional side of the financial markets is going to suggest that you can consistently outperform the stock market without hard work and great effort. Money managers don't generate high commissions by telling their clients that equities investing is *easy*, that the stock market is fueled by logic, that any Fool can do better than the majority of the umpthousand mutual funds peddled today in newspapers, magazines, over telephones and online computer services, in banks, insurance agencies, and brokerage firms. *They* may not tell you, but now you know. Be a Fool: Manage your own money and beat the market and the experts without spending your every waking hour worrying about the investments somebody else picked for you that you know nothing about.

Further, if you can ignore the siren calls of hype stocks and the impassioned importunings of the "Have-I-got-a-stock-for-you" brokers and look instead to the examples of Warren Buffett, Peter Lynch, and Michael O'Higgins—the three most important investment instructors of the late twentieth century—you can see that the task is not impossible. Using a few simple principles easily duplicable by anyone with discipline, each of these paragons has more than doubled the stock market on an annualized basis.

With this goal in mind, we first showed you how to use the Dow Dividend Yield model, stressing the Foolish Four approach to the group of high yielders. For more than two decades running, the approach has compounded over 25 percent annually. From there, we demanded nothing less than returns superior to those of the Foolish Four. If you can't beat them, don't waste your time. The Motley Fool Investment Portfolio from inception to final printing of this text, was up 61.66 percent versus S&P 500 returns of 26.41 percent. How? We focused on growth, on the Fool Ratio, on internal cash generation, on dispassionate, numerical valuations, on professional accounting standards, on collaborative research in our forum, and on beating high-yield Dow investing. Can you do that too? Yes!

Will we compound 50 percent-plus growth every year? Can you? Certainly not. Will we beat the S&P 500 *every* year? Unfortunately, no. Hall of Famer Cy Young didn't win every game he pitched, and neither will you. (In fact, Cy actually *lost* more games than any other pitcher.) The Foolish aim with stocks is to double the market's annualized return. Be twice average, we say, and then aim higher still.

Be Aggressive, Too

You're not going to make a million overnight unless you start with *much* more than that. The investment strategies you've found here are for those willing to look to the future and wait while their money and the market do the work. The most attractive aspect of the long-term approach to investing in stocks is that it eliminates day-to-day risk and worry. If you're generating in excess of 20 percent annual growth on disposable income, sleeping peaceably, and reflexively saving money, you can *and should* constantly open up your model, challenging yourself to do better. Far too much of our nation's financial psyche is weighted down with thoughts merely of spending and saving, like a dieter who forgets that exercise is the key to staying in shape. Be aggressive in investing your money once you've learned how to run the numbers, how to weed out fabricated growth, how to account for your returns against your Dow holdings, and how to be patient and disciplined.

We certainly don't think—and we know how loudly Wall Street will protest this claim—that 30 percent annualized growth is out of the realm of possibility for the individual investor. That's a 4.5 percent improvement in annual returns over the Foolish Four, the model that demands 5 minutes of your time per year. The question, of course, is how much time it would take, and how much it's worth to you.

Permit us then to run some numbers one last time. Let's take $25,000 as our nest egg. To that, we'll add $2,500 in new savings per year. We will tax our investment growth at 28 percent per year. And we'll compound out 30 percent in annual growth. How long until that initial $25,000 has turned into $1 million? Seventeen years.

So, where are you going to be in 2013?

"But where am I going to get that kind of nest egg?" you ask. Well, if you concentrate on saving 10 percent of your salary each year, as well as working on nailing down other income alternatives, you should be able to put away $25,000 in seven years. This takes real preparation; saving 10 percent of annual income means fewer beers, compact disks, and new clothes, it means some home-cooked meals instead of elegant restaurant dining, and you and the family stick with the old jalopy instead of springing for a new car. Finding the right investment strategy and the right stocks is easy compared to this, but the final reward is worth it.

To get there, you'll need to draft a plan for your savings goals. If you bring in $20,000 per year today, what's it going to take for you to save $2,000 per year? You might have to take on some contract work on the weekends to meet those targets. And if you're halfway through the year, it's June, and you haven't tucked away $1,000 yet, maybe it's time to drag out that lawn mower and float through the neighborhood. You've trailed your estimates, and the market doesn't like underperformers. Set to!

Once You Have It, Give It Away

Information, that is. When you have your saving and your investment strategies down cold, give 'em away. Share them with others like you. Join our gang online or form your own.

Giving information away is just what The Motley Fool has committed itself to doing into perpetuity: distributing financial information and analysis on the cheap. For a paltry sum relative to the amounts that publishers charge institutional investors, our readers can access some of the most sophisticated, most comprehensive, and most timely research on the stock market. And a year's supply of superior investment models presented Foolishly online will cost less than it does to take a family of four to the ballpark. In the multitrillion-dollar financial industry, it's a rather radical notion that you could actually skip the occasional ball game, nachos and all, and spend that money instead on mastering stocks, nailing down extraordinary growth for your savings, and actually enjoying the entire process. For the Wise to compete, they'll have to explain their models as we have, account for their returns without flaw, and convince us all that they can consistently outperform the S&P 500. If they do, amen to that. If not, heck, amen to that!

One Last Thing

We consider this tome our single proudest achievement to date, but that's not to say this medium doesn't have its limitations. The primary one is that anything in print simply cannot keep up with the speed of change in the online world.

You know, the market could actually tank this year. Or someone may invent an investment gadget that tops the fabled Dow Dividend Yield strategy. And you better believe that working as a group, our readership will locate some new undiscovered small-cap winners. In each of these cases, the book you hold in your hands may not offer the *latest* help you can get from friends and Fools online. But until you've mastered what's in here, the latest help probably wouldn't be much help at all. Let this book serve as your textbook; let the new medium be your life's continuing education.

One of the great paintings of the Italian High Renaissance came out of a commission from Pope Julius II, who hired a twenty-five-year-old man named Raphael Sanzio to redecorate certain of his rooms in the Vatican. Raphael went on to create for him his famous painting *The School of Athens,* depicting a crowd of philosophers from antiquity up to Raphael's time milling about outside Athens' Academy. In the center are the two great philosophers of all time: Plato and Aristotle. Their two poses perfectly evoke the fundamental distinction in their beliefs . . . and in ours. Plato is pointing upward, in reference to his doctrine of perfect Forms, which all earthly imitations purportedly fail to emulate. Forms have no verifiable existence, though perhaps they do make good foundations for endless ivory-tower dispute. Aristotle, on the other hand, juts his right hand forward as if to say, "Whoa there. Let's look carefully not at the sun, but at the world around us for our answers." Practical man. The founder of formal logic.

We're with Aristotle because Aristotle, you see, was a Fool. Like him, we shall continue to look to the world around us to evaluate our investment decisions, using every means possible—annual reports, financial statements, product analysis, even common sense. In today's dynamic investment world, the Aristotelian approach may eventually result in minor or global changes to our entire investment strategy, if we find the market starting to go Wise on us. We reserve the right to an open mind; we must all be flexible and must welcome change, the proverbial "only constant." Meantime, we'll let dreamers like Plato look to the constellations for astrological reasons as to why the world behaves as it does, and why you should probably just assume that reason cannot beat the market, that the market is going to crash anyway, that—we seem to be hearing—only a Fool would dare to think things out.

But being Foolish is not just about being prepared for change. It also means sticking to your guns. Even if the market bombs altogether this year or next, we'll be there buying right into the bottom, knowing that the market will always come back, and our stocks back stronger with it.

The Wise will continue to offer you their sophistical ramblings and their many-splendored mediocrities. The whole point of this book is to brush off the worldly wisdom, point not up but *out* at the world around us, and find the next damn winner.

Folly forever.

APPENDIX A

. . . . .

Stocks 101:
A Primer for Those
Who'll Admit They Need It

So, you've decided to do it, to get out of your mutual fund, strike out on your own, and buy some stocks. But what do you do *next?* There are hundreds, nay, thousands of self-proclaimed financial experts churning out newsletters telling you *what* stocks to buy, *why* to buy them, and always *when* to buy them (which often is right after they do). But these mavens rarely if ever tell you just *how* you might go about buying stocks.

Many investors plunge right into the stock market, using the first brokerage firm recommended to them or the first one to catch their eye with a cheesy advertisement in their financial daily. Taking the time to think about boring stuff like tax-deferred investment vehicles and commission schedules might seem like an unbearable tedium. And guess what? It is. But if you take time to familiarize yourself with some of these concepts, you may end up saving time, money, and heartache.

What *Is* a Share of Stock?

Funny how common it is for investors, individual *and* institutional, to jump into the equities markets without understanding why and how businesses are built, why they issue stock, and how they grow.

Growth: That's the first matter at hand; businesses are launched in expectation of growth. Tomorrow's profits will allow for higher salaries, more employees, increased opportunity, prosperity at work and home—all the good news we hope for. Of course, there are hoards of other reasons that businesses sprout, bud, and blossom; some aspire to serve customers, others to exploit them, others to serve a larger corporation, others to fund trips to Lake Tahoe. But one thing's true of 99 percent of them: They aim to expand.

How? Sometimes a company has a great new product, like Broderbund's 1993 CD-ROM game Myst. Other times it's recognized a niche for the provision of a great new service, like Internet-access companies. But often, whatever the driving force is—products, services, or whatever—the company lacks the money to drive the operation forward.

Let's cursorially examine FlubSoft, the brand-new software company that you and we just started together that specializes in virus-protection applications. Office space, phone services, networked computers, health insurance, salaries—kicking off this new operation is a costly undertaking. It's no wonder the vast majority of start-up businesses go belly-up within 5 years.

To survive these initial costs, FlubSoft has two traditional alternative sources for funding. First, it can ankle down to the nearest bank, lay out its financial statements and projections, and plead for a loan. Often, this may not work; the less established the company, the less likely a bank is to lend it money. And even when loans do come through, they can do more damage than good. How? Well, risky loans demand higher interest rates. And the higher the rate, the greater the possibility that our company won't be able to pay it down. Never a borrower be, some say.

FlubSoft could instead sell chunks of itself to investors willing to take a shot at a big payout down the road. Conveniently, we would thus avoid costly debt financing, while now sporting business partners who are cheering (to understate the situation) for our virus detection and defense software.

The best of start-up companies—and we wouldn't have started this baby, you and The Fool, if we didn't aspire to superiority—can generate upward of a million dollars by selling off 30 to 40 percent of their equity to venture capitalists. In this situation, we'd create shares of ownership in our company and sell them off. We could pick a number out of the sky and say that 100 shares of stock makes up FlubSoft in its entirety. The number is insignificant; the percentage of the company's total value is what matters. If we sold 40 percent of our company to VentYour Capital Inc. for $1 million, we'd keep 60 shares and VentYour would take 40 shares. Our company wouldn't be listed on any of the

U.S. exchanges, like the New York Stock Exchange, but we *would enjoy* the same sort of "shares of ownership" as Microsoft, Wal-Mart, or General Electric.

Now, how do we get from being anonymous little FlubSoft with twelve employees, a decent infrastructure, and impressive sales growth, to gargantuan FlubSoft with five hundred employees, a square block of office space, national and international distribution, and tens of millions in annual sales? *We go public,* again selling more ownership in our company. This time, however, we'll be selling shares to a base of millions of investors, and taking our spot on one of the major U.S. exchanges.

The Public Company

There are three main ways that shares of ownership in American corporations wind up in the hands of former nonowners. The first is the initial public offering (oft-abbreviated "IPO"). Companies aiming to go public work through a brokerage that does investment banking to sell their first batch of shares to investors. They become, for the first time, a publicly owned entity that trades every day on two stock exchanges.

The second way is for those public companies that have already had an initial public offering to acquire *more* capital to fuel future growth. They make a "secondary offering." No matter how many more times a company offers shares, the sale will be called a secondary offering. Issuing more shares dilutes the existing value of the shares held by the previous owners, as it creates more units of control, but for a growing company this is normally not a problem. If we at FlubSoft need another $5 million to finance a new venture into entertainment software, we could sell another load of ownership, believing that the growth from our new project would far outweigh the share dilution. Most of the companies with a couple hundred million shares started out with only a few million. They kept going back to the well for more cash, though (and splitting their stock).

The final way that stocks get issued is directly to employees, either officers of the corporation or workers, through various profit-sharing and compensation plans. The board of directors, which represents the shareholders, figures that paying the company's officers in stock and not just salary gives those people a little extra impetus to improve the stock price. Giving the employees stock instead of just a paycheck gives them an interest in making an extra effort as well. Plus, companies are able to lower their salary overhead by partially compensating employees with stock.

The Principal Exchanges

Public stocks are traded in public markets, organizations that create outlets for trading equities. Each market has various requirements that a company must meet before it can be listed—minimum asset value, minimum annual sales, maximum management ownership limitations—all designed to prevent manipulation of a stock's value.

The three largest markets in the United States are the New York Stock Exchange (NYSE), the American Stock Exchange (AMEX or ASE), and the NASDAQ Stock Market (NASDAQ).

The New York is the oldest exchange and has the strictest requirements for listing. Its typical member is a more established company— the giants that have been in business for decades. Many in the investment community perceive it as a sign of status when a company "makes" the NYSE.

The American Stock Exchange contains smaller, more speculative companies than the NYSE and has less strict listing requirements. It is actually a leftover from the days before telephones and other rapid forms of communications. The AMEX has five supporting member exchanges: the Pacific, Cincinnati, Boston, Philadelphia, and Chicago stock exchanges.

The NASDAQ is the youngest and most dynamic. It is best known for offering fast-growing technology companies, although it lists stocks in every industry. The market has no central location, but rather is a network of brokerages that move stocks to one another via a computer system. The brokerages that participate are called "market makers." They sign up to fulfill orders for individual companies. Thus a certain brokerage might "make a market" in Microsoft (NASDAQ:MSFT), but not in Intel (NASDAQ:INTC), which means that if you want to buy some Microsoft they'll find the shares in *their* inventory, but if you want to buy some Intel, they'll have to phone up another firm and borrow the shares. This has absolutely no effect on you as an investor; you'll probably never know who makes the market in your stocks.

Lastly, how do these market makers make money? They make it off of the bid-ask spread, or the difference in the prices at which individual investors can buy or sell a stock. They'll quote you one price to buy, and another price for someone else to sell, and pocket the difference themselves. The NASDAQ has been criticized—and even investigated—in the past for setting its spreads too wide, thereby earning an unreasonable profit.

The Traditional Brokerage

Now that we have an idea of what stock is and how companies go about issuing it, we can talk about how you purchase shares of your own. The most common way that investors purchase stock is through a brokerage. A brokerage is an institution licensed by state and federal authorities to buy and sell securities (a fancy word for stocks). Brokerages join the various exchanges and are policed by them as well as by the Securities Exchange Commission (SEC). Brokerages take many shapes and sizes. Knowing a little bit about how brokerages work can help a Fool decide which one is the "right" one. That's the spirit in which we proceed.

Although they might stress their uniqueness, the largest, most renowned *full-service* brokerages are by and large cut from the same mold. The traditional big-name brokerage is broken down into a retail division, a research division, and an investment banking division. These firms also have a "back office," where all the number crunching for customer accounts is done, and a "trading desk," where customer orders are processed and communicated to the various stock exchanges.

The retail part is the one with which you're—perhaps, unfortunately—already familiar, or about to become acquainted. This is the one with all those salesmen (brokers) who make nagging calls to individuals or institutional clients, trying to get them to buy or sell the firm's recommended stocks. They make money for themselves and their firms by generating commissions off trades. This is sometimes referred to as the "sell side" in the industry. It's a little-known fact that most big-name brokerages actually lose money in their retail operations. "What?" you say. "Why have them at all?" We'll make that clear in a bit.

The research side is made up of all the analysts and their assistants who write reports evaluating individual companies. The firm recommends them as a "buy," a "hold," a "market performer," et al. You'll almost never see a firm labeling a stock a "sell." Why? As we noted earlier in the book, research firms rely on their relationships with every company they follow; they don't want to jeopardize those ties by motivating investors to sell. We remember hearing an analyst at one of the big brokerages saying, on PBS's *Nightly Business Report:* "Banker's Trust has fallen from $75 to $50 in a matter of months. When the stock was at $72, we labeled it a 'hold.' So we were right on this one." Right? To *hold* for a 30 percent loss? *Hold* in analyst-ese usually means *sell*.

The investment banking side of a brokerage is the most important part for the big firms. This is where they make all of their money. When companies want to make initial public offerings (IPOs) or companies want to issue more shares as an alternative to borrowing money, it's the investment banking people that do the multimillion-dollar deals. And the firm will leverage its alternate businesses to their favor when they bring companies public. How? Read on.

Conflicts of Interest at a Traditional Brokerage

As we noted above, an investment banking relationship with a company is a very lucrative one for a brokerage firm, one that it's loath to jeopardize. This relationship has a profound effect on a brokerage's retail and research divisions. Firms keep their retail operations—even if they're ostensibly losing money—to serve as a sales channel to push initial public offerings and secondary offerings. When Rydholm's Taxi Service, Inc. (NASDAQ:LATE) issues 2.5 million additional shares, the firm that helped with the offering often immediately puts LATE on its Hot Weekly Buy List. Nice research. Then legions of brokers call all their clients, asking if they want in on this Midwestern cost-cutter, Pinto-cab operation. So keep in mind, when a broker gives you a call recommending a stock, it's not always because he thinks it really is a great buy. Sometimes the firm needs him to sell it.

The research people are not immune to this pressure either. When a firm has an investment banking relationship with a company, instead of having its analysts issue that dreaded "sell" recommendation when they think the stock is overpriced, many firms tacitly persuade their analysts to mumble "hold" instead. All the professionals know it's Wall Street doublespeak, so that the company doesn't have its feelings hurt by that nasty "sell" word.

'Course there may be interesting reversals where a "hold" actually might mean a buy, as the firm is looking to keep the price a bit deflated to get its clients in on the cheap. How pronounced a problem all of this is, is open for debate. We'll look for you at the Fool's Galactic Gathering for Debate on the planet Jupiter in 2012. Between now and then, though, we can all agree that *no Fool* should ever buy or sell stocks based on the qualitative parts of a brokerage recommendation. Keep your eyes on the numbers . . . who cares about the names?

Discount Brokerages: A Revolution on Wall Street

Before the days of lightning-fast electronic communication, full-service brokerages and the brokers they employed were a fairly vital link between individual investors and Wall Street. When you needed to communicate to someone down on a stock exchange trading floor regarding which stocks you wanted to buy or sell, you needed an agent. That's how the commission system, on which most brokers' pay is still based, evolved. Commissions are the fees that you pay to a broker in order to have your request to buy or sell a stock fulfilled. Because of the time and trouble that it took to place an order—sending a runner to the exchange to communicate to the brokerage's agent on the trading floor—compensation was pretty substantial.

But with the changes in technology, Wall Street has lost the stranglehold it once held on investors. Now with Touch-Tone telephones and online communications, the balance of investing power has shifted toward Main Street. It is now as easy for an individual investor in Anchorage, Alaska, to send in an order to buy or sell a security as it is for a well-paid broker in the Big Apple. Yet the oldest brokerage firms on Wall Street still do business in much the same way they did one hundred years ago, charging equally substantial commissions.

What specifically happened to break the control that the traditional brokerages held over the investment world? The watershed moment occurred in May 1975, when the Securities Exchange Commission, the federal agency that has been charged with policing the investment world, decreed that the traditional fixed system of commissions would be repealed and brokerages could charge whatever they wanted, within certain guidelines. Thus, with pricing variables, the price wars began and the so-called discount brokerage business was born.

A "discount" brokerage is one designed to serve the individual investor. The "discount" label means nothing other than that the brokerage doesn't launch initial public offerings (IPOs) and probably doesn't have any in-house analysts. All it does is buy and sell stocks.

The hodgepodge of discount brokers offers varying fee schedules, benefits, and account minimums. The two main kinds of discount brokerages are a normal "discount brokerage," which does the same retail-side stuff as a traditional brokerage—providing news, some research materials, and a few perks at low cost—and a "deep discount" brokerage, which is essentially there only to take your order and execute it with the fewest possible frills.

It's difficult to generalize about "deep discounters" though, since each offers a different combination of services and features, including cheap commissions, services, locations, and hours. Some try to undercut the "discount" brokerages a bit and still try to offer as many services; others let you trade for free with a $500,000 or greater account; others give you great rates if you type in your trades over your own computer; still others charge you very little to trade but are open only from 9:00 A.M. to 5:00 P.M.

Many people believe that discount brokerages are riskier than regular brokerages and might fold in a stock market crash, but that's mainly just full-service industry scare tactics. To the extent that they offer the same minimum account insurance that full-service brokers offer, discounters are just as secure. The government-sponsored Securities Investment Protection Corporation (SIPC) insures accounts up to $100,000 cash and up to $400,000 in other assets. (Obviously, double-check that your perspective broker is SIPC insured.) If your account is larger than $500,000, ask your discount broker how you can go about insuring it further. This shouldn't be a problem.

Boutique Brokerages and Money Management Firms

Most of us divide brokerages into two camps, so-called full-service brokerages and discount brokerages. Although this is definitely a useful distinction, there's a class of brokerage firms that falls somewhere between the full-service and discount flavors. These are the so-called boutique brokerages, or money management firms.

These are regional brokerages, licensed to trade securities that focus on certain regions or certain types of investors. These firms typically charge somewhere between what a full-service brokerage and a discount brokerage would cost, depending on their research, their individual service, and the convenience of their locale. Typically, these firms have in-house analysts and might even do some investment banking and market making but derive the majority of their money from the retail operations.

So, Which Brokerage?

The first major decision you need to make when investing is what kind of brokerage you want to use. The use of full-service brokers must be considered, under most circumstances, quite UNFoolish. Consigning your money to the houses of Merrill, or Shearson, or Dean Witter is as much as to say, "Do it for me yourself, Harry (or Janice, or Joey, or whatever your full-service broker's name might be). I think you can manage my money especially well, and I'm going to pay you extra to do it for me. In fact, I'm going to pay you a premium for *every* trade you make on my account, since you're going to be coming up with virtually all my investment ideas. Finally, I may further pay you an annual management fee as a kind of goodwill gesture acknowledging the fine job you're doing for me."

Basically, what you're saying is that you're willing to pay up for what might well be a market-underperforming portfolio, and what most probably will be a Dow Dividend–underperforming portfolio as well. That's not Foolish, that's dumb.

Some investors, due to time constraints and a fear of going it completely alone, find having their own broker very amenable to their needs when starting out. The assistance that the right, dedicated broker provides can be a valuable commodity. The idea of having someone whose everyday duty is to watch the stocks in your account and call you whenever there is any news about them can be a real comfort to many a fledgling investor. Also, for busy people who have neither the time nor the inclination to do their own research, the notion of a broker giving you advice that comes from the firm's professional analysts can be downright exciting.

Typically, having a full-service brokerage means having a broker who is yours and yours alone, through whom you make all of your trades. This broker is supposed to know about you and your goals and to advise you about what stocks may or may not be appropriate. He or she will supply you with scads of research, newsletters, and model portfolios developed by the brokerage in order to give you some ideas about what you should invest in.

Most investors, however, mistakenly think that all this activity will lead to market outperformance. If you're going to use a full-service broker initially, be sure to stack her returns against the S&P 500 and Beating the Dow—the two no-research approaches to the stock market. If she can't beat Beating the Dow—after deducting *all* commission and research costs—you won't be needing her assistance.

Cautious or Confident?

Depending on the amount of money you have, how often you plan to buy stocks, and how much of your own research you plan to do, you'll make a choice somewhere on the continuum between price and service when picking a brokerage. And there are two typical roles that a Fool plays at the start, the "cautious" and the "confident" investor.

If you're a cautious beginner who's concerned about going it alone and would like to start slow, you can find a lot of ways to do this without relying on the big-name, high-priced firms. The most satisfactory option is the regional or boutique brokerage that can offer you competitive commissions, low account minimums, solid advice, and accountability. The less involved they are with investment banking, the better. To find one of these, you simply need to talk to friends who invest, scour the message folders in The Motley Fool, and/or make a couple of local phone calls and see who offers what. Remember, if you're going to take things this route, you have to expect your broker to outperform the S&P 500 *and* Beating the Dow, which keeps doubling S&P returns every year. Setting expectations right from the start with your broker is essential.

Always remember: Any broker who gives advice is basically a salesman shopping around his brokerage house's stock or fund picks and getting paid a percentage (the commission) for every "sale" he makes. What's really at issue here is not how good the salesman is, but rather the quality of the wares. Do the ideas your broker is selling you make good money or not? If you have a good full-service broker who is driving your account to market-beating returns, then clearly this person is earning you additional dollars. If your broker beats Beating the Dow, celebrate him, deify him, pay for his Thanksgiving turkey.

The Confident Investor

Fools are most at ease when they have the opportunity to demonstrate their expertise by making their own investment decisions, using only a discount brokerage. However, even when you've decided that you need no advice from brokers and no analysts' reports, you should keep in mind that there is still a wide variety of options left to you.

Many investors believe that simply because they're paying the lowest amount for transactions at a trading center, they're doing well. It ain't necessarily so. If you can't get your order in on an active trading day, or if a brokerage is so understaffed it's putting your order in late, then you might well lose the monies you saved with the lower commission waiting to get your order executed while your stock is jumping up or falling down in price.

Also, there are a number of premium services that a more expensive discount brokerage can provide, including checking accounts, credit cards, and *S&P Stock Guides* mailed to your doorstep. Although you might pay a little more per trade, sometimes these small perks are enough to make an investor choose Charles Schwab over, say, National Discount Broker. And remember, all the free trades in the world may not really make up for a lost opportunity to buy or sell a stock because your discount firm didn't answer the telephone.

As convenience is always an issue, check to see if the brokerages you are looking at have a Touch-Tone service or an online trading service available. If they do, check it out and see how easy or difficult it is to use. Using these two little perks can often shave 10 percent or more off of your commissions, as your orders are directly entered into the trading system sans any human involvement save yours.

The Motley Fool's Online Portfolio was originally launched with Charles Schwab, as we enjoyed the convenience of being able to call a Schwab representative and ask what, if any, news there was on the stocks in our portfolio. For our $50,000 portfolio, however, the price of the Schwab commissions became a little ungainly, and we were getting most of the news we needed online. So we looked around for a "deep discount" brokerage that had a reputation for giving timely executions with minimal mistakes. The Fool settled on a deeper discounter that charged half the price of a Schwab trade, but with the loss of a representative to call and ask for news. The final deciding factor for this move was not price per commission, but rather what percentage of our portfolio was being used to pay commissions. Of course, as a company, we continue looking and listening to our readers. Maybe we'll find something even better.

If you're in the market for a discount broker, we think the best place to start your search is our Consumer Rap message board on America Online, where there are active discussions of a dozen discount and deep-discount brokers. Get the information sent to you by a number of them, ask questions online, and make your decision. Below is a Foolish list of considerations when searching for a good discounter.

Finding Your Discount Broker

1. Advertisements can be misleading. Like any ads. When you read about an incredibly cheap rate to trade stocks, read the fine print. Often, you'll be reading only a sample detailing *one* sort of trade (like stocks over $50 purchased in 5,000-share lots), as opposed to *all* trades. Some brokers "forget" to mention their minimum charge, while others print out-of-date claims. "SMOKEY DON'S DISCOUNT BROKER HAS CHEAPEST RATES OF ALL, says industry study," reads the ad, with a footnote. Locating the footnote text at the bottom of the circular, you see in 5-point type: "As of 6/30/93." Read carefully. Also, hey, what sort of industry study is that . . . one carried out by Smokey Don's uncle, Smokey Dan?

2. Commission schedules vary considerably, depending on the trade. While deep discounters' overall rates may look similar, individual trades may not look the same at all. The most Foolish way to go about this is to match your trading style with the broker who offers

the best rates for it. So what's your typical trade? If you most typically buy 1,000 shares of stocks below $10 a share, use this typical trade as a test of your prospective brokers. See how much of a commission you'd pay for this hypothetical trade using each of your several prospects. If you trade a lot of bonds, check those. You get the idea.

3. If you trade foreign stocks, which we don't generally counsel doing, make sure your discounter is set up to trade them. That's because some deep-discount brokers, particularly those offering the least services, are very poorly equipped for handling such transactions. You'll be sorely disappointed if you've just transferred your account to an outfit that can't meet your needs.

4. If you want to use a margin account, which allows you to buy stocks with money borrowed from the brokerage, you're in luck, because discounters generally offer cheaper margin rates than full–service brokers. Make sure you inquire about the current margin rate of interest charged by each of your prospects. Keep in mind, this rate fluctuates from time to time and will probably be based on how much you're borrowing (the greater the amount borrowed, the lower your margin rate). Oh, and The Fool never recommends going more than 25 percent on margin.

5. If you like to keep up day-to-day with your own stocks, we highly recommend a broker that offers some sort of free automated quotation service. That's part of the reason The Fool used Schwab initially; it's a nice way to start. Eventually, you'll have access to all the news online.

Tax Deferment: IRAs and 401(K)s

Entire boring books can be written about the vagaries of tax-deferred retirement vehicles. These are the accounts you can set up and trade on without paying any taxes until you're old enough (fifty-nine and a half) to withdraw and use the money. We can, however, make a couple of observations which you can apply as your situation permits.

First, always try to avoid penalties for early withdrawal. If you want to stuff money in an Individual Retirement Account (IRA), make sure it is money you are not going to need until you are fifty-nine and a half years old. All the tax deferment in the world does not help you if you have to remove the money early and pay a 10 percent penalty. The IRS has a fixed 10 percent penalty on *all* money withdrawn from tax-deferred accounts before retirement age, whether annuities, IRAs, or 401(K)s . . . so think a little before you tuck it away.

Incidentally, tax-deferment is not the same as tax-free. Tax-deferred investments allow you to pay the taxes on your investments at some future point, letting them grow without taxation until your retirement. This deferment can be a very powerful tool, but only if you let the money sit still and only if you continue to add more money on a regular basis. However, do not add anything beyond the stated limits to your IRA or other tax-deferred retirement account or you'll have a nasty little 6 percent excise tax taken off the top. And of course if you have an IRA, don't think you have to use a mutual fund in order to have it in stocks. A self-directed IRA allows you to invest directly in stocks, making changes whenever you like. Almost all brokerages will set these up for you with an annual fee between $25 and $35 per year, depending on your account balance.

If your employer offers to match your contributions to a 401(K) or 403(B) plan, by all means, take the guaranteed 100 percent return. Free money is very difficult to pass up. Even if you do not plan to stay on the job until retirement, you can always simply roll over your 401(K) into a self-directed IRA at a brokerage firm and use that money to invest in common stocks as well through the tax-deferred instrument.

Lastly, if you have a choice between putting into your self-directed IRA stocks that pay a dividend and stocks that do not pay a dividend, *always* go with the stocks that pay a dividend. As dividends are taxed at the rate of income and not subject to a maximum, long-term capital gains tax, you can gain the most advantage out of tax deferment if you use it to shelter dividend income until you retire.

The Dividend Reinvestment Plan

For investors who don't have a lot of money and can't afford to open a brokerage account, there's still an alternative to your average underperforming mutual fund. Direct Purchase Programs (sometimes called Optional Cash Purchase Programs) are almost always offered as a feature of a company's Dividend Reinvestment Program (DRIP). These little gems provide shareholders with a simple and cheap way to purchase stock without incurring brokerage costs. You just buy stock directly from the company.

DRIP arose for two reasons. First, most companies have employee stock purchase programs. Since these companies have already undertaken the necessary steps to sell stock in-house, they figured they might as well offer it for the benefit of shareholders (the nominal owners of the company). The second reason was an attempt to decrease the volatility of the stock. If investors own shares in their name rather than having brokers hold their shares, these investors have to jump through some hoops in order to sell.

When you own shares in your name through a DRIP, in order to sell you need to contact the DRIP plan administrator, mail in the certificates, and have them sold on the specific sell day set by the plan. Or you have to take your certificates down to a brokerage and have the broker do some paperwork. The structure of DRIP investing promotes long-term holding, very much in the companies' best interest . . . and in our minds, often very much in the interest of the individual investor, who ought to buy quality companies and hold on to them tight.

With Direct Purchase Programs, you can put small amounts of money, as little as $25 or $50 at a time, into the common stocks of companies that you believe are superior long-term investments. Over 850 companies have these plans, and many, many of them have excellent long-term prospects. Nearly every high-yielding Dow stock has a DRIP plan, so you can wallop the market without paying commissions.

The best place to go if you want to learn more about Dividend Reinvestment plans and Direct Purchase Programs may be your local library. Or you can try The Motley Fool Online, where some of the leaders in the DRIP industry sit in, waiting to answer your questions. We don't want to tout ourselves too much—we mean, of course, we want to tout ourselves! But while we don't want to overdo it, we have to close this chapter by emphasizing how well The Motley Fool and its tens of thousands of readers can answer your questions promptly, thoroughly, and without the tangled conflicts of interest that many in the industry are tied to for their survival.

Happy Foolin'!

APPENDIX B

. . . . .

How Investment Publishers *Should* Report Their Numbers

To be honest, we entered the financial publishing world licking our chops. That's mainly because the status quo was so clearly crying out for reform and Fools have always enjoyed affecting the reformer's lilting tone. Here was the crux of it: Not only was the available advice generally wanting, but also much of it was extremely poorly—and in some cases, shadily—accounted for. The two are not unrelated. It stands to reason that those offering mediocre investment advice would do their best to obscure the consequences. So going in, we knew that even if Ye Olde Printed Foole offered just plain, run-o'-the-mill stock picks, if we accounted fairly and straightforwardly for what we were doing, we would instantly join an elite minority.

In this appendix, we would like to share briefly the accounting standard we have adopted and attempted to popularize.

We write here for two audiences. For readers, we encourage you first to learn and then expect—nay, *demand*—the accounting standards put forward below. Any newsletter or investment service that you come across that does *not* follow our Foolish principles is skimping . . . probably for reasons that favor *them* and put *you* at a disadvantage. If you encounter such situations, we encourage you to do the right thing: walk in the opposite direction.

For publishers, we encourage you to adopt the practices herein expounded. We'll be compiling a list online of all investment publications and services that publish their numbers Foolishly, making it available to our readership with our stamp of Foolish approval. We do, of course, hope to include you on the list.

1. Use Real Money

We consider this a necessity. The Fool Portfolio contains our own money, giving the reader a very strong sense that ours is exactly where our mouth is. Every single trade ever made on the Fool Portfolio was done with real bucks. Why would you, or we, or anyone else want to follow investment counsel that wasn't backed by the hard-earned greenbacks of the adviser?

This doesn't mean that the adviser should have bought before you did, however. If she has bought her own picks but traded in *advance* of making her recommendation public for the purpose of profiting off of others' attempts to get in, she is guilty of "front-running." Readers should make sure they get an explicit statement from any advice giver that that person does not, as a policy, front-run. Front-runners are effectively using you to boost their own portfolios.

2. Deduct Commissions

Okay, now that we know we're dealing with real money, we must accept—and *reflect*—the real costs that all investors face. Let's begin with commissions. Almost all investors pay their broker a fee for executing their trades. (The only general exceptions are those rich people—who typically have half a million or more—who hold accounts at discount brokerages that enable them to trade commission-free.) The Motley Fool Portfolio has always and will always reflect the expense of making each trade . . . we do not consider our portfolio exempt from something that everyone else has to deal with. The amazing thing is that we're about the only financial publishers we know of who deduct commissions costs from our returns.

It's not hard to figure out why. By ignoring the cost of commissions, investment newsletters can make their returns look better than they actually are. When you consider that most investment newsletters aim to help you make good money in stocks and that they market themselves based on their performance numbers, every little bit helps. Who would notice a tiny little thing like the cost of trading, anyway?

Why, a Fool, of course.

Frequent trading incurs high commissions; high commissions can kill you. Anyone who takes the time to run a few numbers can see how true this is. Let's pretend that you have a $20,000 account, and you hold a balanced list of ten stocks, with $2,000 in each. Further, let's assume that you wish to "day trade" this account, because you think "day trading" is a good idea. (You're wrong; it's a bad idea. Hope you've read part VIII, "Here Be Dragons: Investment Approaches to Avoid," where we run numbers very similar to these.)

For our purposes here we'll assume that you average one switch per day . . . one old sell and one new buy, which would mean that you hold each of your ten stocks, on average, for 10 days (many day traders hold them for something more like 10 hours, not 10 days). Anyway, a switch a day makes about 600 trades a year, give or take. Let's continue to try to make your case look as good as possible by saying you're trading through a deep-discount broker, at only $20 a pop (an extremely good rate). Time to do some math. You're paying $20 a trade, and making 600 trades a year: That looks like $12,000 you're spending in commissions. After 1 year, the cost of trading will have eaten up 60 percent ($12,000 divided by $20,000) of your original investment! That's horrible! Good luck ever trying to beat the market on a consistent basis when you're "playing" like this. Maybe it works with big sums for institutional shareholders—maybe—but for average investors it's a real waste of cash (to say nothing of time!). You'll have to earn a return on your stocks of 70 percent a year just to equal the annualized market-average return of 10 percent.

It is the above scenario that makes "Hot! Hot! Hot!" 900-number day-trading hotlines ("Just $3.95 a minute!") so costly . . . and here we do not refer to your phone bills—which will be bad enough—but to your overall investment peformance, which will be worse. These sorts of services are generally the most blatant violators of responsible accounting. Most don't show any overall numbers for their performance at all, let alone actually publish returns with commissions deducted. Fax 900-number services generally appeal to people who feel they need a new investment idea to trade in and out of every day; many of them are not smart or experienced enough to recognize that this sort of investing done over any intermediate- to long-term commitment should be considered their worst enemy. They get caught up in the adrenalin of the BIG DAILY TRADE and pay $7.90 for the privilege of dialing 1-900-HOTLUCKY to hear the two-minute report on Lucky's Hot Stock of the Day. This is sucker money . . . these are the same people who are just handing away money to their state government for the privilege of losing the daily lottery. Only in this case, the money isn't getting plowed back directly (supposedly, anyway) into public works.

All average investors who trade real money in the stock market face the natural consequences of their actions: a commission of typically $50 or more on every buy and every sell. Any investment service that conveniently neglects to account for these costs is working against—not for—you. Of course, it's especially easy for them to hide these costs when they're not dealing in real money. (See item 1 above.)

In the coming year, we hope that some investment newsletters and services will join us in acknowledging the realistic costs of trading. It's awfully lonely right now, out here on our own.

3. Account for Spreads

Ah, but we can't leave off right there. Commissions are not the *only* cost of buying and selling. A second hidden cost, which can often *exceed* the amount paid in one commission, is the bid-ask spead elaborated upon earlier in the book.

To summarize, every stock actually has two prices, not one. Most people see just the "last trade" in their newspapers and figure that stocks have only one price. Nope. Every stock has a "bid price" and an "ask price." As we explained earlier, the "bid" is the price you get when you sell a stock; the "ask" is the price you pay when you buy a stock. The asking price, for reasons that will become obvious to those who spend five seconds thinking about it, is always higher than the bid. (For those who couldn't spare the five seconds, imagine what life would be like if the price you paid for a stock—the ask—was lower than the price you could turn right around and sell it at—the bid. Instant money!) The reason that two prices exist is that the guy who matches buy and sell orders, the person who is effectively "making the market" in a stock, pockets the difference for his salary. He's the middleman, no different from any furniture salesman or bookie. He deserves to be compensated for the time and the risk that he is taking in holding an "inventory" of shares and orders waiting to be matched and executed.

Stocks trading on the NASDAQ have historically featured higher spreads. That's because these securities have typically been more thinly traded, requiring fewer "market makers." Fewer market makers mean less competition between market makers, which equates to wider spreads. After all, when there's only one guy matching orders, you can bet he's going to skim more off the top than when he has four other competitors to worry about. Let's take an example of a typical NASDAQ situation: We'll call it Acme Thingamajigs Corp. (NASDAQ: STUF), a stock that bids $10 and asks $10½. Let's say you want to buy some 'jigs . . . you can expect to get the stock at $10½ when you put in your immediate market buy order. The moment after it's executed, STUF will now be worth $10 to you—that's the bid, what you'd get when you sell it. In other words, you've just given away 4.8 percent of your money

($½ divided by $10½ equals .0476). That's steep . . . for many trades, that 5 percent will come out to more than you gave away in commission.

Given what we learned in item 2 above—that investment newsletters try to sell copies by publishing attractive-looking returns—do you think the same guys who ignore commissions will actually account for spreads? Of course not. If they're going to blow off the 2 to 4 percent that commissions typically represent for a trade, they're certainly going to ignore the additional 2 to 5 percent paid on spreads, as well. Whether you wish to call this flat-out dishonest is up to you; it is certainly intellectually dishonest, at the very least.

The Motley Fool Portfolio, as it is *real money* moving in *real trades,* always accounts for the spread. We buy at the ask, and sell at the bid . . . there's no other way around it! Contrast this with newsletters that will claim, using the above example of Acme Thingamajigs, to have *bought* at $10, at the bid—as if you could buy at the bid. They'll point to a "last trade" in the newspaper of $10, and hey, that may well have been the last trade; the person who got $10 on that last trade was a seller, however, not a buyer. You simply cannot *buy* STUF at its bid. For investment publishers to use the "last trade" figure to suggest they entered a new long position at $10 demonstrates what a fantasy world they're living in . . . a fantasy that they hope *you'll* make believe in too, when you consider subscribing to their stuff.

Ingoring spreads (and commissions) is cheating. It is also currently rampant among newsletter "gooroos." It may take a Fool to spoil this party, but then again, who would feel safe masquerading with these people?

4. Compare Performance Numbers to S&P 500 and NASDAQ, Daily

Above, we solved The Case of the Missing Expenses. Now it's time to turn our magnifying glasses onto the ever-sinister Case of the Failure to Compare One's Returns to the Market. The game's afoot!

It may seem obvious that the performance of any investment should be placed in the context of the overall market's. But it's clearly not obvious to financial publishers, most of whom would rather that you *not* compare their numbers to the general market's return. In fact, financial newsletters were so loath to make themselves accountable that an entire new *business* sprung up undertaking to track and report on their performance, since in many cases they wouldn't. We refer to *The Hulbert Financial Digest,* a newsletter that tracks how other newsletters do. *The Hulbert Financial Digest* has consistently demonstrated just how few investment rags even *equal* the market. That's not surprising, given that the vast majority of mutual funds underperform the averages. It is surprising, though, looked at in light of the grotesquely inflated claims that some investment newsletters make.

Mark Hulbert qualifies as one of the mavericks of money publishing for his lone efforts to match the *actual* returns of investment newsletters to those that they *claim*. In the process, Hulbert has ended up one of the financial world's more beloved figures by individual investors and one of the more hated by financial publishers. (He must be doing something right.) We love and admire Mark's efforts to keep up with the shenanigans of some whose advertisements would have you believe they earned a "100 percent-+ Annual Return!!!" when in fact they had just one great month and then annualized that figure to produce the fictional 100 percent figure. This sort of chicanery is too typical, brought to you by the sophists of our modern era.

We report on The Fool Portfolio's progress *daily,* posting not just our numbers but a full written recap of the session's news and goings-on with our stocks. Our numerical report includes the portfolio's performance as of market close every day measured against two key market benchmarks, the widely followed Standard & Poor's 500 and the NASDAQ. This comparison of investment returns to the market averages on a daily basis should become standard practice for any publication or service trying to solicit subscribers looking for investment information and stock-picking advice. The model here is mutual funds, which update their value and performance at the end of every market day. Mutual fund companies use computers to run their numbers; so do we; so do many newsletter publishers . . . in fact, who would trust one that didn't? If we're all using these computers every day, why not appoint them to track our investment performance, and report accurate numbers (expenses deducted) contemporaneous with the close of market business every day?

The answer, for too many, has been that such exposure would make their poor performance relative to the averages so glaringly obvious that they might have to go out of business. Right.

5. Report Longs at the Bid; Report Shorts at the Ask

And while we're on the subject of reporting numbers and accounting for bid-ask spreads, The Fool Portfolio reports its prices each reporting period (each day, in our case) in the most conservative manner possible. That means that we represent our long holdings at their bid price, since that's what we'd get for selling them. And we report our short-sale holdings at the ask, since that's what we'd have to pay to cover our short. To report one's prices (and therefore performance) any other way would be unrealistic. However, we once again have thought and thought of who else out there in the big, wide world *also* reports their numbers this way; perhaps we have a limited imagination, however, since we could think of no one.

6. Make Trades When Your Readers Do

The next charge relates not to how numbers should be presented but to how a business should be run: Namely, that those who pick stocks publicly should make their trades *at the same time,* not before, their readers do. We got into this a bit earlier, when we mentioned front-running. The subjects are related, but different.

Have you ever subscribed to an investment newsletter that gave you stock picks in the mail . . . 1 week *after* the newsletter writer had already published and *acted upon* his picks? You may have found that the hot new stock up for recommendation had already risen a point or more. Is that useful to you? If you find this a regular event with a rag that you currently take, you'll also no doubt find the publisher claiming significantly better returns than you the subscriber could ever expect. That's neither useful nor fair.

The Motley Fool Portfolio makes a strong point of announcing all its trades publicly the night before . . . the next morning, we execute our trades at the exact same time that the most earnest component of our readership does. The aim has been, and always will be, to make our returns completely duplicable by anyone Foolish enough to pay attention.

7. Refrain from Ridiculous, Misleading Advetisements

The final Foolish standard of accountability regards the advertisements that publishers draw up to market their products. We want to see good, accurate ones. (We know, we know, we're hopelessly naive . . . but then we're just wet-behind-the-ears kids in our twenties.) Of the existing lot of financial ads on TV and in print, many violate common standards of accountability and respectability, and to anyone who knows investing, are also very, very lame. Of course, these ads aren't composed for anyone who knows investing. Quite the opposite. They're written for suckers unable to recognize any of the following: artificially annualized returns, Mickey Mouse investment approaches invented to exploit back-testing, unrealistic "one-shot-deal" investment bonanzas, and much, much more.

Let's look at these.

How about artificially annualized returns? We've already referred to one such typical scheme above. What happens is that an unprincipled stock picker has a great month or quarter, then begins to advertise that performance by projecting it out over a time period far beyond that month or quarter. Let's say you yourself, dear reader, just finished a *great* first quarter, your investments returning you 24.6 percent. It was a bull market—the Dow was up 12 percent—and your stocks stampeded over the market averages and made you a very happy Fool. Okay . . . now let's pretend you're the typical unprincipled financial publisher. What you might well do, if temptation overcame you, is to publish an ad with the following garish headline:

ARE *YOU* MAKING
141 PERCENT ANNUALLY?

What an eye-grabber. Of course, all you've done—you sly devil—is to "annualize" that quarterly return; you've projected a 24.6 percent return on an annual basis, as if this were realistic or fair. Would *anyone* be well advised to search you out for 141 percent investment returns in *any* year? Not you, and not us either. Not anyone, actually; anyone with this sort of consistent performance would own most of the world's GNP after one investing lifetime.

So what do you think of an operation that would do this? We don't think much of it, either. The only ones who do are the ones who can't figure out what's going on. As usual, ignorance is vulnerability.

Then there's always the magic of back-tested returns. "You would have turned $10,000 into $39,160,394 since 1980 by using Dr. Stephen Leeb's Master Key (trading strategy)," the fateful ad read. We say "fateful" because it was this advertisement that led to an SEC investigation of the otherwise uninteresting investing career of Stephen Leeb, editor of the financial newsletters *The Big Picture* and *Personal Wealth*.

How was this "Master Key" invented? Back-testing. In other words, using past results, somebody essayed to develop a formula that succeeded in identifying the optimal times to buy and sell stocks over the past history of the market. Beginning with a basic premise for when to buy and when to sell, the resulting formula would then be tweaked any time it didn't work. Let's say the back-tester formulated things this way: Buy on Mondays, sell on Tuesdays. He would then begin back-testing until he hit a snag in which it was actually better to buy on Tuesday and then sell on Monday. Let's say that first snag came in August 1994. The back-tester would then tweak the back-tested formula to say, "Buy on Mondays and sell on Tuesdays, *except* in August 1994 when you buy on Tuesdays and sell on Mondays." And so on. Once you go back far enough and invent enough exceptions, you can end up devising a perfect market-timing formula. Unfortunately, you would have wasted your time; such a formula has no predictive value or useful application (other than to unscrupulous advertisement copywriters).

Let's sample a bit more of Leeb's text: "The information in this letter can make you rich in five years, starting with a small stake. False modesty aside, I've discovered the secret to forecasting the stock market."

Ironic use of the word "false."

The third and final example we'll include of bad financial ads intending to hoodwink the novice and the unwary comes to us from the Wall Street headquarters of Data Broadcasting Corporation. Publishers of a real-time quote service called Signal, Data Broadcasting is notorious at Fool HQ for cranking out ads like this one:

> "I made an average 78 percent return using Signal!" says David Baluh, Oklahoma Signal User. "I support my family—5 kids under the age of 7—with the money I make in the stock market. I'm a day trader and in the year I've had Signal, I'd say a conservative estimate of my return would be over 78 percent."

How did the esteemed Mr. Baluh earn this return? Who knows? One suspects options, and anyone can have a good year in options, then lose twice as much the year later . . . the year the ads never tell us about. This is a classic example of unrealistic "one-shot-deal" investment bonanzas trying to grab your eye with sensational claims. But when we look more closely at the claim, it's even lamer than we first noticed:

"I'd say a conservative estimate of my return would be over 78 percent."

It's clear from this text that Mr. Baluh probably does not have any precise idea of how his investments are performing. He's having to give an estimate, qualifying it with "I'd say." That Data Broadcasting has to tout someone about whose returns they can make no claim for accuracy suggests a certain paucity of candidates. The selection of the non-round number "78 percent" is a very nice touch; it attempts to imply an accuracy possibly lacking from the statement itself.

You know, it continually miffs us that more newspapers and magazines don't play watchdog and make a big point of exposing the trumpery of this tripe. But then we conk ourselves on the head and roll our eyes . . . how could we be so silly? These are the very same newspapers and magazines whose businesses rely on taking in these advertising dollars. Geez, what were we thinking?

◆ ◆ ◆

We've now gone through the basics of portfolio accounting, championing the position that always enthusiastically accepts the handicaps of honesty. The conventions presented above are not difficult to understand or to implement; in fact, they're merely common sense. But as of this writing, we don't know of a single financial publisher other than The Motley Fool that adheres to these standards. This may be because The Motley Fool introduced and implemented these standards; it may also be because common sense poses a threatening prospect to a large portion of the financial publishing world.

To repeat, the aim at Fool HQ has always been to make our numbers duplicable by *anyone.* Everyone has to pay commissions and spreads—we do too—so we account for them. And hey, because we interact with our readers online every single day, we couldn't "get away with" anything less. Getting away with much less has been a commonplace for the past several decades of "one-way publishing," where publishers could impose their own standards and coventions—legitimate or otherwise—without fear of retribution. Welcome to the 1990s, where your readership has now become its own community, able to communicate and organize itself with the ardor and coherence of a grassroots political party. Subterfuge just became that much more difficult.

That's all right with us: We're all for rectitude in the first place.

APPENDIX C

· · · · ·

Zeigletics:
The Penny Stock
That Never Was

Long before we launched *The Motley Fool* (a.k.a. Ye Olde Printed Foole) printed publication—which had us throwing down dollars to lay out, print, and mail off our rag, burning the leftover loads of inventory afterward—long before this, we learned age-old lessons from our grandparents and parents about wolves and lambs, lions and antelope, snakes and individual investors. No matter how much we wanted to believe that everyone out in the field was there to assist us, to improve our investment returns, to serve our financial needs, the fact remained that not everyone was looking out for our best interest. And they're still not. Not ours and not yours.

Just as evolution taught the antelope to run in herds to survive the attack of a lioness, individual investors have been forming investment clubs around the country to help them keep a tight hold on their capital. Places like The Motley Fool Online now offer that opportunity for collaboration, only now it's a twenty-four-hour operation, and it's nationwide.

But we didn't just start talking up survivalism and herding after getting online. We spoke of it back in the days of Ye Olde Printed Foole: The best investors pool their informational resources and their analytical expertise to wallop the market average. As has been noted in this guide, many investment clubs have outperformed the S&P 500 for years running.

But the lions are never far away, offering up expensive financial information that often hurts portfolios more than it helps them. We ran into scenarios that were, in fact, far more grisly than the provision of overpriced information. Some outfits were actually profiting by *mis*-leading individual investors in the offline and online world. Whole businesses that were fashioned to hype and manipulate the value of nickel-and-dime stocks were taking their operations from the analog to the digital world, where they could reach large audiences instantly. Of course, unfortunately for these schemers, online communications also allowed the herd of Foolish investors to assemble, and then assess and speak out against this sort of nonsense in the forum—an option none of us had had as individuals on the other end of brokerage cold calls.

We weren't quite aware, and still aren't, to what extent the systematic and deliberate hyping of penny stocks on- or offline is prohibited, so you won't see us batting around terms like "legal" and "illegal." That's not our thing. While this style of investing would seem to be a wrong-headed way to play the market and something regulators ought to keep a close eye on, we've always been content to let the authorities sort it all out.

What follows now, though, is an abridged version of a parody we did on penny-stock hyping. We conducted this parody on a national online service. It wound up in our 1994 April Fool's edition, for which we invented our own hypester complete with an imaginary penny stock to hype. Below is our account of the creation, success, and demise of the legendary Joey Roman. We begin with an overview of the process.

The Compleat Hypester, Revealed

"By right means, if you can, but by any means
make money."
Horace—(B.C. 65–8)

Customarily, the companies promoted by the compleat Hypester—on-line *and* offline—are bantam operations with insufficient prospects to qualify them for any of the major U.S. exchanges. The potential reasons include: grim financial statements, a stock that is too thinly traded, a share price that is too low, and a management team that owns too large a chunk of the company.

These disqualifiers are used by the major U.S. exchanges in part to complicate any efforts to manipulate share prices. For example, a company with 1 million total shares that trade at $0.10 per stub will have a hard time getting listed on an American exchange. The entire value of its stock—the value of the company, therefore—is a mere $100,000 (1 million shares x $0.10 per share = $100,000).

Imagine the push that can be exerted on the share price by a hypester who manages to induce 500 online acquaintances to each buy $1,000 worth of the stock. This $500,000—equivalent to five times the market's value of the *entire* company—will quickly and dramatically push up the share price, whatever the actual merits of the stock or the company. It's just such situations that can prove so lucrative to those interested in using the power of a new medium—online computer communication. For the first time ever, a single person can get the attention of thousands of others merely by posting a message on a public forum (anonymously, if desired) with the click of a button.

The operation is simple. First, the Hypester purchases thousands of shares for himself at a bargain price (usually a few dimes). Next he signs on to one or more online services and writes rhapsodically (though, in practice, illiterately) of the company's outstanding prospects. Some novices are swayed to buy, pushing the price up. The hypester shouts *"Buy!"* louder. More people buy, the trading volume goes through the roof, and the price follows in tow. At some confidential point in time, the Hypester simply parts with his shares, selling them to the very people he'd duped into buying. That he could actually foist off his shares on someone else at such a dear price is a testament to the power of the imagination, since it's the sensationalized, often exotic story that so dependably attracts these novice investors.

What sort of profits could be turned? A $5,000 investment in a stock that moves from 25 cents to $1.50 in a month would net the investor a tidy profit of $25,000. Now, compound that monthly. Yes, that sort of stock price appreciation *was* happening. Incidentally, $5,000 compounded at 500 percent monthly turns into pretax profits of over $78 million in 6 months. No wonder these guys were fired up!

'Course it was all highly unethical and a fine example of poor business. But they went on flipping in and out, buying and selling stocks, and would have continued ad nauseam absent some interruptive Foolishness. To run interference, though, we had to deconstruct the system piece by piece.

The Fairy Tale—Hyping the Company

The Grimmsian accounts of company operations that one can read in online hype necessitates, even from the dimwitted, a mild (sometimes *wild*) suspension of disbelief. More often than not, the stocks trade on wildcat Canadian exchanges, and the "corporations" (which may be nothing more than two- or three-man operations) are primarily doing business in countries that the average American citizen couldn't place on a map, making the business story that much harder to follow (a bonus for the Hypester). Invariably, at least one Hypester claims both to have flown to the distant country to view operations *and* to be in communication with management on a twice-daily basis. This go-between speaks confidently of his access to inside information, and drops hints (sometimes even correctly) regarding the timing of upcoming news announcements.

And what types of business are these companies doing abroad? Well, take Wye Resources, the Canadian owner of a Zairean diamond mine. Despite, to our knowledge, its failure to secure enough crystallized carbon to inlay a single diamond hairpin, Wye—a "hot issue" that was promoted on several online services and broadly across the Internet—witnessed a 500 percent gain in its stock in less than 1 month before regulators stepped in and halted trading.

And consider March 1994's "hot stock," Interlock Consolidated Enterprises (ILS), a company said to be providing materials for prefabricated housing to the "exciting" Russian market. The excitement largely surrounded an announcement of multimillion-dollar contracts with Russia for unbuilt houses planned for returning Red Army soldiers. Whatever. A quick buzz over to ILS headquarters turned up only this: Interlock received no money up front and would not comment on the pending contracts. So, what was the name of the Russian company involved? That too had to be kept secret. And each of ILS's press releases ended with a disclaimer never seen on those of listed U.S. companies: "This press release has neither been approved or [sic] disapproved by any Exchange or Regulatory body."

Hmmm . . . convenient.

Hype: Buy Now! Now! Buy!

But that won't stop a Hypester! Exclamation and exaggeration are the twin pillars of stock manipulation, and any news—the less verifiable, the better—that he can scrounge up provides the framework for his tale. He routinely hops from one online service to the next, posting semiliterate, fully exaggerated growth claims for each chosen peewee company. With millions of people now online—many of them looking for help on how to invest their money—it doesn't take too much noise to rally a profitable group of inexperienced investors.

ILS, the apparent homebuilder in the former Soviet Union, like many other hyped stocks, had a half dozen bulletin boards on the Prodigy online service where investors posted hourly quotes. Therein they dreamed aloud about the stock's prospects as the company crept across Central Russia, and then the potential for monstrous profits once ILS began supplying the components for millions of prefab homes in Africa—though no such deal had materialized. Oh, and had any such deal been announced investors would've been greeted with that standard disavowal:

"This press release has neither been approved or [sic] *disapproved by any Exchange or Regulatory body."*

Hmm.

Buy Zeigletics! (Hurry?): Our Foolish Hoax Recap

Into this online arena stepped our man Joey Roman, penny stock superman, walking April Fool's joke, and full-fledged parody. He launched a massive national online propaganda blitz, just like all the other penny stock Hypesters, only the company he celebrated didn't exist, nor did the exchange on which it purportedly traded. But Roman was better than all of his competitors, even if he didn't have a real company to hype. Roman had always bought all of the competing hypesters' stocks for a dime less, always pushed them up a few nickels higher, and he claimed to enjoy the gushing admiration of the entire penny stock world. Roman was a disgusting extreme.

The fifty some-odd messages published by The Fool on Prodigy over a 1-week period were read by thousands of investors. And the notes occasioned a couple hundred responses in just a few days. Told in the voices that created it, what follows are a dozen of Joey Roman's online notes, which detail his brief but meteoric rise and fall. Likewise, we provide a full description of his hotcakes, sugar-dumpling recommendation: Zeigletics—Canadian manufacturer of linked sewage-disposal systems for the Central African nation of Chad, trading on the most conservative of Canadian stock exchanges, our cloud-built Halifax Exchange. Zeigletics made Roman, and Roman made ZEIG.H.

The Story (as told by Mr. Joey Roman in online postings)

Post #1: Roman Emerges

Zeigletics (ZEIG.H) trades on the Halifax Canadian Exchange at $0.37 x $0.39—a HUGE bargain!

That's because the company has introduced portable toilets *(Zeig-Lo-Pots),* bathroom deodorants, and other septic accessories to Central Africa, specifically Chad. Sounds pretty unusual, huh? But Central Africa is just introducing linked-sewage disposal. So this is a MAJOR growth industry; cleanliness is next to godliness. It's a sizzling market, and Zeigletics, based out of Ludlum, Canada, is capitalizing on the possibilities.

Just between Roman and you, there *are* no other septic-accessory suppliers currently in Chad, or neighboring Sudan. Management is right now in N'Djamena, the capital of Chad, installing the first few hundred thousand Zeig-Lo-Pots, complete with bathroom deodorants. Roman spoke with the Chief Financial Officer yesterday—collect call—and the day before, and the installations are beating all company estimates!!!! The Zeig-Lo-Pot is the envy of the Central African region. Why do you think the stock has six-bagged in a week!?

But the real kicker is plungers. Last autumn's streamlined installation of portable toilets in Libya did not include plungers. The recent sewage debacle in Southern Libya was the direct result of inadequate declogulation apparati. (Basically, they needed plungers, and they had none.) The African infrastructure is so dated in these areas that more clogulation crises will definitely continue to occur at alarming rates. It's happening right now in Zaire, where (Tip, Tip!) Zeigletics has even now shipped (get this!) over a million plungers. BIG BUCKS that you don't have to wait for! This one has been going up, up, up, and will keep at it all the way to $5. Roman's taking it to 5. *Routine for Roman.*

According to the president of ZEIG.H, in Africa the name Zeigletics is virtually synonymous with toilets. The company recently sponsored the Sudanese equivalent of the Boston Marathon, where hundreds of fans were waving plungers at the finish line!!! Chad is at the dawn of its Septic Age, and Zeigletics is the only player in the region.

You want numbers?!

How 'bout 700 percent sales growth in the last 6 months? Our conversations with management (insider info) suggest a CONSERVATIVE estimate of $1.22 per share (Canadian) by fiscal year ended July. THE STOCK IS AT 37 CENTS RIGHT NOW!!!!!!!!!!!!!!!!!!!!!!!!!!

Where does it trade? On the Halifax Canadian Exchange, one of the smallest and most conservative of the Canadian exchanges. It has stricter reporting requirements than any U.S. market, rejecting 9 out of 10 listing applications.

You gotta get in on this thing right NOW. The Canadians don't even know about it yet! The only people who know are Roman and the few others who've ALREADY made 600 percent in 1 week. Roman knows management, and management loves Roman.

This company is an overnight Canadian success story, and you're getting it just after twilight. Hurry! Hot, Hot, Hot! Sizzle. Hotter than an egg on the roof of my new Porsche in mid-August, when it's at $7. (My third new one.)

I already have seen the buy-side volume premarket Monday, and it's pushing the ask envelope on this one past 53 cents. Stochastics have it oscillating in the 80-cent region (no joke!) by midday. Stochastics don't always work; they can err too high or too low. But they have NEVER erred on the low side for one of Roman's stocks in his 17 years of penny stock brilliance. 'Nuff said.

Post #2: Roman Hypes the Issue

BUY ZEIGLETICS!!! MAJOR HEAT! A special one just for you, folks! Up from $0.06 to $0.37 just this week!

People on this service brag about five-baggers in a month . . . Bah! How about a six-bagger in a week? That's Routine for Roman (the name of my newsletter as well). I have to laugh at these other investors. What did ILS do on Friday? Bah! My picks go up and KEEP GOING UP!!!!!

Nobody EVER sells my stocks until I've made my sextuple! I've made my players a bundle. Did you see the coverage on me and my letter in *Penny Stock Player* last month, entitled PINK SHEET SUPER-MAN!?

Routine for Roman: "Most successful penny stock investor of the decade."—Roman

Post #3: Inside Info

Management report expected at about noon on toilet salts deal with Central African Republic. This one's DEFINITE. Just got off phone with Lars Saah, the president of Zeigletics!!!!!!!!!!!!!!—Roman

Post #4: Roman's Reach

Routine for Roman is the most successful publication BY FAR in the penny-player industry. I'm the only one to have earned regular CABLE TV time nationally, on local-access cable. My players are going public with the approach, finding little-known conservative exchanges with HOT HOT HOT companies, like Zeigletics, the African toilet products manufacturer. ROMAN HAS COME TO PRODIGY. When with Roman, do as Roman does—Roman, *Penny Stock Superman*

Post #5: FDA Approval!

Just got off the phone with Lars Saah, Zeigletics's president and also a petty-office holder in the government of Chad. Guess what? News is great!!!

Here's the scoop: Zeigletics has received permission from the federal Food & Drug Administration of Chad to sell its Zeig-Lo-Pots directly to the market!!! Previously, the Zeig-Lo-Pots were sold through middlemen who charged stiff commissions for distribution outside the Lake Chad region. What this means is hundreds of thousands of savings in Chad francs, the country's currency. This justifies Roman's writeup in the March 15 issue (6 days ago) of *Routine for Roman:*

"Look for Chad's eventual permission for the direct marketing of Zeig-Lo-Pots throughout the country on or about March 21st."

This is a stock that our readers bought at 6 cents at the beginning of last week; it closed Friday at 37 cents!!—Roman

[Editor's Note: Over the next 3 days, Roman led the multitudes down the primrose path, while desperately trying to keep the gag alive.]

Post #6: ZEIG.H—Monday's Action

$1.12 x $1.14!!!! Up $0.75 today!!!!

This baby just tripled, in ONE DAY!!! Roman's now taken this one up from 6 cents last Monday to $1.12 now! Thanks to all online Prodigy readers for your support . . .

Routine for Roman: Nobody sells. Our stocks never go down. If you haven't bought Zeigletics yet (Halifax Canadian Exchange, symbol: ZEIG.H), you're no player at all.

—Joseph Roman, Investor

Post #7: ZEIG.H—Tuesday's Action

Zeigletics, quote as of 12:21 P.M., Tuesday: $1.74 x $1.76. Whew!!!! Roman's made big money once again! *Routine for Roman:* The shorts have been squeezed like an orange on a strainer, and Roman's the one who's squeezin' 'em.

To anyone who hasn't bought yet: Isn't it time you listened to *the* player, superman penny stock picker of the decade?—Roman

Zeigletics closed Tuesday at $1.92 x $1.93, UP $0.80 on the day! Thanks to all for hurrying into this one! I'll keep you posted; meeting with Lars Saah here in Manassas tomorrow. Big announcement about Madagascar should come tomorrow at about 1:56 P.M. Buy more, if you want to make more.—Roman

Post #8: Zeigletics—Wednesday's Action

At the open, $1.55 x $1.57, DOWN $0.37.

What's up here, people? Let's keep the shorts on the run. Roman's stocks *never* go down. We all need to stay in to get this to work. BIG NEWS coming soon! The Madagascar deal should be announced today. Keep your eyes peeled on Reuters. You just watch. ROMAN SAYS BUY!!! BUY!!! BUY!!!

Looking for it to go back over $2 today. I think $3 is reasonable by the end of the week. $$$$$$$$$—Roman

(Two hours later . . .)

Post #9: Ssshhh! SELL!

Joey Roman and *Routine for Roman* put out a sell order on this one this morning. The stock right now is down $1.00 to $0.92 x $0.94. We told you to get out at $1.92 [yesterday's close] and if you did you made big money on this one . . . you did better than 10 times your money in 10 days. Zeigletics is a good company; we'll keep our eye on this one. Meanwhile, buy RUMR.H on the same exchange. That's where a lot of *Routine for Roman* readers are moving their money for the next few days.

We made big money, people! $$$$$

I'm lookin' out for ya.—Roman

Post #10: ZEIG.H—Wednesday's Closing Comment

Zeigletics had a bad day, closing at $0.68 x $0.70. If you got out when we told you to, you made a bundle on this one. We sold at $1.92, and moved the money into our new pick, RUMR.H. We bought it this afternoon at .12. Closing quote? .23, on 1.4 million shares (average daily volume: 2,000 shares). ROMAN STRIKES AGAIN!!!! $$$$$$$—Roman, Superman

Fly and Swatter

Along the way, Mr. Roman received loads of fan and hate mail. Below we publish some of the notes sent to Roman, as well as his responses, all in our Foolish fly and swatter format.

Fly

Hype has been taken to a totally new level. Roman, if you have been having this type of success for 17 years, you would be the richest man on earth—Geaty

Swatter

Sure, but there's no reason on earth why I shouldn't keep working. *Routine for Roman.*

Hey, did you just ask about my newsletter? *Routine for Roman*—the premier penny stock player letter!!! Most people can't afford it, because subscription is $2,000/year. We do that on purpose, to price out nonplayers. We have a lot of BIG players, trust me, but we never reveal the names. We have a couple of people you routinely see on national network television, a couple of professional athletes, a couple hundred mutual fund managers (of international hedge funds mostly), and some average Joes too.

Our readers don't care about the subscription cost, especially when they make $20,000 in a month. They thank Roman for his tips, and we get several invitations to Christmas dinners every year!

Routine for Roman has been called "the Penny Stock Bible" by the MAJOR movers and shakers in pink sheets. And that doesn't mean small-time online service players. We're talking NAMES, people you see in the newspaper and on TV. Thanks for your interest. —Roman

Fly

Roman, if you really are legit, I will issue a public apology on this board. But PCFN, the discount broker, had never heard of the Halifax exchange either. So first, you need to give us some phone numbers. What's the phone number for this company? How does one go about trading on the Halifax exchange if one's broker has never heard of it?

Since you're new to Prodigy, you will have to excuse our skepticism.

If you really are legit, then it will be great to have you on board. There are a lot of nice people here. But, first, some phone numbers, please.—Juanita

Swatter

Roman is in constant (everyday) contact with the half dozen companies featured in *Routine for Roman.* Our one stipulation is that they deal with Roman, and Roman *only.* We don't work with anyone who won't work with Roman exclusively. WE HATE P.R. FIRMS AND 800 NUMBERS, and Roman doesn't need pipsqueaks to move these stocks UP UP AND AWAY. A lot of companies won't work with us, because we demand exclusive access to the story and numbers.

That's fine with Roman. *Routine for Roman* only picks one maybe two hotcakes an issue, and again, WE HAVE EXCLUSIVE ACCESS TO OUR COMPANIES. Their phone numbers are UNLISTED; they DElist their phone numbers when Roman initiates coverage of their stock. So only Roman has the phone number. It's the best arrangement for *Routine for Roman and* its players. All news gets forwarded through Roman before the market catches wind of it. . . . It's all part of the deal.

Would you complain about Leaf Tectonics if YOU'D bought it at 15 cents (like Roman players did) last November and it was $3.43 at Friday's close? Roman doesn't think so. We laugh (hahahaha) at people who invest in other penny stock companies that don't offer exclusive access to one individual. That's the best way to make money in stocks. But you have to know the right people, big-time money managers who gain exclusive access to company stories and numbers. Like Roman.—Roman

Threats and Insults

Then, in the succeeding days, Roman's mailbox and posts in the folders were deluged with follow-up responses. Some came to praise him, many more to bury him. Why many more? Because, as online services allow more than one screen name per account, angry penny stock hypesters logged on under multiple aliases and beat up our poor promoter and his newsletter. After a while, it was time for Roman to answer to his detractors. Many of them had taken to tossing out vile threats, even dialing into Fool HQ with strings of invective and threats. We've chosen not to reprint them here. Not worth your time. Roman's reply *is,* though:

Roman Responds

It's sad that some people invest large portions of their time trying to knock down Roman. Some of the saddest cases actually become *consumed* by it. But that's the price of greatness. Check it out in the history books: Every beloved figure over the course of human history has had some mosquitoes buzzing around his ears. Heck, George Washington had an entire country out for his head!

Roman on Roman—Let me ask all of you this: Is your broker able to quote securities off the venerable Halifax Canadian Exchange? Has he ever heard of Zeigletics (Halifax: ZEIG.H), which was up over 3,000 percent in 8 days??!!! Can he come up with shares of ZEIG.H at 2-cent spreads in any lot you request? Roman's guess is that your answer to these questions is an emphatic *no.*

But that doesn't surprise Roman, because long ago he came to accept his own superiority to *all other investment advisers.* And Zeigletics is just the latest in a 15-year-long litany of MONSTER stocks that Team Roman has taken up to stratospheric heights in a matter of days.

The respected industry publication *Penny Stock Player*—that seasoned observer of pinks and pennies—wouldn't have given its Lifetime Service Award to Roman haphazardly, would it? And hey, Roman can't help it if *Micro-Stock* magazine insists on calling him (February 1993 issue) ". . . the Minnesota Fats of micro-cap, thinly traded foreign stocks with large spreads. He calls the shots and then he sinks 'em." These ARE NOT paid advertisements, just unsolicited praise for a great investment technique, and a great man.

Roman will keep to his brilliant, can't-lose investment formula, keep making disgusting amounts of money for his loyal followers, and will keep giving away 75 percent of it to charity (this past year saw the erection of the Joseph Roman Empire Library at Roman's alma mater). The way my life is going, I don't think it'll take very long for a larger-than-lifesize statue of Roman to be erected in Roman's hometown.

And probably in yours, too.

—*Joseph Lincoln Roman, Sr., American*

The Illuminati

We've decided to share the wrap-up commentary on the Zeigletics April Fool's Joke that we thought the most eloquent. We have no idea who Mr. Hughes is but, to our ears, his note pretty well and Foolishly summarized the 1-week plunge into the squash of online penny stock manipulation.

This is the funniest exchange I have ever seen on this board. Come on, people, think! Toilet seat exports? Clogulation? Crowds of cheering plunger wavers?

The point Joey Roman is making is pretty clear: It is so easy for a fast-talking hypester to establish a position in a low-volume stock, rattle off a bunch of crap that sounds plausible enough to convince a novice, let the price pop due to uninformed amateurs flying in, and sell into the rise, laughing all the way to the bank.

Dear people, learn to evaluate and think for yourselves. There are some legit stock pickers on this board, and good ones at that, but please check their records and do your own research before buying someone's rec. The risk/reward ratio of buying something you haven't checked yourself will get you torn to pieces, so don't buy into hype. Intelligent investors (and prudent speculators) can and do get rich. But patience is critical, and risk must be calculated and limited as much as possible, and that only comes through knowledge and education. Read Peter Lynch, Warren Buffett, and Ben Graham.—Hughes

Wrap-up: Shakedown

And there you have it: a condensed report of our Foolish send-up of on- and offline pyramid schemes tied to foreign-listed penny stocks. It didn't take any great stroke of genius to peer into and see through the system—a pretty transparent promotional strategy, no?

The Motley Fool was then featured in *The Wall Street Journal* and *Forbes* magazine in the weeks ahead, and many other traditional media operations have since taken an interest in the story. What is, unfortunately, not oft-reported is that this sort of racket has and will continue to thrive over the telephone for many years to come. It isn't merely an online phenomenon.

In fact, not only is the online world not the breeding ground for penny-ante scamsters, it's their graveyard. The Motley Fool continues to work with state securities regulators in the months succeeding this Folly, and we believe that greater scrutiny is now tied to online financial services than any other mode of communication. We love it! When individual investors by the tens of thousands can gather to share information and advice about full-service brokers, discount brokers, mutual funds, aggressive bank salesmen, insurance salesmen, car salesmen, realtors, et al., the information is going to be the commodity; the service is going to be the distinguishing factor. Foolish investors like the sound of that!

In the meantime, the Foolish catchword is *patience.* Any investment vehicle with which you're not entirely comfortable or familiar is an "opportunity" to let slide by. Remember that rogue traders bring down multibillion-dollar banks *because* the banks aren't familiar with the rogue's investment approach. The same happens right down the food chain, with individuals watching their money evaporate in the hands of a financial manager whose strategy they did not understand and whose accounting system they couldn't untangle.

We hope our Investment Guide has well taught Fools to understand what they've invested in, to account for investment returns profession-ally, and to compare overall growth to the S&P 500. Stick to those con-cepts, and Joey Roman and his fellow hypesters will make for nothing more than a couple good laughs around the barbecue.

Acknowledgments

One thing we've learned in this whole messy process is that doing a book requires a tremendous team effort. We have many to thank, but we'll keep this short and sweet. Susan Jensen, as our assistant agent, receives our highest Foolish praise for "discovering" us and guiding us to ICM to get us started. We wish you the best of future success, Susan. Suzanne Gluck, our turbo-high-powered agent with spikes on her gauntlets, receives Foolish kudos for thoroughly squeezing the New York publishing world for everything it's worth. She's a great agent, and has an even better sense of humor. Then there's Bob Mecoy, our editor at Simon & Schuster, the guy who first described himself to us over the phone with the felicitous words, "I have big hair and little glasses." Would that every editor were as easygoing, humorous, and patient; the world would be so much more . . . er . . . easygoing and humorous (and patient)! Also at Simon & Schuster, Brian McSharry, Isolde C. Sauer, and Patty Romanowski were all a pleasure to work with as we explored together the limits of modern facsimile and electronic mail technology.

Closer to home, we'd like to thank the highly capable Randy Befumo for his thoroughgoing research on this book and general personal finance savvy. Further, we'd like to thank our company staff—local and remote—for keeping The Motley Fool running shipshape while we wrote the book each night from 2 A.M. to dawn. Our greatest appreciation and admiration go out to Erik Rydholm.

And finally (almost), we thank our families—the one that got us started, and the ones that we've started—for providing incredibly attractive, fruitful, and loving households that so strongly account for why we're able to do stuff like this in the first place.

And *finally,* to our online readers, thank you for teaching us more than we ever taught you. Together we are creating, as somebody once said in one of those space movies, "Something wonderful."

Index

Getting to The Motley Fool on America Online

We're in the enjoyable position as authors of being able to keep the book "alive" for our readers by answering your investment questions *right now* if you like, online.

Whether you're hoping to find additional research for the stocks in your portfolio, new investment ideas, information about your 401(K) plan, weekly updates on the latest Dow Dividend picks, minute-by-minute stock quotes, or just a place to talk to other individual and institutional investors, The Motley Fool has all of that and more on America Online 24 hours a day.

If you're already on AOL, just draw down the Go To menu to Keyword and type in FOOL.

If you're not yet online, but have a computer and a modem, you can dial (800) 592-3131 to receive a FREE disk to try out America Online (for Windows or Mac) for 10 FREE hours.

Get Foolish!

About the Authors

DAVID GARDNER, architect of The Motley Fool, is a former writer for *Louis Rukeyser's Wall Street Week,* is married and the father of a perfect child, and was a Morehead Scholar at the University of North Carolina. His brother, TOM GARDNER, voice of The Motley Fool, is a graduate of Brown University, an ex–girls basketball coach, and taught business and investing at the University of Montana.